THE
WHOLE-FACULTY
STUDY GROUPS
FIELDBOOK

For our spouses

Marilyn K. Lick

Joseph A. Murphy

*with grateful appreciation for their love, care, patience,
support, and encouragement for our efforts on this book*

THE
WHOLE-FACULTY STUDY GROUPS FIELDBOOK

Lessons Learned
and Best Practices From
Classrooms, Districts, and Schools

EDITORS

DALE W. LICK • CARLENE U. MURPHY
FOREWORD BY HAROLD M. BREWER

CORWIN PRESS
A SAGE Publications Company
Thousand Oaks, California

For information:

Corwin Press
A Sage Publications Company
2455 Teller Road
Thousand Oaks, California 91320
E-mail: order@sagepub.com

Sage Publications Ltd.
1 Oliver's Yard
55 City Road
London EC1Y 1SP
United Kingdom

Sage Publications India Pvt. Ltd.
B-42, Panchsheel Enclave
Post Box 4109
New Delhi 110 017 India

Printed in the United States of America.

Library of Congress Cataloging-in-Publication Data

The whole-faculty study groups fieldbook: lessons learned and best practices from classrooms, districts, and schools / editors, Dale W. Lick, Carlene U. Murphy.
    p. cm.
Includes bibliographical references and index.
ISBN 1-4129-1324-1 (cloth)—ISBN 1-4129-1325-X (pbk.)
    1. Teacher work groups—United States. 2. Teachers—In-service training—United States.
3. School improvement programs—United States. 4. Academic achievement—United States.
I. Lick, Dale W. II. Murphy, Carlene U.
LB1731.W475 2007
370.71′5—dc22

                            2006002984

This book is printed on acid-free paper.

06 07 08 09 10   10 9 8 7 6 5 4 3 2 1

Acquiring Editor:	Rachel Livsey
Editorial Assistant:	Phyllis Cappello
Project Editor:	Astrid Virding
Copyeditor:	Kristin Bergstad
Typesetter:	C&M Digitals (P) Ltd.
Indexer:	Nara Wood
Cover Designer:	Audrey Snodgrass

Contents

Foreword

As I begin this task of writing a foreword for a work that has earned my full support for its commitment to quality education and professional development, I share with you that I am a fellow sojourner on the journey focusing on school improvement. Whether you have just begun your journey or are well along the way, you will hopefully find, as I have, that what school improvement should seek, year in and year out, is an understanding of (a) what we need to do to help our students improve their learning and (b) how our systems need to align to serve the needs of teachers.

Over the past thirty-five years, I served in a number of roles, each with its own perspective of school improvement and the change process. As a teacher, the goal was right in front of me daily in the presence of between twenty-five and thirty-five students. As an assistant principal and principal, school improvement was all around me in the form of working with students and teachers to meet diverse needs and the location of scant resources. As assistant superintendent for instruction, school improvement was centered on the curriculum and policy development. As a superintendent, the goal was in the eyes of every student, parent, teacher, business owner, and community member I met: It was about meeting the needs of individual students and serving the needs of the community. Standards guided us and assessments measured us. At times, school improvement was reduced simply to year-end assessments. However, we know that school improvement is much more. For the professional educator, school improvement is in the process of designing, implementing, assessing, and reflecting and acting on our ever-increasing awareness of what our students need.

I learned to ask a question of instructional teams and others: "What evidence do we have that this system has the capacity to perform at the level of our expectations?" That question focused on reality and the essential needs. Assessing capacity should be a regular component of data-based decision making. Building capacity is fundamental in the Whole-Faculty Study Group (WFSG) System. The WFSG approach aligns the professional learning needs of teachers with data on the students they teach, and then provides a process to meet the needs of learners. The key to higher performance embodied in the WFSG model is the work of planning, doing, assessing, and reflecting as an ongoing process.

I have found that there are many distractions to claim the attention of faculty, making it highly challenging to focus and sustain conversations on teaching and learning. Consequently, the WFSG approach embeds the change process in the school plan and supports the faculty and the school in addressing student needs and skill development for success. It means taking precious time to develop our skills to meet identified goals, but it is no longer acceptable to say we are doing the best we can unless we can show how our practice is improving student achievement on a daily basis.

In my experience, there are few models that successfully promote authentic collaboration among teachers, focus clearly on student data for instructional improvement, and set a higher expectation for success as the WFSG System does. It is a student-centered and a teacher-driven model that refocuses the conversation and culture of the school. Throughout this fieldbook you will have the opportunity to view the model from many different perspectives and experience the WFSG model and general school improvement through the eyes of practitioners at all levels. Here are real-world examples of the model that have the potential to guide the conversation toward core values, effective teaching, and improved student learning.

Where do you go from here? The choice is yours. Start in any chapter that meets your needs. The experiences shared in this fieldbook will be helpful in improving schools and in your use of the WFSG System. As you will see, successful implementation of this model requires a commitment to people development, collaboration, and improved professional practice. It is not for the faint of heart, but worth every minute. Good luck!

—Harold M. Brewer
Senior Vice President for Programs
The Centers for Quality Teaching and Learning, Raleigh, North Carolina

Preface

The *Whole-Faculty Study Group Fieldbook: Lessons Learned and Best Practices From Classrooms, Districts, and Schools* is the natural companion book to the editors' earlier three books on Whole-Faculty Study Groups: *Whole-Faculty Study Groups: A Powerful Way to Change Schools and Enhance Learning* (1998), *Whole-Faculty Study Groups: Creating Student-Based Professional Development* (2001), and *Whole-Faculty Study Groups: Creating Professional Learning Communities That Target Student Learning* (2005). As Whole-Faculty Study Groups (WFSGs) and their application have been refined since their creation in 1987, many especially effective WFSG initiatives have emerged as excellent real-world examples of WFSG models. In its 31 chapters, The *WFSG Fieldbook* provides an array of successful WFSG and WFSG-related initiatives, providing a comprehensive collection of relevant and helpful illustrations and models of the WFSG System in action in the field.

The Whole-Faculty Study Group (WFSG) System has spread to school systems across the country, and the implementation and work of study groups has now become a daily occurrence in many schools, districts, and school systems. Because such work is continuous in these schools, the process and its refinement are constantly evolving. What one study group does has the potential to affect other schools that use the WFSG System.

In addition, as Murphy and other consultants travel from school to school around the country in their consulting role and Lick continues to research the application and theoretical bases for study groups, new ideas are generated that help strengthen the WFSG System. These changes accumulate over time and lead to major adjustments that make the process even more effective. In the eight years since the first WFSG book was written, several hundred schools have implemented the WFSG System. This translates into several thousand individual study groups. From these and continuing groups, new insights into the WFSG approach have created a wealth of new and helpful material.

If the study group model were a paper-and-pencil design, it might stay in a fixed or rigid state. Because the model continually evolves from how teachers actually work together in schools, it is fluid and readjusts itself. As leaders in schools chronicle the movement of study groups, we examine why some are high-performing groups and others struggle. What we learn is shared with schools already involved in WFSGs and those that are considering or just beginning the process. This fieldbook offers snapshots of numerous successful WFSG initiatives and provides a valuable addition to the literature for keeping schools up-to-date with a broad base of findings on what is working best in the field.

NEED AND PURPOSE

School reform and school improvement are on the minds of everyone today, including school administrators and teachers, parents and students, those in business and industry, and the general public. The concerns of all of these people and their organizations will not go away easily or quickly; it will require school reform processes and improvements well beyond anything that this nation has ever seen (see Chapter 31). Consequently, effective transformational processes will be essential to successfully reforming and improving schools and transitioning them so that they meet the students' and the country's future needs.

The WFSG System, as described in Chapter 1 and discussed in more detail in *Whole-Faculty Study Groups: Creating Professional Learning Communities That Target Student Learning* (2005), has been shown to be one of the most successful school reform and school improvement processes in the country. When applied properly, it has resulted in extraordinary school and student results.

The purpose of this fieldbook is to deepen administrators', teachers', parents', students', and others' understanding of and ability to use effective school reform and improvement approaches, especially those of the WFSG process, to significantly enhance the potential of their reform and improvement efforts. The many concepts and approaches modeled and illustrated, along with the numerous examples and illustrations, will provide a dramatically enriched collection of new understandings and tools for implementing major and successful school reform and school improvement. There is no other such resource now available in the marketplace. It will be relevant not only to those using the WFSG process, but also to others involved in or preparing for school reform and improvement undertakings.

In particular, the fieldbook will: (a) demonstrate how critical concepts can be applied in a wide variety of school reform efforts; (b) provide a broad array of relevant strategies, concepts, and activities; (c) help readers bring ideas to life by illustrating how to use and apply them in their "real-world situations"; (d) contain first-hand case studies that highlight the details of how concepts worked for a variety of activities and in different settings; and (e) offer tips, strategies, and lessons learned on a wide range of pertinent circumstances, approaches, processes, problem areas, and concepts and ideas.

WHO SHOULD READ AND USE THIS FIELDBOOK?

The primary audience for this book is everyone involved in school reform and school improvement in the country, as well as in other countries. The most natural audiences and potential users of this fieldbook would be all of those who have been involved or are becoming involved with our earlier WFSG books (e.g., school systems and districts, individual schools, administrators, teachers, parents, and their community leaders), and this now represents a sizable proportion of the school and general population. This fieldbook would be a particularly valuable addition to their library and in their WFSG applications now under way.

In addition, since this fieldbook will provide a wide variety of experiences, examples, and illustrations of concepts and approaches common to *most* school reform and school improvement efforts, this fieldbook should be especially of value to anyone seriously involved in or interested in other school reform and improvement undertakings. Specifically, this fieldbook will be unique in its approach, broadly understandable, and relevant to those who want to lead, be involved in, or support school improvement and reform movements going on around the country now and in the foreseeable future.

Organization and Contents

The fieldbook is organized with chapters conceptually grouped into eight major sections, called Parts, reflecting their commonality and logical placement under the specific section title, and with sequencing of Parts appropriately following in a natural order. The titles of the eight Parts are, in order: Getting Started, Leadership and Sponsorship, Study Groups and Learning Communities, Key Success Elements, Instructional Strategies, Perspectives for Teachers and Teaching, State and National Initiatives, and An Overview of School Reform.

The contents include the key elements in WFSG and change processes and their implementation, along with a large number of real-world examples and illustrative cases. The fieldbook is written so that it can serve as a textbook, a detailed reference book, or a stand-alone guide for many effective conceptual initiations and implementations, and successful completion of the WFSG approach to staff development and major improvements in schools.

Part I. For those who want to gain a better perspective on school improvement in general or develop an overview sense of the WFSG System, the three chapters in this section provide: (a) a detailed introduction to study groups and effective faculty and school development for using them; (b) an explicit application of WFSGs in a typical school; and (c) an overarching perspective on the pivotal role professional development standards play in school improvement.

Part II. The three chapters in this section illustrate authentic leadership and sponsorship situations, one relating to principals as leaders and sponsors, one with the school district as sponsor, and one with union collaboration to strengthen leadership and sponsorship. These chapters: (a) focus on practices of principals who help their teachers and WFSGs experience success, while enhancing the principals' effectiveness as instructional leaders; (b) unfold an implementation sequence that began centered on student learning, moved to process alignment at all levels, and continued with district-level support for quality implementation and an uncompromising expectation for results; and (c) describe given circumstances and how schools and the union can partner in future relationships to enhance progressive change efforts for significant school improvement.

Part III. This section contains three chapters that discuss (a) research on the effectiveness of study groups and learning communities in school improvement and

(b) examples of special types of study groups, i.e., student and principal study groups, and their applications.

Part IV. This section contains six chapters that give important insights into the key issues affecting school improvement. In particular, these chapters: (a) provide a comprehensive rubric for understanding and generating professional learning communities; (b) show how to build commitment for effective study groups and create and sustain learning communities; (c) use study groups and the WFSG process to bring about necessary and meaningful changes in the school culture; and (d) discuss in detail the process of data-based decision making and its application to enhance student achievement.

Part V. This section contains five chapters devoted to illustrating the successful application of *instructional strategies* in the WFSG process for improving student achievement in the classroom. The chapters in this section: (a) cover primary, elementary, middle, and high schools; (b) focus on such things as: strategies and activities, application of ideas in "real life," first-hand case studies, implementation of the WFSG System, action plans, rubric development, gap closing, data-based decision making, creation of quality teaching, lesson development, instructional troubleshooting, examination of student work, peer observation and mentoring, effective and ineffective lesson sharing, current literature, and action research; (c) contain several content areas, including reading, mathematics, English Arts, and languages; and (d) have among their success factors: a consistent and supportive administrative team, strong instructional leadership from within, a belief that study groups work, a decision to bring in "expert voices" for writing instruction and sound practices, use of data to drive instructional decisions, a commitment by all faculty members to make a difference in the life of a child, a study group intent on content "that matters" and an instructional focus.

Part VI. This section contains five chapters that offer perceptive stories relating to teachers and teaching. In particular, these chapters: (a) tell how meaningful professional learning for teachers is required for effective student learning; (b) explain how changing teachers' beliefs about students and learning can positively impact student learning; (c) recount a teacher's first-hand point of view of the transition and journey toward achieving school success; (d) describe team efforts of a principal and instructional specialist in planning and implementing school improvement that led to true collaboration, different learning styles, opposing viewpoints, and clashing personalities, all uniting together at one school for the purpose of improving teaching and learning and student achievement; and (e) introduce teacher evaluation into a model of sustained teacher collaboration that integrates expectations for self-directed professional growth and elements of shared instructional leadership, empowering both processes and providing a consistent and cohesive focus for increasing student achievement.

Part VII. This section contains four chapters that deal with state and national initiatives. These chapters: (a) unfold the story of how Louisiana and educators throughout the state are implementing in 170 schools, through their Learning-Intensive Networking Communities for Success (LINCS), an effective multidimensional

professional development process to support improved teacher and student performance; (b) tell how Georgia, in cooperation with business and nonprofit organizations
in the state, created the Georgia Leadership Institute for School Improvement, providing unique approaches to leadership development, policy influence, and research
and development that are positively affecting systematic changes with long-term
implications for student success; (c) relate insight into the roles and responsibilities
of the Georgia Department of Education and the significant potential they have to
influence proper school development; the critical ingredient being statewide dialogue followed by true, meaningful, long-term collaboration with and among all
education stakeholders, particularly schools, unifying ideas to ignite and sustain the
required change to perpetuate far-reaching, future-oriented school improvement;
and (d) describe the National Whole-Faculty Study Group Center, whose mission is
"to ensure student achievement through the authentic application of the WFSG
System in schools worldwide," accomplished through people, programs, products,
and resources.

Part VIII. School improvement and reform are both "significant local, state, and
national issues" *and* "truly global issues." What happens in this global arena will
become a critical part of the foundation for the long-term future growth and development of each member-nation in the world community. The chapter in this section
discusses both sides of "school improvement and reform" issues and then tries to
illuminate the positive and negative factors and circumstances for us for today and
tomorrow, as we attempt to prepare our people and country for the long-term future.

As a final editors' comment, the chapters in this fieldbook have been written by
thirty-five different people and offer a comprehensive content and wide variety of
perspectives. Consequently, we have tried to keep the "voice" of the authors in each
of the chapters so as to capture their essence as if they were talking directly to you,
the reader.

Acknowledgments

We acknowledge all of the members of the faculties and administrations who have implemented, sustained, and advanced the various elements of the Whole-Faculty Study Group System since its initiation in 1987. These people, individually and collectively, are silent heroes in the school-improvement movement across the nation. We continue to marvel at the richness of learning going on in their schools as a result of the committed leadership, effective work, and deepened understanding, persistence, and creative successes of these dedicated professionals.

We acknowledge, with great appreciation and respect, the thirty-five authors of the chapters in this fieldbook. Each of them, even under the stresses of complex employment responsibilities and demanding professional obligations, has been a committed partner in this fieldbook effort. They have created especially perceptive insights into critical aspects of nationally important school-improvement initiatives and unfolded in their chapters interesting, relevant, penetrating, and valuable professional stories for their readers to see, feel, understand, and use. Our authors have been the heroes in this fieldbook story.

We acknowledge our editors at Corwin Press, Rachel Livsey and Phyllis Cappello, for their strong initial encouragement for us to take on this fieldbook project and for their unwavering support during its development. Their wisdom and advice along the way proved to be both helpful and enlightening.

The contributions of the following reviewers are gratefully acknowledged:

Allan Alson
Superintendent
Evanston Township High School
Evanston, IL

James Kelleher
Assistant Superintendent
Scituate Public Schools
Scituate, MA

Charles F. Adamchik, Jr.
Corporate Director of Curriculum
Learning Sciences International
Blairsville, PA

About the Contributors

Lynn K. Baber has been an independent consultant for six years, during which she conducted staff development on Learning Styles and Teaching Styles, Communication Skills-Effective Writing Skills and Reading Strategies, Designing and Implementing Curricula for businesses and education, Team Building and Whole-Faculty Study Groups, and, in association with the National WFSG Center, launched and supported schools using the WFSG approach to school improvement, including ATLAS Community Schools and High Schools That Work. She worked in the Richmond County (Georgia) public schools, as a classroom teacher for seventeen years and an Instructional Technology Specialist for three years, providing support to elementary, middle, and high schools on the integration of technology with instruction and curriculum.

Gwendolyn Baggett is the Assistant Principal of the Richard R. Wright Elementary School, North Philadelphia, Pennsylvania. Prior to 2005, she was a teacher, Small Learning Community Coordinator, and Assistant Principal of the Eugene Washington Rhodes Middle School, Philadelphia, Pennsylvania. She, with Robin Cooper, developed Student Study Groups, mirroring the WFSG process. As a graduate of Temple University (BA), Antioch University (MED), and Cheyney University (Administrative Certificate), and an ordained Minister, she also served as the Site Director and Academic Coach for Freedom Schools, National Children's Defense Fund. Her passion is that "Every Child Can Learn and Will Learn" when we CARE!

Charlotte Ann Buisson is a professional educator who has devoted 30 years of her life to teaching and learning. As a classroom teacher, she learned the value of student portfolios and dedicated her teaching to finding ways to motivate students to become lifelong readers and writers. She holds National Board Certification in Early Adolescent English Language Arts, has been an educational consultant at the state and national levels for more than twelve years, and currently serves Louisiana as a Regional Coordinator for the Learning-Intensive Networking Communities for Success, a statewide program where she teaches model lessons and facilitates Whole-Faculty Study Groups in fifteen schools.

Karl H. Clauset is a Whole-Faculty Study Group Consultant with the National WFSG Center. Since 1999 he has helped many schools launch and implement WFSGs. He also assists district offices to align and support reform efforts in schools. Previously, he worked in standards-based reform and international education development at the Education Development Center, was on the faculty at the Boston University School of Education, and served as an elected school board member for six years. His dissertation, on effective schooling, received the 1983 ASCD Outstanding Dissertation Award. Earlier, he taught in secondary schools in Philadelphia, Indonesia, Zambia, and Tanzania.

Robin P. Cooper is the Principal of Leslie Pinckney Hill, a large elementary school in Philadelphia, Pennsylvania. She has served as a sixth- to eighth-grade teacher, administrative assistant, assistant principal, union representative, and project director for Children's Defense Fund. Recently, she was the 2005 recipient of the prestigious Dr. Ruth Wright Hayre Outstanding Achievement Award for her work in urban education. Currently, she is in doctoral studies in Saint Joseph's University. An avid believer that students must be challenged, she won local and national acclaim with her creation of student study groups, a program that focuses on student leadership, teachers, administrator transformational leadership, and Whole-Faculty Study Groups.

Angela S. Dillon has been the principal of Samuel E. Hubbard Elementary School, a six-year Title I School of Distinction, since 2000. She began her teaching career in 1981 and moved to the field of administration as an instructional assistant principal in 1994. She is the mother of two children, ages thirty-one and twenty, and lives in Forsyth, Georgia, with her husband of thirty-four years.

Beverly A. Gross is a third-grade teacher in Emporia, Kansas. She started her teaching career in St. Mary's, Georgia, in 2001 at Crooked River Elementary School. It was at Crooked River Elementary that she became a member of the original Focus Team for Whole-Faculty Study Groups in the fall of 2003. She has attended many different trainings and conferences for WFSGs. Since her move to Emporia, she has been a liaison for WFSGs and assisted the local professional development team and high school in the implementation of WFSGs.

Gale Hulme is an educator with twenty-nine years of experience, including high school English teacher, department chair, director of leadership development, executive director of organizational advancement, assistant superintendent of instructional services, and executive director of professional development. She has served with distinction on professional organizations, such as the National Staff Development Council's Board of Trustees (2002–2005), and was honored with the UCEA Excellence in Educational Leadership Award (2005). As Program Director for Georgia's Leadership Institute for School Improvement, she leads GLISI's systemic initiatives, including Leadership Preparation Performance Coaching (LPPC) and its core training offerings, Base Camp and Leadership Summit.

Terri L. Jenkins is an educational consultant working with schools and school systems providing guidance and staff development in Whole-Faculty Study Groups as well as a variety of instructional areas. She has worked with Carlene Murphy since 1988 and was a member of the first Study Groups formed in Richmond County seventeen years ago. A teacher for fourteen years, she amassed experience at all levels of K–12 education. She served an additional two years as an Instructional Technology Specialist for the Richmond County Schools in Augusta, Georgia. She holds a master's degree in Administration and Supervision and is currently a doctoral student at the University of South Carolina.

Steve Keyes has been staff development coordinator at Destrehan High School for the past nine years. Prior to that, he was a Spanish teacher at the same school. He has presented on many topics in several states and foreign countries.

Anita Kissinger has served as the staff development director for Springfield (Missouri) Public Schools since 2000. She is a summa cum laude graduate of Missouri State University and a graduate of the National Staff Development Council's Academy XIV. During her service as staff development director, the professional learning programs for teachers and leaders in Springfield Public Schools have been featured in NSDC publications (*Results* and *The Learning Principal*). She is an experienced facilitator and presents locally, regionally, and nationally.

Andrew E. Koenigs is Associate Superintendent for Academic Affairs at Andover Public Schools, Andover, Kansas. He earned his undergraduate teaching degree from Kansas State University and his master's and doctoral degrees in Educational Leadership from Wichita State University. His doctoral dissertation, *The Affects of Whole-Faculty Study Groups on Individuals and Organizations,* evaluated a districtwide implementation of Whole-Faculty Study Groups. In August 2007, he will begin his nineteenth year in education. He taught high school mathematics, served as a high school building administrator, and has eight years of experience in Curriculum and Instruction at the district level.

J. Patrick Mahon is a retired educator with thirty-seven years of educational experience. He served as a high school principal for twenty-three years, taught school law as a part-time assistant professor at the University of Georgia and Georgia State University, and was a Site Developer for ATLAS Communities from 2001–2005, where he worked with schools implementing Whole-Faculty Study Groups as part of the ATLAS process. He has published over twenty professional journal articles and the book, *School Law for Busy Administrators* (2005), by the Education Law Association. The Georgia Association of Educational Leaders presented him with its Outstanding Educator Award in 1991.

Michael Murphy is the Director of the Institute for Excellence in Urban Education. Earlier, he was Director of Product Research and Development Art, Westmark Systems; Executive Director of the Principal Assessment and Action Center, a collaborative of the Region 10 Educational Service Center, Dallas Independent School District, and Dallas Institute for Urban Leadership; Executive Lecturer, University of North Texas; and Director of Programs, National Staff Development Council. He has extensive experience in school districts in Texas as a teacher, principal, and assistant superintendent; lectured and facilitated strategic planning and professional development seminars; and published numerous journal articles and contributed to several educational books.

Julie J. Nall started her career as a fourth-grade teacher at Park Elementary School in Baton Rouge, Louisiana, and is now a curriculum writer/trainer for the East

Baton Rouge Parish School System. Earlier, she spent six years as a LINCS (Learning-Intensive Networking Communities for Success) Regional Coordinator for the Louisiana Department of Education, where she supported more than thirty schools in five school districts in implementing the WFSG System; modeled standards-based, technology-rich lessons; and provided coaching on research-based instructional practices proven successful with poor, low performing children, all empowering teachers to improve student achievement with components enduring in the school culture. She has been an Instructor for the Louisiana State University/LaSIP partnership (Mathematics Project) for the past seven years.

Deb Page began her career as a high school English teacher in Georgia, eventually transitioning to HR/Training with a passion to help adults succeed in their careers. She has managed broad-based curriculums, led business improvement projects, implemented a corporate university, served as a Senior Vice President for Citigroup, been recognized in several national magazines, and founded Willing Learner, Inc. In 2002 she became the first Executive Director of Georgia's Leadership Institute for School Improvement (GLISI). In this role, she leverages her more-than twenty years of experience to lead research/evaluation, policy influence, and performance-based training for educational leaders, research, and evaluation to support student achievement.

Sherman H. Parker is a retired Superintendent of Schools at Lake George Central in New York state. Since retiring, he has worked as a Site Developer for ATLAS Communities, consulting in a number of schools in the Albany, New York, area.

Xochitl Perez Castillo is a Special Education Bilingual-Spanish teacher at the John F. Kennedy Elementary School in Boston and a Research Associate for the Teacher Union Reform Network (TURN) of American Federation of Teachers (AFT) and National Education Association (NEA) Locals. She earned her Ph.D. in Social Sciences and Comparative Education from UCLA. She currently serves as a Faculty Representative on the Boston Teachers Union; is a candidate for the National Board for Professional Teaching Standards; and has been a delegate to the Conventions of the American Federation of Teachers, the Coordinator of the Supporting and Sustaining Teachers Project, University of Washington; and on the TURN/Broad Foundation's "Improving Student Achievement Through Labor-Management Collaboration" initiative.

Jill Potts is the Principal of the Coal Mountain Elementary School in Forsyth County, Georgia. She has been a teacher, an assistant principal, and a principal in Forsyth County since 1993. She received a bachelor's degree in English Literature from the University of South Florida, a master's degree in Early Childhood Education and an Education Specialist degree in Educational Leadership from Georgia State University, and is currently pursuing a doctoral degree in Instructional Leadership at the University of Alabama.

Stephen M. Preston is Director of Professional Learning in the Georgia Department of Education. He has served in the Department of Education (DOE) for over thirty years, primarily in leadership and teacher development; he led the Research and Evaluation Division, managed the Research and Development Utilization Program, and led the DOE in its strategic planning process under two state superintendents. He received the Distinguished Staff Developer Award from the Georgia Staff Development Council in 2003. Earlier, he was a teacher and a middle and high school principal for a total of nearly forty-two years of experience. Beyond his primary DOE role, he has taught in a public school or college for thirty-eight years.

Ann Proctor entered her career in education in 1971 as a Health and Physical Education teacher. Twenty-one years later, she became Superintendent of Schools in Camden County, Georgia. On her journey to becoming superintendent, she served in several administrative capacities at the elementary, middle, and high school levels; and she worked as a Director of Special Education, an Assistant Superintendent for Curriculum, and a Deputy Superintendent. As Superintendent, she focuses on improving student achievement through the use of the WFSG System and data, collaborative decision making, and open communication.

Kim Reynolds-Manglitz has a master's degree in Middle School Education from the University of Georgia and taught middle school science and language arts for six years before becoming a gifted collaborator and working for several years with sixth- through eighth-grade teachers to incorporate gifted strategies into classroom teaching. She is currently the Instructional Lead Teacher at Clarke Middle School.

Teri Roberts is a dedicated educator who is highly knowledgeable in the elementary mathematics curriculum. Standards-based lesson planning with constructed-response assessments is her area of expertise. She is skilled in helping administrators and teachers grow professionally. Students are the focus of all of her well-planned lessons and professional developments. Therefore, analyzing student work is her passion. She is an accomplished mentor in the Whole-Faculty Study Group Process in twenty-eight Louisiana schools. She has presented at the local, regional, state, and national levels.

Michael L. Rothman is cofounder of the Project for School Innovation (PSI), a nonprofit organization that uses school-to-school faculty study groups to help educators share their successes and drive school change. Under his leadership, as Executive Director from 2000 to 2005, PSI involved more than 250 educators in peer-learning networks through which they published fifteen books, produced seven videos, and developed more than 100 workshops to share their effective practices with educators everywhere. He holds a B.A. from Brown University and a M.P.P. from Harvard University, and served as a Jane Addams Fellow at Indiana University.

Kenneth Sherman has been Principal at Clarke Middle School in Athens, Georgia, since 1996. He is a native New Yorker and worked in the New York City Public Schools for ten years before moving to Athens in 1991. He earned a master's degree in English and American Literature from New York University in 1986, and a doctorate in Educational Leadership from the University of Georgia in 1997. He is married to Dr. Sherrie Gibney-Sherman, Associate Superintendent in the Jefferson (Georgia) City Schools system, and they share three children, Mollie, Alexandra, and Kellen.

Danette R. Smith is a school counselor for Paulding County Schools in Dallas, Georgia. Over the years, her dedication to student learning and awareness of the school environment's influence upon learning led to career decisions resulting in the completion of an Ed.D. in School Improvement from the University of West Georgia. Her dissertation research focused on professional learning communities and study groups as a means of generating learning communities. Currently, she is a middle school counselor fulfilling her dream of making a difference in the lives of those she serves.

Lisa S. Smith is a former elementary school principal, assistant principal, media specialist, and high school English teacher. Under her leadership, her school implemented Whole-Faculty Study Groups, resulting in vast improvements being made in student achievement, attendance, and parental involvement. She also has been involved in comprehensive school improvement efforts as part of the Georgia Governor's Office of Education Accountability and the Office of Student Achievement Standards and Grading committees. She is currently a school improvement consultant with a Georgia Regional Education Service Agency and serves on the Regional Support Team for the School Improvement Division, Georgia Department of Education.

Beverly S. Strickland is currently the Curriculum Director for Camden County Schools in Georgia. She has served the Camden County Schools as a classroom teacher, instructional lead teacher, assistant principal, and principal of St. Marys Elementary School. While at St. Marys Elementary School, she introduced her faculty to the Whole-Faculty Study Group System; the faculty embraced the concept and continued the work. She also authored materials for a chapter in the WFSG book by Murphy and Lick (2005).

Adam Urbanski is president of the Rochester (New York) Teachers Association and a Vice President of the American Federation of Teachers. A former high school teacher and college professor, he earned his Ph.D. from the University of Rochester and is an active proponent of change in education. He is the director of the Teacher Union Reform Network (TURN) aimed at creating a new vision of teachers' unions that supports needed changes in education, and has served as a trustee of the National Center for Education and the Economy, as a Senior Associate to the National Commission on Teaching and America's Future, and on the Federal Department of Education Board of Directors of the Fund for Improvement and Reform of Schools and Teaching.

Ronald D. Walker is the Associate Director of ATLAS Communities. He shares responsibility with the Director for leadership and management of ATLAS activities and staff and for outreach, marketing, and fundraising and development efforts; oversees the delivery of services to selected districts; identifies and negotiates strategic alliances; and has primary responsibility for the development and management of the annual Principals' Institute. He is the recipient of the Black Educators Award for Professional Service in Education (1995) and the Liberating Vision Award, presented by the National Council of Negro Women (Greater Boston), and a Harvard University Gates Fellowship for senior-level education-change coaches.

Emily Weiskopf is currently teaching fifth grade at her children's neighborhood school in Jacksonville, Florida, and, as a former teacher, academic coach, and district instructional specialist and an experienced staff developer in whole-school improvement, is consulting for the National WFSG Center, ATLAS Communities, and the

Springfield (Missouri) Public Schools. In an earlier position in the Springfield Public Schools in 2001–2004, she was instrumental in districtwide implementation of WFSGs, helping with the formation of WFSGs for Principals, which focused on current practice and new innovative approaches to coaching teachers, and reflected on instructional leadership and overseeing the development and implementation of School Improvement Plans.

Marcia R. Whitney is currently fulfilling her career goal as a professional development specialist as the Coordinator for School Development for the Washington-Saratoga-Warren-Hamilton-Essex BOCES in upstate New York. With more than thirty years devoted to the educational profession, she has held positions as an art teacher, special education teacher, educational and special education administrator, consultant, supervisor of student teachers for the State University of New York at Plattsburgh, and Site Developer for ATLAS Communities. Throughout these years of service, empowering teachers, students, and administrators through teaching, example, and leadership has remained her focus and guiding force.

Jeff Zoul is Principal of Otwell Middle School in Forsyth County, Georgia. He holds degrees from The University of Massachusetts, Troy State University, and The University of Southern Mississippi. He began his career in 1982 as a first-grade teacher, taught at the middle school and high school levels prior to serving as a school administrator, and has extensive experience in working with Whole-Faculty Study Groups. His educational passions include school climate and culture, classroom management, learning communities, and teacher morale.

About the Editors

 **Dale W. Lick** is a past president of Georgia Southern University, University of Maine, and Florida State University and is presently a university professor in the Learning Systems Institute at Florida State University. He teaches in the Department of Educational Leadership and Policy Studies and works on educational and organizational projects involving the Whole-Faculty Study Group System, school reform, school improvement, enhancement of student learning, transformational leadership, change creation, leading and managing change, learning teams, learning organizations, distance learning, new learning systems (e.g., the HyLighter Learning, Assessment and Collaborative Document Preparation System), strategic planning, and visioning.

Included in over fifty national and international biographical listings, he is the author or coauthor of six books, more than ninety professional articles and proceedings, and 285 original newspaper columns. Two of his recent books are *New Directions in Mentoring: Creating a Culture of Synergy* (with Carol A. Mullen, 1999), and *Whole-Faculty Study Groups: Creating Professional Learning Communities That Target Student Learning* (with Carlene U. Murphy; Corwin Press, 2005).

 **Carlene U. Murphy** is founder and director of the National WFSG Center and the principal developer of the Whole-Faculty Study Groups® system of professional development. In August 2007, she will begin her fiftieth year of work in public schools. She began her teaching career in 1957 as a fourth-grade teacher in her hometown of Augusta, Georgia, and retired from the district in 1993 as its Director of Staff Development. During her fifteen years as the district's chief staff developer, the district received many accolades, including Richmond County receiving the Award for Outstanding Achievement in Professional Development from the American Association of School Administrators and Georgia's Outstanding Staff Development Program Award for two consecutive years. She was awarded the National Staff Development Council's Contributions to Staff Development Award and served as the National Staff Development Council's chairperson of the annual national conference in Atlanta in 1986, president in 1988, and board member from 1984 to 1990.

Since retiring from the Richmond County Schools, she has worked with schools throughout the United States implementing Whole-Faculty Study Groups. She and her colleagues established the National WFSG Center in 2002, sponsoring annual National WFSG Conferences and WFSG Institutes and providing technical assistance to schools. She has written extensively about her work in *Educational Leadership* and *Journal of Staff Development*.

PART I

Getting Started

During the past twenty years, school personnel and boards, governmental agencies, and people across the country have been struggling with how to realistically "improve schools and enhance student learning." What they found was that there is just no easy or quick solution. Frankly, most educational reform efforts have been, at best, marginally successful, or they have failed to meaningfully increase either learning productivity or quality.

This section of the Fieldbook, *Getting Started*, introduces a major faculty-driven, school-change system for schools that has the potential to make a significant difference in productivity and quality for the schools in which it is effectively implemented. For those who want to gain a better perspective on school improvement in general or develop an overview sense of the Whole-Faculty Study Group (WFSG) System, the three chapters in this section provide: (a) a detailed introduction to study groups and effective faculty and school development for using them; (b) an explicit application of WFSGs in a typical school; and (c) an overarching perspective on the pivotal role professional development standards play in school improvement.

1

Introducing Whole-Faculty Study Groups

Carlene U. Murphy

Dale W. Lick

There is an old saying, "I didn't know what one was, and now I am one." That saying pretty much describes Whole-Faculty Study Groups as professional learning communities. Whole-Faculty Study Groups (WFSGs) did not begin as whole-faculty study groups. WFSGs began in 1987 as a part of a training design to support all of the teachers at a school who were implementing new teaching strategies in their classrooms. We wanted every student in the school to perform at higher levels. WFSGs began before they had a name. They also began before the phrase *professional learning communities* was the Number 1 topic in educational journals, conference presentations, and books. What seemed to us a commonsense strategy in 1987 is now "the thing to do." A few state departments of education have even gone so far as to mandate that schools have some form of professional learning community in place in schools. We have gone from hearing early in the WFSG work that "expecting every teacher in a school to be a member of a study group was undemocratic and unrealistic" to hearing today that "you (leaders in WFSG schools) are only doing what the research says to do." Guess what? We were the groundbreakers in research on professional learning communities (Joyce, Murphy, Showers, & Murphy, 1989; Murphy, 1992, 1995; Murphy, Murphy, Joyce, & Showers, 1988; Showers, Murphy, & Joyce, 1996). We are proud of the work we have done, and we are even prouder that we have remained true to our purpose in having a whole-faculty form of study groups focused on student needs. Twenty years later, WFSGs are still a structure to support teachers implementing new materials and strategies in their classrooms to address specific instructional needs. We have not shifted our focus, even though we have adjusted a few of our procedures based on feedback from schools. However, we have not lessened our expectations. Over the years, we have strengthened our spirit and our will to make the WFSG process one that exists for the *benefit of students.* This chapter unfolds a professional overview of the WFSG System and its application to create professional learning communities, improve schools, and enhance student learning.

WFSG SYSTEM DEFINED

The WFSG System is a job-embedded, self-directed, student-driven approach to professional development. It is a professional development system designed to build communities of learners in which professionals continuously strive to improve schools and increase student learning. This is accomplished by practitioners: (a) deepening their own knowledge and understanding of what is taught, (b) reflecting on their practices, (c) sharpening their skills, and (d) taking joint responsibility for the students they teach.

"Whole-faculty" means that every faculty member at the school is a member of a study group focusing on data-driven student instructional needs. In such a context, a study group is a small number of individuals, three to five, joining together to increase their capacities to enable students to reach higher levels of performance. The collective synergy of all the study groups advances the whole school.

The essence of the WFSG system resides in the following two "grounding" or "fundamental" questions:

- What do students need for teachers to do so that teachers will have a deeper understanding of what they teach?
- What do students need for teachers to do so that teachers will be more skillful in how they teach?

WFSGs are student based! Consequently, the "essential" or "overarching" question that guides the WFSG system is:

What are our students learning and achieving as a result of what we are learning and doing in our study group?

WFSG PRINCIPLES

The WFSG system is based on the following five guiding principles:

1. *Students are first.* WFSGs provide an approach to staff development that overtly puts the needs of students first. The theme "what do students need for us to do" runs throughout the WFSG books (Murphy & Lick, 1998, 2001, 2005) and throughout the WFSG process. Teachers in WFSG schools routinely examine student work collaboratively, listen to students, observe students in each others' classrooms,

and pay attention to a wide variety of student data. The *student voice* is heard and is the factor that makes what teachers do in study groups authentic.

2. *Everyone participates.* Every certificated person is a member of a study group with three to five members. Members of a study group may: teach at the same grade level or at different grade levels, teach in the same department or in different departments, and be special area teachers or regular classroom teachers. If teaching assistants have instructional responsibilities, they may also be members of study groups with teachers, or they may form study groups that have only teaching assistants as members. In some schools, nonteaching personnel form study groups to investigate ways they can support the instructional programs. Principals most often are members of study groups with other principals.

3. *Leadership is shared.* Every member of a study group serves as leader on a rotating basis. An *instructional council* consists of a representative from each study group and meets every four to six weeks as the primary study-group communication network. Members of study groups also rotate in attending council meetings.

4. *Responsibility is equal.* No one person in a study group is more responsible for the work than any other person. Everyone is equally responsible for every aspect of the group's work. Group norms are established at the first meeting, and every member holds every other member responsible for respecting and adhering to the norms.

5. *The work is public.* All the work of study groups is *public.* Action plans are posted in the school on clipboards or electronically. This is also true for the study group logs. Any teacher can ask a teacher in another study group about the work of a group. There are whole-faculty sharing times and printed summaries of what every group is doing. Sharing study group work is on the agendas of faculty meetings, grade-level meetings, and department meetings.

THE WFSG SYSTEM AND STUDENT NEEDS

The WFSG System is grounded in student instructional needs. The system is governed by a WFSG Decision-Making Cycle (DMC; see Murphy & Lick, 2005, p. 109). The DMC is a seven-step process. In Steps 1 through 4, the whole faculty meets to analyze student data and to specify student needs that study groups will address. Steps 5 through 7 occur after the study groups are formed and work begins.

WFSG PROCEDURAL GUIDELINES

The WFSG system is a framework or structure consisting of fifteen procedural or process guidelines. The guidelines make the expectations clear and also manage the group dynamics, defining relationships and behavioral norms. Study groups that routinely use the Checklist for Procedural Guidelines (Murphy & Lick, 2005, pp. 87–101, 239) to confirm adherence to the operational rules are much less likely to go astray.

THE WFSG RUBRIC

A rubric for WFSGs is presented in Chapter 10. This rubric analyzes the WFSG System and describes the expected behaviors. The rubric is divided into three components: Context, Process, and Content.

WFSGs for Whole School Improvement

Making the school better for all students is a constant function of every study group in the school. It is the collective energy and synergy generated from the study groups that propel the school forward. In particular, a student does not excel as a middle-school student because he or she had a great fourth-grade teacher. The more likely reason is because the student had outstanding learning opportunities as a kindergartener and first through fifth grader. Similarly, the middle school continues to excel because the students' teachers have an extensive repertoire and are masters of their content. The cumulative effect of good teaching over years of schooling produces a graduate who does well and can be expected to continue as a learner. When every teacher in a school is in a study group that targets effective teaching practices, an important range of schoolwide needs can be met. To focus on a schoolwide need, data and the effectiveness of curricula must be examined from all grades. For example, the fourth grade is not singled out because it is the grade in which the state tests are administered. If the standardized tests administered in the fourth grade indicate that reading comprehension is a problem, then that is a problem for all grades in the school.

In forming WFSGs, the faculty goes through a process of analyzing student and school data to identify student needs that study groups will address. When the needs are determined, groups form based on these needs. Each group then determines what its members will do when the group meets to address a specific student need. Often, this means examining what will enable teachers to use new and refined instructional practices and materials effectively in the classroom. Teachers also decide how they will support each other and the use, at the impact level, of new practices and materials. As study groups implement new and more effective practices and materials, each classroom improves, resulting in improvement in the whole school.

The goal of WFSGs is to focus the entire school faculty on creating, implementing, and integrating effective teaching and learning practices into school programs that will result in an increase in student learning and a decrease in negative behaviors of students, as reflected in related, relevant data sources.

WFSGs bring individual and institutional needs together in an organizational setting. Teachers become more skillful, knowledgeable, and confident as their study groups progress and gain competence and as their students become more skillful, knowledgeable, and confident. The power in the WFSG process rests in the promise that teachers will become more knowledgeable and skillful at doing what will result in higher levels of student learning. Study groups that function simply to satisfy interests of group members often lack adequate content focus to boost the goal of the school. The primary goal of schools is to meet student needs; therefore, it is the collective energy and synergy from the study groups and the whole faculty that propels the effectiveness of the school forward.

To our knowledge, the documented effects of study groups on students and the learning environment are limited to situations involving WFSGs' focusing on instruction. Schools that have successfully implemented the WFSG approach have many differences, such as those reflected in student age and level, location (e.g., rural vs. urban), socioeconomic circumstances, and size. Even with the many demographic differences in schools, we have not seen such factors make significant differences in how adults in schools work together in study groups.

Presenting the WFSG System to a Faculty

Faculties resist beginning "another new thing." The feeling of overload is so strongly felt by teachers that there is an immediate, automatic negative response to any new structure added to the already full day. WFSGs are presented as a way to facilitate what the teachers already have to do. Teachers already must design lessons using new curricula. In study groups, teachers work together on designing lessons using new curricula. Points that strengthen the cause for a new collaborative structure are that WFSGs are:

- A vehicle for collaboratively doing what teachers have been doing alone
- A structure for implementing the School Improvement Plan or a process for ensuring that targeted school goals are being addressed
- A structure totally devoted to how teachers teach and what teachers teach
- A place to work on the work of teaching and learning
- Not another program to be implemented in the classroom

The above points have softened the most entrenched resistors. However, the biggest hurdle by far is finding time for study groups to meet within the contract day. Within the past few years, more districts and schools are finding ways to release teachers for professional development. When we started this work in 1986, we could find very few, if any, schools that found time within the school day for teachers to collaborate. In 1994, the first school in Georgia to release students one hour early on Wednesdays for teachers to engage in professional development was a school implementing WFSGs in Americus, Georgia.

WFSG Results

Where properly implemented, the WFSG process has been unusually successful in facilitating schoolwide change and enhancing student learning (see, e.g., Joyce et al., 1989; Murphy, 1992, 1995; Murphy & Lick, 1998, 2001, 2005; and other chapters in this book, e.g., Chapter 5 and 7). The driving force in the WFSG process is its self-directed, synergistic comentoring learning teams (see Lick, 1999a, 2000, 2006). Such teams creatively:

1. Produce learning communities and set common goals, support member interdependence, empower participants, and foster active participation.

2. Plan and learn together.

3. Engage broad principles of education that modify perspectives, policies, and practices.

4. Construct subject-matter knowledge.

5. Immerse everyone in sustained work with ideas, materials, and colleagues.

6. Cultivate action researchers, producing, evaluating, and applying relevant research.

7. Struggle with fundamental questions of what teachers and students must learn, know, and apply (Murphy & Lick, 2005, p. 13).

The focusing question for study groups is: What is happening differently in the classroom as a result of what you are doing and learning in study groups? With that vision, "study groups are motivated, work harder, and take responsibility for the successful implementation of required processes and procedures" (Murphy & Lick, 1998, p. 18). The benefits include the following:

- Improvement is seen in the student needs areas that study groups target
- Culture shifts from isolation to collaboration
- Data are prominent in making instructional decisions
- Principals are more instructionally focused
- New teachers are in comentoring groups surrounded by support
- Teachers see themselves as action researchers
- New instructional initiatives are implemented sooner and more thoroughly
- Multiple initiatives are more coherent and integrated for maximum effects
- All teachers are viewed as leaders
- Behavioral norms for faculty become standard
- Looking at student work in collaborative settings becomes the norm
- Teachers take full responsibility for students represented in a study group

General Success Factors

WFSGs, by themselves, have little power to change anything. They are only a structure, a set of guidelines. The WFSG System is a job-embedded approach that gives teachers the opportunity to focus on specific student needs and how to reduce those needs. WFSGs are like a basket. The basket is only as good as what is put in the basket (e.g., guided reading) and where the goods are taken (e.g., classroom). The heart of the WFSG System is what teachers do to develop understanding of what they teach, what teachers do to become more knowledgeable about what they teach, what teachers investigate, and what teachers do to become more skillful in the classroom with students. Those "whats" are the content of study groups, and without appropriate content, the process is empty. Without intellectually rigorous work, the process is boring and can be a waste of time. It is substantive teacher work that requires teachers to immerse themselves in searching for deeper understandings of what they teach that creates high-performing, motivated study groups.

Members of WFSGs determine what they are going to do when study groups meet. If the work is boring, they determined it to be boring. If the time spent in study groups is a waste of time, they determined it to be a waste of time. If they determined it to be meaningful work, they determined it to be meaningful work. We have heard teachers blame course instructors, workshop leaders, and guest speakers for disappointing and uninspiring professional development. In WFSGs, members of study groups hold the key to either disappointing or inspiring work!

The WFSG process, centered around multi-level synergistic comentoring study groups is, in fact, a massive change management process. It is one of the most practical and effective approaches presently available in the literature.

In particular, the study-group process dramatically increases:

1. *Focus on imperative changes,* as determined by school personnel.

2. *Change sponsorship effectiveness,* both project and schoolwide.

3. *Preparation of change agents,* including the principal, faculty, and others.

4. *Commitment of targets and the reduction of resistance.*

5. *Positive advocacy,* including that of the school board, superintendent, principal, faculty, students, parents, and others from the general community.

6. *Individual, group, and school resilience,* enhancing stakeholders' change-adaptability.

7. *Knowledge of change and change principles for stakeholders.*

8. *Organized processes for transition,* including integrated, cocreative learning experiences that are teacher- and student-centered, experimental and research-oriented, reflective, supportive, and inspiring.

9. *Group synergy, comentoring, and learning team development,* setting new school operational and relationship norms for action research and improving learning systems.

10. *School and educational culture modification,* allowing a critical reexamination of basic assumptions, beliefs, and behaviors and required learning systems and practices (Lick, 2000; Mullen & Lick, 1999).

The WFSG process, through the above ten elements for leading and managing change, generates collective and inspiring vision and creates a high level of synergy and comentoring, allowing substantive learning, change, and continuous improvement to become the norm in the school workplace and culture.

IT'S NOT ABOUT THE MEETINGS

Even though the WFSG system may appear to be centered on study-group meetings, it is not. The system's heart is what teachers do between meetings. This may be the major difference between WFSG and other professional learning communities' designs. Think of a heart monitor. If groups meet, meet, meet, with little or no action in between the meetings, it is like the beep, beep, beep sound a heart monitor makes when someone dies or the flat lines that appear on the screen. When a patient is alive and well, the monitor shows a "▲" between beeps or between the flat lines. In WFSG, the upward movement is the action between meetings. A study group meets to plan and reflect; members go into their classrooms and take action on what was planned; the group meets to plan and reflect on what happened in the classroom; members go into their classrooms and take action on what was planned; the group meets to plan and reflect on what happened in the classroom; members go into their classrooms and take action on what was planned. The WFSG monitor looks like:

The meetings have no value without the action that occurs when members are in their classrooms. If meetings are boring, most often it is because members are not basing their work on what they do in their classrooms. The more action there is in the classrooms, the more meaningful are the meetings.

SUMMARY

The writers of the chapters in this book have presented the WFSG System from all directions and perspectives. They have magnified the weaknesses as well as the strengths. We did not attempt to temper their words. Some readers may focus on the weaknesses and use those negatives as a reason for not moving forward in determining whether WFSGs are right for their school. Some readers may focus on the strengths and positives of the WFSG System and want to know more about how to get started. The complexity of the WFSG System is made obvious through the examination of the WFSG Rubric, discussed in Chapter 10. Integrating WFSGs into an established, traditional school has many challenges and many rewards. As we have said before and repeat here: such work can lead to powerful results, but it is not for the fainthearted!

2

Applying the Whole-Faculty Study Groups Framework in Schools

Ann Proctor

During a 2003 superintendents' meeting, I listened intently as Carlene Murphy delivered an overview of the Whole-Faculty Study Group System. As she explained the process, I began to think this would be an excellent tool for the districtwide initiatives that were under way in Camden County. In my opinion, the Whole Faculty Study Group (WFSG) process was the perfect framework for formalizing our work because it provided the structure for the initiatives that Camden County Schools had begun. These initiatives already included making data-driven decisions, offering extensive professional learning, and totally revamping the instructional and curriculum design. Data indicated that each school had unique needs, and within the schools were teachers who had unique needs. Clearly these needs could be effectively addressed using the WFSG model.

THE SETTING

The philosophy behind Whole Faculty Study Groups and our own districtwide philosophy, which upholds the importance of school-based decision making, seemed to compliment each other very well. In addition, our overall philosophy was shifting from a hierarchy of leaders to a successful network of leaders who embrace effective communication, collaboration, and collegiality. WFSGs provide a formal structure to facilitate these essential elements.

Prior to Carlene Murphy's presentation, I had already come to the realization that the sharing of ideas and even more collaboration was necessary for establishing a unified focus. I felt we had already taken our first step in beginning to develop a similar approach as all principals and central office administrators were involved in a five-hour instructional effectiveness course. Out of this course came the notion that our schools should be more learning focused based on specific identified needs. Principals understood the expectation that they were to be the instructional leaders of their schools. Throughout the course, assignments were given that required administrators to become more involved in the instructional program based on their schools' needs. We found that the instructional effectiveness syllabus was very similar to the Brazosport model, which validated what we were already doing while pulling us together as a team. This model gave us an opportunity to experience the effectiveness of the collaborative process. Once the participants understood the benefits of collaboration, the expectation that the process would work was an easy sell. Collaborative efforts at the system level were effective and served as a successful model for the school level. Thus, my work began.

EXTENDING THE INVITATION

Carlene Murphy was invited to present her model of professional development to the administrators and central office personnel of Camden County. In keeping with our school-based decision-making process, principals were offered the opportunity to implement this professional learning model in their buildings. Adhering to the WFSG suggestions, principals were encouraged to implement WFSGs in their buildings under the condition that 80% of their teachers wanted to participate in this schoolwide initiative. Key to implementation of any program is acceptance by stakeholders. I feel that willingness to embark upon the WFSG journey was due in large part to the culture and philosophy of our learning community, which is built on a variety of belief systems. Practiced daily, these belief systems, consisting of open communication, collaboration, collegiality, and data-driven decision making, reinforce our commitment to increase student achievement. Because we had these systems in place, along with a climate of trust and teamwork, we could successfully implement WFSGs. I was delighted when more than 50% of Camden County's elementary schools chose to implement the WFSG model.

SUPPORT FOR THE PROCESS

As leaders of schools were asked to make commitments to increase student learning, I also made a commitment. I would support the work of the schools by designating Tuesdays as professional learning days for schools. Districtwide meetings were prohibited on Tuesdays in an effort to protect this important professional learning time. This turned out to be one of the most important norms set to meet the needs of the model. Schools that chose to implement WFSGs were provided financial support for professional learning as well as the materials needed to begin the process.

The process began when administrators and other faculty members from each school formed focus groups that met with Carlene Murphy to learn about the content, context, and process of WFSGs. They found that commitment to the process created stronger commitment to the content. The focus groups found that certain conditions, such as action plans, group size and norms, shared leadership, regular meetings, looking at student work, and utilizing resources, were nonnegotiable. The focus groups then took the work back to their respective schools and so the process continued.

WORKING ON THE WORK

Our school personnel knew that data analysis and disaggregation were the catalysts for our work. Our vision focused on continuous instructional improvement. In fact, our central office personnel had already begun book studies with school administrators, and I conducted a book study with members of our board of education. Although this was not the WFSG model, it was an insightful precursor to the process. We had begun the process of strategic planning at the district level, and we knew this planning must include those who were closest to the work. Curriculum had been aligned to meet district and state learning standards. Staffs had been provided with the support, resources, information, and training needed to align the curriculum and support student achievement priorities. The key was that teachers, as critical stakeholders, needed to analyze and disaggregate the data themselves for the data to be more meaningful. They needed to work in small groups in order to generate a supportive relationship, feel more responsibility for the work, and participate more in the process of instructional improvement.

DEFINING GROUPS AND SHARING LEADERSHIP

In our school system, a critical feature of the WFSG process was how group membership was determined. By gathering and analyzing assessment data, key stakeholders identified several areas in need of improvement. Once the needs, or study topics, were identified, participants chose the topic most relevant to their needs. Thus, study groups were formed. Next, participants requested norms from their administrators, and the administrators upheld those norms. Groups, as well, set their own norms and revisited them regularly. In discussions with administrators, I learned that shared leadership fostered group member accountability. "The principle of shared leadership is based on the belief that all teachers are leaders. The current norm is not expecting all teachers to be leaders" (Murphy & Lick, 2005).

ACTION PLANS AND LOGS

Another key feature of WFSGs was that of developing action plans and making them available to the school community. Making the work public seemed to give impetus to the work itself. By researching the problem, making a plan, practicing a new instructional strategy, and reporting on the effects of the strategy, the process of continuous improvement was formalized. It was important that administrators check the pulse of the work. They did so by providing feedback to all groups as their action logs were regularly submitted. When feedback is given and the work is made public, it is deemed important and given a higher priority. Stakeholders proudly exhibited WFSG work in their schools, which promoted its importance.

The action plan cycle followed the other models of learning by including the "plan, act, and reflect" format. "Each cycle of learning takes the study groups to higher levels of learning and deeper understanding. A study group experiences ongoing cycles throughout the school year" (Murphy & Lick, 2005). As teachers began to experience the plan, act, and reflect cycle, they began to experience the importance of the work. They began to understand how to search for best practices. These practices were implemented in classrooms, and then teachers were able to give each other timely feedback on how well those practices worked. Adjustments in instructional strategies were guided by the successes of the action plan. Teachers began to ask themselves the guiding question: *What are students learning and achieving as a result of what teachers are learning and doing in study groups?* They also began to understand the importance of the five WFSG guiding principles:

- Students are first
- Everyone participates
- Leadership is shared
- Responsibility is equal
- The work is public

MONITORING

Accountability is the buzzword in education today. Carlene Murphy keeps the administrators accountable in a tremendously favorable manner. Murphy continually seeks feedback from the schools and offers suggestions for improvement. The components of WFSGs naturally lend themselves to monitoring, and the action plans and logs, viewed and responded to by principals, provide an avenue for continual monitoring. The action plans and logs are not, of course, for evaluation; they provide direction for the group and allow the principal to make suggestions and provide resource information.

THE RESULTS

As a result of the WFSG process and the positive outcomes evidenced by the schools that participated in 2004, I am proud to state that the remaining schools are participating in WFSG orientation as this chapter is being written. Our achievement scores increased and all principals and schools who were involved in this unique professional learning process in 2004 are continuing the efforts this year. Data have been collected and disaggregated, and new study groups have been formed.

As I reflect on the comments made to me by the WFSG school administrators, I hear echoing themes. Camden County Schools have experienced teacher collaboration for years; however, most collaboration was experienced at grade levels or in special areas. Principals reveal that the collaboration and communication among teachers with similar interests and needs have been exceptional. Teachers and administrators are learning and sharing through this professional development strategy like never before. Most important, I hear about the collegiality demonstrated by school personnel. WFSG schools have become adult learning centers, where everyone participates and has shared leadership roles. Murphy and Lick (2001) state, "The unique strength of study groups comes from their functioning as self-directed, synergistic comentoring teams, setting common goals, working interdependently, empowering one another, and, in a balanced fashion, openly sharing their ideas and perspectives" (p. 153). The schools involved in the comentoring process experienced the following as predicted by Murphy and Lick (2005), who stated that teams creatively:

1. Produce learning communities and set common goals, support member interdependence, empower participants, and foster active participation

2. Plan and learn together

3. Engage broad principles of education that modify perspectives, policies, and practices

4. Construct subject matter knowledge

5. Immerse everyone in sustained work with ideas, materials, and colleagues

6. Cultivate action researchers, producing, evaluating, and applying relevant research

7. Struggle with fundamental questions of what teachers and students must learn, know, and apply

I believe all schools found this to be true of their comentoring teams. The authors (Murphy & Lick, 2001) add, "Through this learning approach, learning becomes an investment, and the norm, common goals, and expectations are set, compelling sponsorship for change is communicated and accepted, and creative synergy is enacted, enriching and enhancing everyone's efforts" (p. 171). This process has proven to provide synergistic energy to schools. It is this energy that has changed instruction in our schools.

MEETING NATIONAL STAFF DEVELOPMENT GUIDELINES

One final note on Whole Faculty Study Groups with regard to the National Staff Development Council (NSDC)—by following the guidelines of the NSDC, schools meet the highest level of NSDC's professional learning standards, which have been adopted by the Georgia Department of Education. I am delighted that all Camden County schools will now participate in a model that takes them to the highest level of national standards attainment.

RECOMMENDATIONS

The Whole Faculty Study Group process has been a venture in which I am proud many of our schools became and are becoming involved. The three essential components of the process and the National Staff Development Council—context, process, and product—are the backbone of professional learning. Each of these components must be considered as the organizational framework for increasing student achievement. I believe in this process and support this student-based professional development philosophy wholeheartedly.

Consider the elements of communication, collaboration, and collegiality and the roles they play in the learning communities. The WFSG process affords the opportunity for these elements to build on each other when teachers begin to reveal and study similar professional needs. Schools may have communication without collaboration or collegiality, but they cannot have collaboration or collegiality without communication. In this context, I believe that the leader must understand that communication must be "two-way" and that listening is essential. The leader must not only listen but must search to find ways to use input that is specific. So, talk with people, listen to their ideas, and use what is said, if possible, when making decisions. This begins to build trust, and leaders must have the trust of the learning community for successes to be realized. As leaders begin to listen and to use the input of others as decisions are being made, the barriers of leadership begin to break down. There will be less emphasis on the hierarchy of leaders and more on the network of leaders that includes administrators, teachers, and parents.

Each member of the learning community must truly feel that he or she has an opportunity to make a contribution. I am passionate about developing an effective learning community. But for me to be passionate about it is not enough. In our learning community, WFSGs are the formal structure that facilitates communication, collaboration, and collegiality that is essential for learning communities.

I am proud that, fortunately, our previous team-building efforts and sense of trust among administrators laid the foundation for the framework of Whole Faculty Study Groups. WFSGs have become the vehicle for our continuous improvement initiatives by providing structure for our efforts.

3

Aligning Whole-Faculty Study Groups With Staff Development Standards

Michael Murphy

Standards-based education has continued to be the rallying cry of education. Indeed, standards-based thinking not only permeates curriculum and assessment but also quality staff development. In thinking about Whole-Faculty Study Groups, then, the "cutting-edge" educator will want to ponder and answer this essential question: Will the design and implementation of Whole-Faculty Study Groups be an effective school improvement design, illustrating the highest standards for adult learning? This chapter attempts to answer this salient question and supply the reader with (a) background for professional learning standards, (b) examples of how WFSGs merge beautifully with quality staff development, and (c) a tool for assessing the effectiveness of WFSGs on the journey to quality adult learning.

PROFESSIONAL DEVELOPMENT AND STANDARDS-BASED THINKING

A key feature of Whole-Faculty Study Groups is in the job-embedded nature of its school-focused informal research and action. Whole-Faculty Study Groups (WFSGs) are a powerful design for professional development when five fundamental principles are present at a school (Murphy & Murphy, 2004):

- Student results are paramount
- Everyone is committed to participate in the WFSGs
- Everyone agrees to assist in the leadership of the WFSGs
- All are willing to share the responsibility for results
- The work of the WFSGs is seen as a publicly professional practice

In every case, the impetus and design of WFSGs should be grounded in the particular nature of that school. In other words, (a) the unique nature and culture of the school, (b) the unique adult learning content to be explored or gained, and (c) the unique method in which the WFSGs are organized and developed must be considered, celebrated, supported, and continually evaluated. Thus, those constructs—context, process, and content—serve as our beginning framework for thinking about WFSGs and the results of WFSGs on the students of the school.

CONTEXT, PROCESS, AND CONTENT

Indeed, the conceptual framework of context, process, and content was first introduced to document the connection between professional learning and student learning (Sparks, 1983). In that article, Sparks introduced the context, process, content framework to organize the results of her research. In essence, the work revealed that the three components necessarily existed in unison to ensure that professional learning was designed and implemented to improve student learning. A brief explanation of these three components follows (National Staff Development Council [NSDC], 2001):

- *Context:* What are the conditions in the school that exist to support professional learning? The idea of context refers to the organizational structures, systems, and overarching culture in the school that may either accelerate or block the school's intended efforts.

- *Process:* In what ways is the professional learning being implemented and evaluated? Process, then, is the "how" of staff development—the methods by which the professional learning is being planned, enacted, institutionalized, and evaluated to ensure that the adults are acquiring their new knowledge and skills and embedding them in daily practice.

- *Content:* What is being learned to promote student achievement? If process is the "how" of professional development, content is the "what." Content, then, refers to the actual skills and knowledge the educators want to gain and implement to ensure that their students are more successful.

THE DEVELOPMENT OF STANDARDS FOR CONTEXT, PROCESS, AND CONTENT

Within each of these three constructs for quality professional learning, the National Staff Development Council has delineated measures, or standards, that further define and clarify either the context, process, or content of quality adult learning for student results. The 12 standards and descriptions (Easton, 2004) are as follows:

Context Standards:

- *Learning Communities:* Organizing adults into learning communities where the goals are aligned with those of the school and the district
- *Leadership:* Requiring, nurturing, and supporting skillful school leaders who collaboratively guide continuous instructional improvement
- *Resources:* Requiring resources to support the adult learning and the collaboration to achieve the goals

Process Standards:

- *Data-Driven:* Using disaggregated student achievement data to determine adult learning priorities and monitor progress
- *Evaluation:* Using multiple sources of information to guide improvement and to demonstrate its impact
- *Research-Based:* Preparing educators to practice and apply principles of informal research to decision making
- *Designs and Strategies:* Using learning strategies that are related to the intended learning goal
- *Learning:* Applying knowledge about human learning and personal change to the goal
- *Collaboration Skills:* Providing educators with the knowledge and skills to effectively and efficiently collaborate for student achievement gains

Content Standards:

- *Equity:* Preparing educators to understand and appreciate all students and create supportive learning environments
- *Quality Teaching:* Deepening educators' content knowledge and providing them with research-based strategies to assist students
- *Family Involvement:* Providing educators with knowledge and skills to involve families and other community stakeholders

The content standards define the nature and scope of school improvement content for educators, such as (a) understanding learning differences, (b) ensuring safe learning environments, (c) planning with high expectations for students, (d) using classroom assessments, and (e) promoting family and community involvement in schooling. While these standards are important to consider when planning for WFSGs, it is understood that the particular nature of the content of the adult learning will depend on the unique analysis of student achievement data at that school.

Of particular interest to those implementing WFSGs are the context and process standards, as the analysis of each of these nine standards can give the leaders of WFSGs ways of assessing the quality of their professional development efforts in action.

THE UTILITY OF STANDARDS-BASED THINKING

The National Staff Development Council Standards for Staff Development, then, can be viewed as measures of relative quality and impact by which designers of WFSGs continually assess the results of this particular powerful design. While all educators devoted to quality professional learning can immediately confirm the value of the NSDC Standards, many staff developers and WFSG advocates frankly do not know what to do with the NSDC Standards once they have adopted them. In response to this need, NSDC, in partnership with the Southwest Educational Development Laboratory (SEDL), developed Innovation Configurations for each standard (National Staff Development Council & Southwest Educational Development Laboratory, 2003). The original concept of Innovation Configuration was developed in the 1970s by a University of Texas research team that was working on understanding change as it relates to people and the change innovation itself. Simply, Innovation Configurations develop and apply word-picture descriptions of what the change can look like at various stages of its change "life" (Hall & Hord, 2001).

STANDARDS AND THE STAGES OF DEVELOPMENT OF WFSGs

When implementing WFSGs, school leaders have a clearly designed framework to follow, including detailed instructions outlined in the WFSG decision-making cycle (Murphy & Lick, 2005). Yet anyone who has been involved in this kind of whole-school improvement effort knows that the tendency to adapt, modify, and mutate aspects of WFSGs is a natural part of the developmental change process; indeed, the implementation of WFSGs depends on implementing the design based on the unique context of the school setting. So, the Innovation Configuration (IC) Maps, organized around each of the NSDC Standards, can detail the various descriptions of different variations of actualizing the particular standard as it relates to WFSGs. Let's take an example:

HOW IC MAPS CAN HELP ASSESS THE PROGRESS OF WFSGs

The first NSDC context standard is Learning Communities. This standard is defined as: "staff development that improves the learning of all students and organizes adults into learning communities whose goals are aligned with those of the school and district" (National Staff Development Council, 2001). It is clear to designers of WFSGs that this standard is inherent, indeed key, to the concept of the principles that undergird WFSGs. The NSDC Standards IC Maps then further break down this standard into "desired outcomes" (NSDC & SEDL, 2003). The desired outcomes for the Learning Communities Standard are:

1.1 Meet regularly with colleagues during the school day to plan instruction

1.2 Align collaborative work with school improvement goals

1.3 Participate in decision-making responsibilities within the school

1.4 Participate in learning teams, some of whose membership extends beyond the school

For each of these desired outcomes, NSDC has provided an IC Map, a continuum of practices and variations, in word-picture descriptions. The Map that has been developed for the outcome 1.1, for example, looks like the following (NSDC & SEDL, 2003): Level 1 describes the most ideal description of this standard in practice. Level 6 describes the most unwanted description of the standard or, in other words, the "null" version of that outcome. As one moves from Level 6 to Level 1, the described behaviors and practices become increasingly more ideal as viewed by the innovation developers or managers (Hall & Hord, 2001). The IC Map for the Learning Communities Standard, Outcome 1.1, *"Meet regularly with colleagues during the school day to plan instruction,"* is shown in Table 3.1.

Here is where the power of Innovation Configuration Maps becomes clear for the Whole-Faculty Study Group leader. The leaders of WFSGs can use these Innovation Configuration Maps to assess the quality of the implementation of WFSGs as a change innovation. These Maps were used recently by a school leadership team at a school I have been assisting. An example follows.

Table 3.1   IC Map for Learning Communities Standard, Outcome 1.1

Level 1	Level 2	Level 3	Level 4	Level 5	Level 6
Meets regularly with learning team during scheduled time within the school day to develop lesson plans, examine student work, monitor student progress, assess the effectiveness of instruction, and identify needs for professional learning.	Meets regularly with learning team during the school day to plan instruction, examine student work, and monitor student progress.	Works with learning team on special instructional projects during planning time.	Works with others on non-instructional issues. Addresses personal concerns, not group issues.	Uses planning time for individual planning.	Uses planning time for non-instructional tasks, such as management and personal tasks.

AN EXAMPLE IN PRACTICE

The school improvement leadership team at Lakeview Elementary School meets monthly to assess the progress of their Whole-Faculty Study Group effort. This year there are nine study groups, each focusing on an aspect of student learning needing improvement. The facilitator of each study group changes periodically, and four times a year the leadership team meets with the current facilitators of the study groups to ascertain variations in the process and to determine the collective status of the groups. To do this, the leadership team has been using the National Staff Development Council's Innovation Configuration Maps for the NSDC Standards. Several actual IC Maps or adaptations of the maps are used for this rich conversation among the members of the leadership team and the facilitators. For this particular meeting, the leadership team has chosen the standard, Learning Communities, and is focusing on Desired Outcome 1.1, "The teacher meets regularly with colleagues during the school day to plan instruction" (NSDC & SEDL, 2003). Instead of using exactly the word-picture descriptions of the six levels published by NSDC and SEDL, however, the team has modified the IC Map to more closely reflect the desired outcomes of this standard in context (see Table 3.2).

The learning team has been using their specifically adapted IC Maps to discern the progress of their study groups and to indicate ranges of quality and fidelity, as well as to continuously describe how closely their study groups mirror their "word pictures" of ideal practice. Each time the team meets with the facilitators, they collectively draw two lines on the particular IC Map indicating benchmarks and ranges

Table 3.2 IC Map in Action

Level 1	Level 2	Level 3	Level 4	Level 5	Level 6
The groups meet regularly during the school day to develop theories about their learning and the impact on students, share lesson plans that show implementation of the strategies, examine student work, and identify ongoing needs for additional professional learning.	The groups meet regularly during the school day to develop theories about their learning and the impact on students, share lesson plans that show implementation of the strategies, and discuss student work.	The groups meet frequently during the school day to read, discuss, and research their focus area and to develop theories about their learning and the impact on students.	The groups meet frequently during the school day to read, discuss, and research their focus area and to discuss some group and some personal issues.	The groups meet sporadically during the school day and after school to read and discuss their focus area.	The groups meet infrequently during the school day and after school to discuss their focus area.

of acceptability. At this point in the implementation of WFSGs, the team recognizes that their expectation is that all faculty members are participating in the study groups and that the groups are meeting more than sporadically, which is why the team has drawn a solid line to the right of Level 4, indicating that all variation to the right has been judged as "unacceptable" ways for demonstrating this standard as it relates to the WFSGs. Similarly, the team also draws a dashed line to show all descriptions to the left of that line that are considered to be "ideal." In essence, the team believes that those behaviors and practices to the left of the dashed line are expectations of the future but not presently descriptions of what they expect to regularly observe when thinking about this particular outcome of the WFSGs. Those practices between the solid line and dashed line are still viewed by the team as "acceptable" and what they would fully expect to see at this point in the implementation.

IMPLICATIONS AND SUGGESTIONS FOR USING THE STANDARDS TO ASSESS THE QUALITY

Leaders of WFSGs, then, can point to the NSDC Standards for Staff Development as benchmarks by which to continually evaluate the effectiveness and efficiency of the study group school improvement design. By crafting such tools as Innovation Configuration Maps, the designers and managers of WFSGs have ready-to-use measures with which to frame their regular conversations with school improvement teams at their schools.

Indeed, leaders might organize to use the Standards, Outcomes, and IC Maps to evaluate not only the effectiveness of WFSGs but also any school improvement effort designed to increase the competency of the adults in the school so students may achieve more. Let's suppose that the leaders of the school improvement team have designed and implemented WFSGs at a school to address some specific student achievement gaps in reading, mathematics, and science. The groups have formed, and all staff members are participating in the groups, attending district staff development training sessions, reading pertinent books, and beginning to implement strategies that they are sharing with others at the school. The school improvement team meets in November, after the start-up in August, and designs a management plan to incorporate the NSDC Standards and IC Maps to assess progress and results, shown in Table 3.3.

CONCLUSION: WFSG SYSTEM PASSES THE STANDARDS-BASED TEST

It is clear, when reviewing the NSDC Standards for Staff Development, that WFSGs are a professional development and school improvement design that seems to mirror the "ideal" practices as indicated by each of the NSDC Standard's descriptions. The implementation of WFSGs, then, can comfort school improvement leaders with the knowledge that this design mirrors the best of what we know about standards-based professional learning. The Innovation Configuration Maps designed from the Standards, then, can be powerful conversation and evaluation tools to

Table 3.3   Standards Management: Year One of WFSGs

November	*December*	*January*	*March*	*April*	*May*
The team meets and discusses the 12 Standards and selects the two-three Standards on which to focus. The team then selects those four-five outcomes that best describe its goals for the first year of implementation of WFSGs at its school.	Taking those four-five outcomes, the team designs IC Maps to illustrate the variation in behaviors and practices for each. The team then devises how it will collect information about the IC Maps and commits to the collection of information for two Maps to share at the next meeting.	The team draws lines to show the range of acceptability for each of the two maps to be discussed and shares that information. The gap between the "expected" and the "actual" is discussed as well as implications for the management of the WFSGs and changes, if any, to the organization or management of the WFSGs.	The team meets and discusses any adjustments to the WFSGs made in reaction to the data collected and discussed in January. The team then determines lines of acceptability for the other IC Maps and discusses information to gather and share at its next meeting.	The team meets and shares the collected information, then discusses adjustments to the WFSGs made in reaction to the data collected and discussed. Decisions to make adjustments or collect more data are made and delegated.	The team discusses any additional data and displays all Maps, detailing where it believes the WFSGs are in their first year of implementation. Decisions and adjustments are discussed for the management and the design for year two.

assess the impact of the WFSG work. In essence, the use of the IC Maps, whether from the NSDC and SEDL publication or school-adapted, takes a snapshot in the overall progression toward standards-based adult learning and practice. When applying the NSDC Standards as a measure of rigor and effectiveness, WFSGs appear to pass the test with flying colors.

PART II

Leadership and Sponsorship

In major change efforts, such as school reform, *leadership* and *sponsorship* are two fundamental essentials. No significant school-change approach should be initiated without having in place strong and effective leadership and sponsorship. As Kouzes and Posner (2002) relate,

> The *leadership challenge* is about how leaders mobilize others to want to get extraordinary things done in organizations. Its about the practices leaders use to transform values into actions, visions into realities, obstacles into innovations, separateness into solidarity, and risks into rewards. It's about leadership that creates the climate in which people turn challenging opportunities into remarkable successes. (p. xvii)

And change expert Conner (1993) similarly reminds us that:

> Effective leaders are capable of reframing [their own thinking and] the thinking of those whom they guide, enabling them to see that significant changes are not only imperative but achievable. (p. 9)

Conner (1993) also tells us about *sponsors* and their importance to change:

> A *sponsor* is the individual or group [e.g., principal, superintendent, or board] who has the power to sanction or legitimize change. . . . Major change will not occur unless the appropriate sponsors demonstrate sufficient commitment. . . . When sponsors don't fully understand a project's implications or are unwilling or unable to take the necessary action, advocates must either convince the sponsors of the importance of the change, be in a position to replace them with people who will provide the needed support, or prepare for the change to fail. (pp. 106, 112–113)

This section of the Fieldbook, *Leadership and Sponsorship,* contains three chapters illustrating authentic leadership and sponsorship situations, two relating to principals as leaders and sponsors, one with the school district as sponsor, and one with union collaboration to strengthen leadership and sponsorship. These chapters: (a) focus on practices of principals who help their teachers and WFSGs experience success, while enhancing the principal's effectiveness as an instructional leader; (b) unfold an implementation sequence that began centered on student learning, moved to process alignment at all levels, and continued with district-level support for quality implementation and an uncompromising expectation for results; and (c) describe given circumstances and how schools and the union can partner in future relationships to enhance progressive change efforts for significant school improvement.

4

Enhancing the Principal's Instructional Leadership Role

J. Patrick Mahon

To say that being a principal is a difficult job is a gross understatement. In the era of No Child Left Behind, the demands on already-stressed school leaders have escalated dramatically. Even under these heavy commitments, though, principals can and must make a world of difference in their schools.

Research clearly shows that job-embedded professional development in the Whole-Faculty Study Group (WFSG) System provides a process that can make a positive and significant difference in the ways teachers teach and students learn. This chapter, therefore, focuses on practices of principals who help their teachers and Whole-Faculty Study Groups experience success, while dramatically enhancing the principal's effectiveness as an instructional leader.

PRINCIPAL AS JUGGLER

Once, when I was a high school principal, I asked an art student to do a caricature. Basically, I asked him to draw me as a juggler and I gave him a long list of the alphabet soup that made up my life as a principal. As it turned out, I was juggling about twenty balls, each one of them labeled with a different program or responsibility. Things have not changed for the principals that I am working with in ATLAS Communities schools.

Standards, No Child Left Behind, Adequate Yearly Progress (AYP), Comprehensive School Reform (CSR), WFSGs, parent and community involvement, school councils, safety and security concerns, the flavor-of-the-month top-down reform initiative, closing achievement gaps, car riders, bus riders—the list goes on and on. Yes, the principal is expected to juggle numerous programs and responsibilities.

KEY FOCUS FOR THE PRINCIPAL

As a Site Developer—a person who works with schools to implement ATLAS Communities (ATLAS)—I now have a much clearer perspective on the primary focus schools and their principals should have. Now, I personally believe that improving student understanding, which is a cornerstone of the ATLAS design for school improvement, is the primary responsibility of the principal. Howard Gardner, David Perkins, Tina Blythe, and their colleagues at Harvard's Project Zero have worked to define what it means to teach for understanding. Blythe's (1998) definition captured the early essence of Harvard Project Zero's definition of teaching for "student understanding":

> Understanding is being able to carry out a variety of actions or "performances" that show one's grasp of a topic and at the same time advances it. It is being able to take knowledge and use it in new ways. (p. 13)

Recently, David Perkins (2004) reframed the concept of "understanding" into a more comprehensive concept:

> The knowledge arts include communicating strategically, insightfully, and effectively; thinking critically and creatively; and putting knowledge to work in what educators sometimes humbly call the "real world." The knowledge arts bundle together deep reading, compelling writing, strong problem solving and decision making, and the strategic and spirited self-management of learning itself, within and across disciplines. (p. 14)

Even in an era of standards, focusing on student understanding helps principals focus their efforts on what really matters. Teachers will sometimes complain that they have so much to cover for the state test that they cannot teach in depth. Newmann's research (Newmann, Bryk, & Nagaoka, 2001) in the Chicago schools puts this concern to rest: "Assignments calling for authentic intellectual work actually improve student scores on conventional tests." A persistent focus on student understanding helps principals juggle the many balls they are trying to keep in the air.

THE POWER OF WHOLE-FACULTY STUDY GROUPS

Whole-Faculty Study Groups (WFSGs) provide the principal with an excellent vehicle for school reculturing that focuses on student understanding. WFSGs provide the opportunity for job-embedded ongoing professional development. They give teachers the opportunity to meet with colleagues on a regular basis in order to look at student work and improve their instructional efforts so that students will gain greater understanding.

Study groups begin with data. What are the student needs that must be addressed? Once the study group develops its Action Plan around identified student needs, the main work of the study group is to examine student work. Using protocols to analyze student work helps the study group determine whether students truly understand.

A teacher brings the work of an elementary student who cannot write legibly or communicate in writing to her study group. The group examines the work. A member of the study group suggests that the teacher highlight in different colors the words she wants the student to copy on the lined paper. This simple suggestion allowed the student to focus on one word at a time. By the end of the year, the student was writing legibly and effectively communicating his thoughts in writing. For the first time in his brief academic career, this student experienced success. He developed a deeper understanding of the writing process. Such is the power of WFSGs!

RECOMMENDATIONS FOR PRINCIPALS

Whether all WFSGs achieve the same powerful results depends in large part on the principal. I see my role as a Site Developer as being the "guide at the side" of principals as they implement ATLAS approaches to improving schools and increasing student achievement. Based on my experience over the past three years, I offer the following suggestions to principals who want to use Whole-Faculty Study Groups to focus on improving student understanding.

Being Involved in the WFSG Process

The principal must be involved in the process. Today's principal must be a reflective practitioner and must model the value of lifelong learning for the faculty, staff, and students. This is not the chicken-and-egg type of involvement. This is the pig-and-ham type of commitment! The Decision-Making Cycle (DMC) in the *Whole-Faculty Study Group* book (Murphy & Lick, 2005) is an excellent process guide for the principal. Reculturing the school to focus on student understanding is, indeed, a process, and the DMC guides the principal through the study-group process, which supports increased student understanding. The principal who visits study groups, reads and comments on logs, and provides resources for study groups to do their work is the principal who will have efficient and effective study groups. All these activities give evidence that the principal is fully vested in the process—fully sponsoring the school's and teachers' efforts to improve student achievement.

Commenting on Action Plans and Logs

The principal's comments on the action plans and logs are critical. Others can comment on these, but it will have much less impact than the comments of the principal. In larger schools, members of the administrative team can comment on the action plans and logs. In such cases, I suggest that the members of the administrative team rotate the responsibility of commenting on logs so that every group gets some feedback directly from the principal during the year. However, "Way to go!" or "I enjoyed reading your log!" are probably not good comments. Comments on the action plans and logs should be robust and follow the commonly accepted norms for providing feedback. Specific comments that focus on sound instructional practices are the most effective.

Keeping Study Groups Focused

The principal must keep the study groups focused on the task at hand. I have seen situations where study groups have devolved into unstructured discussion groups or committees because the principal did not hold their feet to the fire. Effective study groups use protocols to examine student work. Protocols give the group members the structure needed to examine student or teacher work in depth. Study groups have to research their essential questions; however, after the action plan is developed, study groups should be spending the majority of their time examining student work with the appropriate protocols. Examining student work enables teachers to improve their effectiveness as they teach for student understanding. I just finished summarizing the WFSG Evaluation forms from the schools where I am the Site Developer. I was not surprised when I got comments that some teachers had much better meetings without all the structural ties imposed by using protocols. Not so! Experience has shown that protocols structure groups to delve deeper into the student and teacher work.

Focusing on Research

The principal must help study groups set aside a segment of their time to do ongoing research. Reading books together, surfing the Web, and watching videos are activities that give study-group members new ideas for improving instructional practice. For example, with regard to printed materials, there are techniques such as jigsawing and The Final Word Protocol (Baron & Averette, n.d.) that can enhance the learning experience.

Using the Decision-Making Cycle

The principal should use the DMC as an excellent tool for bringing together various components of school improvement. The schools I have had the privilege of working with, such as in Cherokee County, Georgia, prepare School Improvement Plans and revise them annually. These schools also have data management teams. The schools often have new curriculum initiatives. The ever-present demands of No Child Left Behind are always lurking in the shadows. State and local testing programs provide valuable data. Using all sources of data about the school, the principal can lead the faculty through the DMC early in preplanning. The data from all sources will help determine the essential questions for the study groups. If the principal manages the process wisely, there will be a seamless connection between the work of the study groups, the School Improvement Plan, the work of the data management teams, and curriculum initiatives. This approach also has the added advantage of not adding anything to the principal's already full platter.

Sharing the Work

It is the principal's challenge to make sure the work of the study groups is shared with those who are not members of the study group. There is some value in posting the action plans and logs. This makes the work public and gives others the opportunity to find out what other study groups are doing; in three years, however, I have never seen anyone reading the posted action plans and logs. Nevertheless, I do know that teachers, central office staff, parents, and community members read the logs when they are posted in a high-traffic area. In smaller schools, principals have found it to be an effective practice to have study groups report on their work at faculty meetings. In larger schools, reporting could be rotated with different groups presenting at the faculty meetings.

Using Data

Principals must reflect to all that data collection and accountability are facts of life in schools today. No longer can a teacher say, "I tried a new technique; therefore, the students must have learned." The teacher must have evidence. Evidence is at the core of the study group process. The newly revised action plan really tightens up the process of gathering evidence of student success.

The principal should work with teachers to provide whatever professional development is necessary for them to get comfortable with using data for improvement and accountability. Accountability must go beyond the data from state testing programs. The tests come out only once a year and often not in a very timely manner.

Supporting Core Practices

ATLAS works with schools on four core practices related to teaching and learning: looking at student work, essential questions, authentic assessment, and curriculum alignment. This is a comprehensive process for instructional improvement. When teachers frame instruction in terms of essential questions, they set up conditions for teaching in depth and enhancing student understanding. Working in study groups, teachers can frame essential questions related to state and local standards. This promotes curriculum alignment. Finally, authentic assessment techniques will tell teachers whether their students understand. Once teachers learn how to use rubrics, portfolios, exhibitions, and other forms of authentic assessment, they will be able to "dipstick" throughout the school year to gather ongoing evidence of student progress. *Principals must grasp these core practices and make sure that study groups are addressing them in their work together.*

Looking Deeper

I was intrigued by a new book by Peter Senge and his colleagues (Senge, Scharmer, Jaworski, & Flowers, 2004). These authors talk about the importance of "seeing" and "seeing deeper." If we have a vision of an educational system that works and provides equity and excellence for every student, *principals and teachers must develop strategies to see things anew, to look deeper, and to address root issues related to teaching, learning, and student understanding.* I recently heard a commentator say that we are spending our time shooting mosquitoes when we should be draining the swamp. What does No Child Left Behind really mean? How can teachers reflectively practice strategies that teach for student understanding for every student? Again, if the principal is not focused on draining the swamp, the teachers will not be focused on that task either. Study groups help teachers to look deeper and work toward a vision of teaching in depth for student understanding.

Dealing With Reluctant Teachers

Principals have to help others see the importance of draining the swamp and of seeing things differently. As change agents for student understanding, principals always face the challenge of coping with those who see themselves as being beyond school improvement. They are quick to tell you that they learned everything they need to know about teaching for student understanding in their undergraduate programs thirty years ago! *Principals should recognize that change is difficult for many people, and teachers are no exception.* I really like Howard Gardner's new book, *Changing Minds* (2004). This book gives principals a framework for dealing with change and different reactions to change.

Every principal has at least a few trailblazers. The principal briefly mentions a new strategy in a casual conversation, and the trailblazers are implementing it the next day! Every principal has homesteaders who are not going anywhere unless they can be convinced. After all, they have survived several principals and numerous flavor-of-the-month change initiatives. If push really comes to shove, the principal can help the hard-core outlaws, who disrupt every change effort, to find other options. Knowing his or her staff, *the principal has the responsibility for bringing staff members along as study groups are implemented.* The materials in the WFSG book (Murphy & Lick, 2005) provide valuable guidance on the change process. The Concerns-Based Adoption Model (CBAM) is a tool that gives pointed guidance to principals on implementing change (CBAM, n.d.)

Celebrating Work and Success

Sometimes we get so serious about school reform and accountability requirements that we become too somber. *It is important for principals to make sure that members of study groups celebrate their successes.* In support of such successful efforts, *the principal must genuinely reward and appreciate the hard work of study group members.* An end-of-the-year celebration is an excellent way to celebrate success. Some of the schools I work with have used a PowerPoint presentation to celebrate the works of the groups. It may be better to do one schoolwide slide show than to have each group do their own; this avoids the time-consuming pitfalls of one-upmanship where every group tries to outdo the other groups. If a group has a newly birthed techie as a member, the slide show will be full of all the bells and whistles and may lack focused substance. For example, each group might submit four slides on the work of the group, and principals will have someone put all of the slides in a common template.

CONCLUSION

In order for WFSGs to be an effective professional development tool in the school, the principal must be involved intimately in the process. Commenting on action plans and logs is a concrete way to demonstrate involvement and interest. Encouraging teachers to examine research by providing up-to-date reports and making sure that teachers make data-based decisions will ensure the effectiveness of the WFSG work. The principal should take every opportunity to make the work of the WFSGs public and to reward teachers for their work by recognizing their accomplishments. Finally, the principal should help teachers develop and maintain a single-minded passion for teaching for student understanding. The study groups will be effective only to the extent that student understanding increases as a result of the WFSG process.

If principals do their jobs and follow the guidelines presented here and in the WFSG book (Murphy & Lick, 2005), study groups will become a powerful tool for school improvement and student achievement. Ultimately, principals will be more effective in their efforts, and students will gain in understanding and be the real beneficiaries.

5

Strengthening School Improvement Plans Through District Sponsorship

Anita Kissinger

"**G**ood," on average, is not good enough! As the third largest school district in Missouri, Springfield Public Schools district performance on state assessments was typically above the state average in all areas. Why a problem with averages? When we looked at the performance of individual schools and our progress as a district, the data told a much different story; our 51 campuses demonstrated wide variances in performance, and we were seeing little districtwide improvement. To fulfill our mission of academic excellence for all students, we needed to face the reality of our data, roll our sleeves up, and develop an effective school improvement system. Thanks to our Board of Education, superintendent, district leaders, principals, teachers, and the community, the results have been nothing short of amazing!

Our story is about an implementation sequence that began with a focus on student learning, moved to process alignment at all levels, and continues with district-level support for quality implementation and an uncompromising expectation for results.

INSTITUTIONALIZING A FOCUS

Keep it simple and clear! Upon the realization that we needed to improve our schools, our Board of Education developed two goals that provided a simple, yet powerful, focus. All schools and programs in Springfield Public Schools would strive to (a) improve student achievement and (b) reduce the drop-out rate. While most people would assume that these goals are the goals of all school districts, we have learned that only when these two goals were articulated and institutionalized with an accountability plan did we truly have a laser-like focus that resulted in improved student performance district wide.

> **Key Learning 1:** *Articulate a clear and uncompromising focus on student learning.*

FACING THE BRUTAL FACTS

It ain't easy! It would be inaccurate to portray the initial leg of our journey as smooth sailing. The challenge of change seems to grow exponentially in relationship to the district size. I often comment that comparing change in a larger district to change in a smaller district is much like comparing the time and fuel it takes to move a cargo ship in comparison to a fishing boat. But as a relatively large district, we desperately needed to quickly move a ship that had been anchored in the status quo sea of satisfaction.

Our anchor in the status quo was first lifted when a district-developed accountability system was implemented. This system uses a statistical process that allows each individual school site to determine whether or not the school is contributing to the performance improvements of its students. The initial result? A sense of urgency to respond to the brutal facts in our performance data was established at all levels in the organization.

> **Key Learning 2:** *Accountability creates a sense of urgency.*

SYSTEMATIZING THE SCHOOL IMPROVEMENT PROCESS

It's got to make sense! An important antecedent to improvement is external and internal alignment. "Making sense" for us meant that our school improvement processes needed to be aligned externally with the two district goals and internally in process. In 2001-2002, district leaders, principals, and teachers in Springfield (MO) Public Schools implemented a new school improvement planning process that was guided by our district goals and driven by the accountability plan.

While requiring site goals to align with the two district goals was a critical step, a data-driven action planning process that focused solely on student performance provided specific navigation charts for school improvement. The alignment within these action plans was accomplished with the requirement for specific, measurable, time-bound objectives that aligned with the stated goals. The resulting action steps aligned with the stated objectives, and performance measures were identified for each action step.

This deep and districtwide focus on planning for specific improvements in student performance necessitated a meaningful reflection on the school and class-room variables most likely to impact the expected performance results. The "ah-ha" for all of us came relatively quickly—using the same content, context, and process we had been using would merely get us the same results we had been getting. Change was on the horizon.

> **Key Learning 3:** *Systematic and well-aligned planning models can cause meaningful reflection and can result in action appropriate for the stated goals.*

DELIVERING THE SCHOOL IMPROVEMENT PLAN

A plan implemented is the only plan worth having! We now had a systematic planning process at both the district and school levels and a clear focus on and accountability for student performance. What we needed was a primary *vehicle* that could effectively and efficiently *deliver* the school improvement plan. Enter the Whole-Faculty Study Group (WFSG) System.

Prior to our 2001-2002 implementation year, we had researched school improvement processes. It was determined that significant school improvement could be realized only by creating a system of professional learning communities. This approach basically provides a structure that focuses each school and the district on student learning and relies on collaborative efforts guided by action research to accomplish measurable goals. As the Staff Development Director, I was also seeking a proven, systematic, site-based professional learning model that would align with our basic school improvement process, respect the professionalism of our teachers, and focus our professional learning efforts entirely on student learning needs. In addition, we needed a model that was content free. Such a model would allow each school to use its own student performance data to determine the content without having to use a different delivery model. In other words, the model could remain and be effective even when the data changed.

During my research and study, I attended an Association for Supervision and Curriculum Development (ASCD) preconference session with Carlene Murphy and was introduced to WFSG. During the first session, it was obvious to me that WFSG was the highly structured, focused model for which I had been searching. The content is driven by student-learning data, and the WFSG study group action plan is nearly a mirror image of our school improvement plan (SIP). In fact, when I introduced the WFSG action planning process to leaders and teachers in Springfield, a common comment was that the WFSG action plan was like a "mini SIP." It makes sense. It is aligned with our processes and with best practices in professional development. It provides flexibility for our sites and teachers without compromising our focus on student performance.

> **Key Learning 4:** *The WFSG system is a systematic and well-designed implementation model for school improvement plans.*

DELIVERING THE DELIVERY MODEL

Timing is everything! As previously mentioned, an immediate sense of urgency resulted from the implementation of our accountability plan and related school improvement planning process. While the ultimate decision regarding "how" educators would improve student performance at their schools was a site decision, the WFSG model was presented to our site leaders (principals) as a "highly recommended" model for implementing their school improvement plans. We attempted to address potential levels of concern and point out the many benefits to them and their staff members. Among the most initially enticing benefits was how the data analysis and resulting determination of student learning needs so easily transitioned into the organization of the study groups. WFSGs solved the dilemma of how to effectively address these needs schoolwide. While the potential reasons for implementing WFSGs were numerous, the bottom line was that the then-current site professional development models weren't getting the job done. Change was necessary. The WFSG System, if implemented as intended, would obviously align site professional development activities with school improvement plans, and using WFSGs would focus the entire school and district on teaching and learning—the exact focus needed to address student performance!

It was my observation that both the sense of urgency felt at the time the WFSG System was introduced and the rationale provided during the orientation encouraged a majority of our site leaders to implement WFSGs during the initial year of our improvement efforts. With or without the accountability and schools' improvement plans, I would have advocated for WFSGs, but it is my belief that the sense of urgency resulting from these plans accelerated the districtwide interest in and implementation of the WFSG System.

> **Key Learning 5:** *A sense of urgency can be harnessed to facilitate change.*

WALKING THE TALK

Talk is cheap! Offering WFSGs to principals as a districtwide, site professional development model does not ensure successful implementation unless there is a systematic plan to provide the necessary organizational changes and support.

In Springfield (MO) Public Schools, the organizational changes included, but were not limited to, (a) reallocating contract time for professional development from district activities to site activities to provide more time for WFSGs; (b) allowing the WFSG action plans to be used as the required professional development plan in our teacher evaluation program; and (c) when possible, allowing schools to creatively schedule time for study groups to meet during the school day.

Ongoing support continued to include a focus on the elements needed for the effective implementation of the WFSG model. This occurred through coaching and continuous training opportunities, including both the general model and specific WFSG processes such as protocols for looking at student work, collaborative skills, and writing action plans. In addition, we wanted to ensure that leaders new to Springfield (MO) Public Schools could effectively maintain the WFSG structure in their buildings and programs. With this in mind, we made WFSG training a required component of our new leaders' induction program.

The combination of organizational changes, ongoing support, and positive outcomes from sites that were first to implement WFSGs has helped encourage the implementation of WFSGs across our district. During the 2003-2004 school year, approximately 90% of our school sites utilized WFSGs as the primary delivery vehicle for their school improvement plans.

> **Key Learning 6:** *District leaders must provide the organizational changes and support necessary for effective implementation.*

REFLECTING ON RESULTS

We have turned the ship! The Missouri Department of Elementary and Secondary Education (DESE) facilitates an accreditation process that results in an Annual Performance Rating (APR) for school districts each year. This APR is based on student performance indicators such as student scores on the Missouri Assessment Program (MAP) tests, drop-out rates, student attendance, and ACT scores. Our total score for 2000-2001 found Springfield (MO) Public Schools only one (1) point above the cut-off for "provisional accreditation." A closer inspection revealed that while our "test scores" generally remained above the state averages, we weren't improving. The accountability plan, school improvement planning process, and WFSGs were implemented in the fall of 2001. On the three accreditation reports that Springfield (MO) Public Schools has received since implementation, the district has been accredited with "distinction in performance"!

> **Key Learning 7:** *Districts can improve when dedicated, focused board members, district leaders, and professional teachers implement effective, well-aligned models.*

SUMMARY

District sponsorship for implementing school improvement plans in Springfield (MO) Public Schools required a systematic approach that had an uncompromising focus on student learning. This approach began with the identification of student needs and a level of accountability that created a sense of urgency. The urgency to act was then met with well-aligned, research-supported models and processes that provided the structures professional educators needed to get results. As we moved our improvement process to the classroom level, the WFSG System was, and is, our primary choice for the delivery of our school improvement plans.

NEXT

Full steam ahead! We won't be dropping the anchor in Springfield, Missouri, anytime soon. As we continue our school improvement journey, the board goals will act as our rudder; our school improvement plans will plot the course; and the WFSG System will continue propelling us toward our destination—academic excellence for all students!

6

Partnering With Teacher Unions for School Improvement

Adam Urbanski

Xochitl Perez Castillo

After nearly two decades of education reform efforts, things today are more like yesterday than ever. The current reforms—such as career ladders for teachers, site-based management, and changes in the evaluation of staff—are necessary but not sufficient to improve teaching and learning substantially. These reforms are getting broader but seldom deeper, and whereas they have heightened the level of comfort that adults have with each other, these reforms often are process fixated and adult oriented. School reforms thus far have had little impact on students and their learning. When it comes to real change, it seems that too many favor reform only as long as it does not require any real change on their part. This chapter discusses such circumstances and how schools and the union can partner in future relationships to enhance progressive change efforts for significant school improvement.

Reform for What?

All of the above circumstances can change, but until now, reforms have not been radical enough. We repair and remodel the same system, rarely reinventing education and learning. As long as reforms remain marginal, we remain permanently perched on the eve of revolution.

The impediments are numerous: too many mandates and not enough leadership, resources, and preparations; too little passion and not enough urgency; too much bureaucracy and not enough involvement of school-level practitioners; too many unrelated programs and assessments and not enough consensus on standards. We have too much emphasis on doing longer and harder what we already do, and not enough emphasis on doing things differently. What's more, we have left teachers and parents with little time for conferencing and almost no time for adult learning. Still, there is much impatience and not enough appreciation for the reality that *real change* is *real hard*, takes *real time*, and needs *real direction*.

Despite the efforts of so many, reform remains rudderless. Virtually anything goes, no matter how minimally grounded in research or validated by what we already know about effective teaching and learning. We *must* focus reforms, and we *must* focus them on *students* and on *learning*.

The Union's Role

Central to any specific efforts to improve our schools is the relationship between school managers and the teacher union. Without labor–management collaboration, even the best efforts of management are tantamount to one-handed clapping. If education reforms are to yield substantially better results, both districts and unions must be open to considering a substantial shift in the roles of central office and union headquarters. Both must be willing to restructure themselves to be primarily service centers to the schools and to support schools by assuring equitable distribution of resources while respecting each school's autonomy. Both districts and unions must involve school administrators *and* teachers in the shaping of policies and in the search for effective strategies for supporting students' learning.

With the support of parents, neighborhood groups, the business community, and political leaders, school districts can and should sustain the existing efforts and build on them by jointly pursuing new and promising strategies. In bringing about change, we must consider balance while we are building on existing efforts, and we must let go of efforts that duplicate work without providing additional improvements. We must be careful to guard against overloading our schools with programs and expectations that leave our students and our teachers overextended in implementation with insufficient time for reflection and learning. It is in the context of a caring community and labor–management collaboration—at the district level, but especially in the schools—that we can best promote the needed reforms in education.

Effects of Unions

Critics of teacher unions have long alleged that student performance and educational progress are often hindered by teacher unions and contracts negotiated by them. All along, no empirical or credible research has been offered to substantiate these allegations. Meanwhile, those of us who believe that collective bargaining is more likely to have a positive effect on student academic performance were also hard pressed to show research-based proof as evidence.

A recent article in *Harvard Educational Review* (Steelman, Powell, & Carini, 2000) offers some strong data in answer to an important question; the article's title is "Do Teacher Unions Hinder Educational Performance? Lessons Learned From State SAT and ACT Scores." Researchers from Indiana University at Bloomington and the University of South Carolina found that "the presence of teacher unions appears to be linked to stronger state performance on these tests." They concluded that their findings "challenge the position that teacher unions depress student academic performance." The pattern is that teacher unions have a consistently positive impact and "this pattern is surprisingly robust."

The study authors point out that the issues cited by critics of teacher unions as "hurdles to educational progress" are in fact the very reason for improved student learning: "Better pay, and more secure working conditions may attract higher quality teachers and foster a standard of professionalism that is conducive to effective teaching," and "Unions also may negotiate classroom changes by pressing for smaller classes, time set aside during the school day for lesson preparations, and lighter teaching loads—factors that some social scientists have suggested are positively associated with educational output."

The authors add: "Additionally, unions may strengthen teacher standards through licensure procedures that eventually boost educational productivity and may lead to changes in administrative practices and styles that prove beneficial," and "Taken together, these possible benefits of unions may enhance not only the status of teachers but also the educational climate to which students are exposed."

In the final paragraph of their article, the authors offer a confession:

> In closing, we must admit that when we began this inquiry, we did not anticipate a positive or negative link between teacher unions and these measures of educational productivity. Rather, we expected no relationship. That we found such a strongly consistent positive relationship across so many permutations of analysis should give pause to those who characterize teacher unions as adversaries to educational success and accountability. (Steelman et al., 2000, p. 466)

Unlike these authors, we are not surprised at their findings. It has always made sense to us that improved teaching conditions translate to improved learning environments. Smaller class sizes afford more students with more individualized attention and planning with the teacher. As is often the case, this research merely confirms common sense. Nonetheless, this important study constitutes a strong reminder to us all that the collective bargaining process could be a principal tool for negotiating provisions that heighten the prospects for improved student success. It also represents a powerful reinforcement for the argument that the scope of collective bargaining should be expanded to include professional and instructional issues.

WHAT MATTERS MOST

Teacher unions and school districts are most responsible and responsive when they collaborate to improve students' learning. The best way to promote such collaboration is to emphasize it at the level of each individual school. Indeed, the two general categories for our joint efforts include *making our schools more learner-centered* and *building a more genuine profession for teachers.*

Learner-Centered Schools

Schools can be most effective when they have the necessary resources, support, and autonomy to serve their students well. But why are some schools better than others? What are the common characteristics of high-achieving schools? Here are some reasons that we would single out as principles that effective schools share. Schools:

• *Must have a consensus about what all students should know and be able to do.* Without consensus, we have no legitimate way to know what adults should know and be able to do, and no basis for knowing how schools should be structured and organized—no agreed-upon purpose.

• *Must have small school essence—small enough so that all students are well known.* Data from a research study funded by MetLife Foundation, conducted by What Kids Can Do, Inc., has turned up troubling incongruence with how students and teachers view their interactions with each other. Surveys included 6,350 high school students and 466 teachers from Chicago, Houston, Oakland, Philadelphia, and St. Louis. Only 27% of students say they received individual attention from their teachers. More than 25% of teenagers surveyed said there was not a single adult in their school whom they felt they could approach with a problem (http://www.whatkidscando .org/studentsasalliesintro.html). We can have schools-within-schools, satellite schools in places of employment, or schools in settings with other enterprises, where each school can be a community of learners—with accountability built in.

• *Must have active, contextualized, and real-to-life learning* rather than the passive and rote learning that now inhibits achieving any worthy standards. Students should learn at their own pace, in cooperative groups, by reading real literature rather than textbooks, using primary sources of information. They should learn "habits of the mind": how to think, not what to think; how to construct their own meaning and raise essential questions; how to see connections and discover patterns; and how to solve problems and make good decisions (Meier, 1995).

• *Must have learning assessments that are diversified and performance-based,* not the paper-and-pencil tests that are based on guesswork. These assessments should reveal what students know and what they can do.

• *Must ensure that those who assist students in learning are knowledgeable themselves.* Teachers must know their subjects well and how to teach them effectively to all students (Darling-Hammond, 1992). Teachers must also value multiculturalism, developmental learning, group learning, and the multiple learning styles and the types of intelligence that students have. They must recognize that, in teaching, excellence cannot exist in isolation and without collaboration and collegiality.

• *Must recognize that without democratic dynamics evident around them, children will not learn how to practice democracy.* We can preach to them about democracy, but if children don't see adults in their lives interacting in democratic ways, they will not believe that democracy is important and possible for all. So all decisions about school dynamics and the instructional program must be shared by all constituencies—teachers, parents, administrators, and, in high schools, also students. Each must have a voice with no one excluded.

• *Must have safety and discipline.* Neither effective teaching nor learning can occur in an environment of fear and disorder. Schools must not tolerate criminal, destructive, or disruptive behavior. Children must be taught self-discipline and how to live in peace.

• *Must work closely with the students' families, accepting the responsibility for participating in the nurturing of students' readiness to learn.* Recognizing that children spend only 20% of their time in school and exist within the context of their families, schools and educators must seek effective ways to involve parents in the education of their children.

• *Must inject into education incentives to do right by kids and disincentives for failure to do so.* Such incentives should represent logical consequences—granting more resources, recognition, and autonomy for successful practice, while correcting harmful or ineffective performance by schools or individual educators. Also, there must be incentives for the learners, so that students don't come to school with the attitude that they have no responsibility for their own learning.

• *Must allow students and their parents to elect the public school of their choice.* Likewise, the school should have the authority to set and enforce behavioral and academic standards. This two-way choice would constitute an accountability system that could ensure responsible and responsive behavior on the part of the clients (students and parents), no less than on the part of the providers (schools and educators).

While there is no boilerplate prescription for making schools effective; there are examples of good practice worth emulating. Since reform is a search—an inductive process—we must maintain a willingness to try different ways to be more effective. New practice may not succeed, but we know for sure that if we always do what we've always done, we will always get what we've always gotten, and the teachers' union can be a strong partner in the effort to improve our schools.

Building a More Genuine Profession

The search for creating such accountable and learner-centered schools must be in tandem with the drive to professionalize teaching. To achieve a more genuine profession, teachers themselves will have to reject the phony choices between compensation and dedication, between unionism and professionalism, and between equity and excellence. When teachers begin to build a genuine profession for themselves, the public can gain greater accountability. To improve the learning opportunities for all students, we must improve the quality of teaching and conditions within which teachers work.

What impedes effective teaching and learning is not that teachers are the problem; it is that teachers work within outmoded, unprofessional systems. By sharing responsibility for redesigning schools and abandoning unexamined practices and policies, teachers can restructure the teaching profession in ways that promise more productive schooling. The challenge is formidable. In fact, if we were to design an occupation that would virtually guarantee isolation from one's colleagues and would lack not only intrinsic rewards but also most of the characteristics of a real profession, we could hardly find a better model than what most teachers face today.

Learning—or failing to learn—their trade by trial and error, new teachers serve no internship and receive little help. Teachers cannot be promoted except out of teaching. Consequently, a teacher's status and responsibilities are not substantially different upon retirement than on the day the teacher was hired. Greater status and pay are reserved for those who leave the classroom. Nonpractitioners make pedagogical decisions. The farther one works from the classroom, it seems, the more authority one has to dictate to those left behind. Teachers are evaluated and assisted by administrators who have little available time and who cannot have expertise in all of the subject areas in which teachers teach. Teachers who lack competence are neither assisted nor removed. Administrators alone are unable in ensure quality teaching. To help change all that, we must first strengthen teaching in ways that emulate the features evident in other, more genuine professions, including the following:

- *Shared Knowledge Base.* Good teachers must know their subjects well and how to teach them effectively, understand human development, and how the brain works and learning occurs.

- *Standards.* Teachers must be involved in setting rigorous standards.

- *Professional Preparation and Induction.* All teachers deserve high-quality preparation programs that include disciplinary and teaching knowledge and merge theory and practice. New teachers should be ushered in under the watchful, supportive eyes of experienced and expert colleagues.

- *Continuous Learning.* Teachers must be learners; "professional development" should become inseparable from their day-to-day work.

- *Promotion.* It should be possible to promote teachers without compelling them to leave teaching. One successful model of a *differentiated roles and pay system* is the Career in Teaching (CIT) plan, implemented in Rochester (New York) Schools. This plan retains excellent practitioners and permits them to achieve leadership roles related to instruction. It includes such designations as: *intern teachers, resident teachers, professional teachers,* and *lead teachers.* Also, knowledge- and skill-based pay systems should provide salary increases for the demonstration of valued knowledge, skills, and professional expertise.

- *Conditions and Accountability.* Teachers need and deserve professional compensation levels, circumstances, and accountability.

Teacher Leadership

The changes that are required for schools cannot be achieved without strong teacher leadership. This represents a challenge and an opportunity for teacher unions to serve as agents of this neglected agenda. To enhance teacher leadership requires a change in the very culture of schools. Like administrators, teachers have become accustomed to hierarchical organizations and have conceded decision making and leadership functions to their supervisors. However, entrusted with making complicated judgments about their work, teachers sense an invitation to unleash their skills and knowledge about schools, teaching and learning, and education-related policy. They view this as an opportunity to forge important new roles that combine teaching and leading, while maintaining the primacy of teaching and the drive toward greater professionalism.

Throughout the nation, teachers, through their unions, have begun to develop models of *teacher leadership.* Toledo, Dade County, Cincinnati, Columbus, Los Angeles, Rochester, and many other cities in America have become known for educational innovations principally because of the leadership provided by teachers and their unions. But, these model examples are exceptions, and not yet the norm. However, the successful models have proven Senge (1990) right: It is possible to *diffuse leadership, to build a learner-centered culture, and to make schools into learning organizations.* An effecive design model for *teacher leadership* is: a focus on learning, engagement, and culture formation, which will require teachers' taking ownership of their own fate and the accompanying challenges and dilemmas. Teachers must, as Meier (1995) put it, "lead the way toward their own liberation."

Implications for Policy Makers

But teachers cannot do it alone. Past experience and lessons learned offer important implications for policy makers:

• *Teachers must be invited to be policy makers, too.* Teachers must want the changes, be part of determining them, and view them as legitimate, or they will use their well-honed skills in "creative insubordination" to either sabotage or ignore them.

• *New roles for teachers as leaders must be multiplied and supported.* Increasing opportunities for teachers to serve as leaders must be matched, at all levels, with the needed support and greater authority.

• *Support for teacher leadership must include more time and increased access to new knowledge and skills.* Teachers—not just leaders—require more time, including time for dialogue, collaboration, and the intellectual life of the school, and greater access to new information and ongoing development of skills.

• *Teacher unions must reinvent and redefine themselves to better meet the professional needs of their members.* This may require expanding the scope of collective bargaining to include educational policy matters, assuming responsibility for the quality of instruction, providing for professional development for teachers, and challenging even the most hallowed practices of the industrial union model.

PROFESSIONAL DEVELOPMENT

If the knowledge and skills of teachers impact students' learning most, then teacher unions have both a responsibility and the best opportunity to affect that critical factor. They can do that best by expanding professional learning opportunities for teachers at the level of each individual school. In fact, our goal ought to be to make schools into places where the adults come to learn as well.

Although there are many types of good professional development for teachers, the best kind is the one that is inseparable from the day-to-day work that teachers do: job-embedded, teacher-driven, and centered on the work of their current students. That is why the Whole-Faculty Study Group System is so well received by teachers and so rapidly spreading throughout our schools. It is respectful of teachers' expertise and experience, eminently grounded in teachers' practical and pragmatic goals, and structured to promote genuine collegiality and collaboration among teachers. In short, it harnesses the collective wisdom of teachers and focuses it all on the academic interests of their own students. By doing so, it diminishes the isolation that has plagued teachers and makes their practice more public—thus also more accountable.

CONCLUSION

Real change is *real hard* and takes *real time*. It can be done; it is just that it cannot be done easily. The prospects for improving education in America's schools can be significantly improved if policy makers nurture, support, and multiply the emerging opportunities for teachers to provide leadership in those endeavors, and for unions and schools to form new partnerships that allow for added respect for each other and a full range of collegial collaboration toward the common goal of meaningful school improvement and enhanced student achievement.

PART III

Study Groups and Learning Communities

Among the common buzz words of the day and as part of the various school improvement initiatives are "study groups" and "learning communities." Unfortunately, many people involved with education readily use these terms, but often don't fully understand them or appreciate their application and significance. What we are finding is that study groups, properly implemented, have the potential to generate "learning communities" in schools, which can then be the mechanism for genuine school improvement and increased student performance.

DuFour and Eaker (1998) discuss the essence of using "study groups" to build effective "learning communities," as follows:

> The most promising strategy for sustained, substantive school improvement is developing the ability of school personnel to function as professional learning communities. . . . The most critical question educators must confront as they consider an initiative to create a professional learning community is this one: Do we believe in our collective capacity to create a better future for our school? (pp. xi, 286)

Although most evidence that supports the meaningful application of study groups and learning communities to improve schools is anecdotal, a recent scientific in-depth study of a school system, by Koenigs (2004), provides insightful confirmation of school change and improvement:

> Professional learning community models, such as the Whole-Faculty Study Group System, show great promise to positively affect teachers' instructional practices and school culture if thought and care are taken during the implementation process.

This section of the Fieldbook, *Study Groups and Learning Communities*, consists of three chapters that discuss (a) research on the effectiveness of study groups and learning communities in school improvement and (b) examples of special types of study groups, that is, student and principal study groups, and their applications.

7

Answering the Question

Do Professional Learning Communities Really Work?

Andrew E. Koenigs

Recently, the literature has been replete with calls for more collaboration among teachers to help form a culture of continuous learning (DuFour, 2003a; DuFour & Eaker, 1998; Hord, 1997; Murphy & Lick, 2005) as a way to reshape entrenched school cultures. These educational theorists claim that schools should transform themselves into professional learning communities in order to improve teachers' professional practice and change the structure and culture of the school.

Professional learning communities are being pushed by many (Darling-Hammond, 1997b; DuFour & Eaker, 1998; Eaker, DuFour, & Burnette, 2002; Hord, 1997; Lick, 2000; Murphy & Lick, 2005; Sparks, 2002) in the field of education as a panacea for educational reform. The Whole-Faculty Study Group System is one of a number of new reform models for professional development that are based on the concept of professional learning communities.

This chapter explores the notion of whether professional learning communities change teachers' instructional practices and whether they facilitate change in the structure *and* culture of the school as an organization. Much has been written about what professional learning communities *should* look like, and this chapter will illuminate how the faculty of one small, Midwestern school district implemented the Whole-Faculty Study Group model of professional development.

CONCEPTUAL FRAMEWORK

Change theory (Argyris, 1959, 1992; Lewin, 1948, 1951; Schein, 1992, 1996) and adult learning theory (Knowles, Holton, & Swanson, 1998) served as the conceptual framework for analysis of this case study. Lewin described change as a process of unfreezing, changing, and refreezing one's own perceptions. Individuals must undergo such a process before true, lasting change is accepted and embedded into their beliefs and values.

Adult learning theory or andragogy is the process of how adults gain new knowledge and expertise. According to Knowles et al. (1998), andragogy is based on several assumptions about how adults learn. These assumptions focus on motivation to learn, life experiences of adults, personal interests, and self-directed learning. Both change theory and adult learning theory were used to inform this research study regarding a districtwide implementation of professional learning communities in one particular school district.

RESEARCH DESIGN AND METHODOLOGY

Various forms of data collection methods were used in this qualitative case study. They included surveys of all teachers in the district; in-depth interviews with a sample of teachers and administrators; observations of schools, teachers, study groups in action, and teacher classrooms; and a document review of pertinent items such as study logs, lesson plans, and student achievement data.

A semantic differential survey was administered to all teachers in the district at the beginning of the 2003–2004 school year. This survey gauged teachers' perceptions of the affects of professional learning communities on themselves and their school structure and culture. In-depth interviews were conducted with all administrators in the school district.

A purposively selected study group from each school was chosen for more in-depth research. The researcher observed each study group in action and conducted a focus group interview with each study group. Classroom observations of each member of the selected study group were conducted to look at instructional practices and teacher behavior. Classroom artifacts, school documents, extensive school site observations, and field notes rounded out the data collection methods.

CONTEXT AND BACKGROUND

This case study took place in the Tigerville (a pseudonym) School District, which is located in a small rural community in central Kansas. It is the only school district in town and is composed of four schools: a primary school, intermediate school, middle school, and high school. The town of approximately 4000 citizens has managed to stay economically viable, despite its rural setting and remote locale.

The demographics have changed from a predominately white, middle-class community with an agricultural base, to a town with growing ethnic and economic diversity (U.S. Census Bureau, 2000). Some companies involved with beef and egg industries recently expanded production and created jobs in Tigerville that have attracted more migrant, mostly Hispanic, workers.

The school district is somewhat of an anomaly for its conservative, rural setting. Tigerville is considered a progressive district with a forward-thinking superintendent. The community is very supportive of the school district, as evidenced by the school district's recently passing a nearly five-million dollar bond issue that included renovations to most of the district's facilities.

Student Demographics

The school district has an enrollment of 940 students. Seventy-five percent of the students in the district are white, 22% Hispanic, and 3% black. The poverty rate of the school district has increased from 38% to 58% in the past decade. The percentage of Hispanic students attending Tigerville schools has increased from 6% to 22% as well (Kansas State Department of Education, n.d.).

History of Professional Learning Communities in Tigerville

Whole-Faculty Study Groups (WFSGs) were implemented in Tigerville during the 1998–1999 school year. During the first year, teachers were asked to meet voluntarily after school each week in their study groups. This was met with much resistance from the teaching staff. After listening to teacher feedback, the administration asked the board of education for released time once a week for study groups the following year. This change helped reduce tension and resistance and improve teachers' feelings toward study groups. Although the times and dates for study groups changed over the years, study groups have been sustained in Tigerville for more than six years.

Study groups in Tigerville have engaged in a variety of activities. The most common activities were sharing ideas, discussing instructional practices and strategies, aligning curriculum to state standards, creating products and projects, discussing books and educational articles, and researching best practice. Sharing was probably the most popular activity in study groups, according to the teachers in Tigerville. Most teachers in Tigerville found great value in using their study group session as a time for sharing. Teachers shared new ideas, instructional practices, lesson plans, personal experiences at school, and student work.

Some study groups in Tigerville shared and discussed student work. Teachers had created a lesson to teach students about technical reading. Several teachers brought examples of the lesson and products that students had created. A teacher discussed the benefits of using study groups for this purpose:

> I think sometimes we also like to show student work because you know we look in a textbook and on paper it looks like it's going to work very smoothly. And logistically things should go the way the book or somebody told us it should go, but in reality it probably does not.

Teachers in Tigerville found benefit from sharing student work. They were able to evaluate the effectiveness of their lesson plans, receive feedback from study group peers to improve the lessons, and evaluate how well students understood concepts and skills.

TEACHERS' AND ADMINISTRATORS' PERCEPTIONS OF WFSGs

Survey results from teachers in Tigerville showed a consistently positive perception of the effects of WFSGs on both individuals and the organization. Teachers felt most positively about study groups' being helpful, supportive, and student focused.

Differences in perceptions about study groups did exist for various teacher groups. Differences existed between male and female teachers' perceptions, indicating that women were more positive toward the study group process. Likewise, teachers at the elementary levels felt much more positive about study groups than those at the secondary level.

Open-ended responses from teachers indicated that they felt study groups were beneficial for sharing, collaborating, collegiality, learning, and growing as a professional and for providing time for teachers to accomplish many of these tasks. On the other hand, teachers did not care for the lack of flexibility over study-topic selection, topics that were not relevant to them, who controlled study groups, when and what day study groups occurred, and attitudes of some of their peers during study-group time.

Effects of WFSGs on Teachers

Most teachers and administrators in Tigerville felt study groups affected teacher attitudes and behavior, changed instructional practices, focused on curriculum standards, and facilitated their ability to collaborate with other teachers. However, many teachers pointed out that the effects of study groups were contingent upon the relevancy of the topic to them and their own classrooms. When topics were perceived as relevant, their effects were perceived more positively.

Most important, teachers and administrators felt study groups had affected instructional practices in the Tigerville School District. They were confident that classroom teaching strategies had changed as a result of study groups. One teacher confirmed this by replying, "I think we have all used the strategies [learned in study groups] and have implemented them in our classroom." One high school teacher noted, "I have found myself using more new techniques in the last five years than I did the previous fifteen!"

Most study participants agreed that one of the positive results of study groups was that they were now more focused on curriculum and standards. One teacher noted that study groups have made teachers more cognizant of standards when she stated, "I think we are more aware [of the state standards]. I think the whole building is more focused on what they are supposed to be doing."

Another effect study groups had on teachers in Tigerville was the opportunity to collaborate with their colleagues. Teachers throughout the district believed that study groups provided time that was not available in prior schedules to work with their peers on curriculum integration and cross-curricular projects. Time for collaboration seemed to be especially important to participants at the secondary level. One participant responded, "I think amongst our staff here at the high school we struggle with time to talk with one another and meet with one another, just even be around one another."

Teachers in Tigerville felt strongly that study groups affected them *if* the topic was relevant to them. In contrast, teachers viewed study groups as a waste of time if they perceived the topic was not relevant to them.

Benefits of WFSGs

Teachers and administrators thought that there were valuable benefits from study groups. They believed that they provided an opportunity for teachers to bond, be collegial, support each other emotionally, build trust and camaraderie, and socialize. Teachers interviewed spoke frequently about bonding, collegiality, and emotional support as benefits of study groups. For some teachers, study groups seemed almost a cathartic experience: "We did a lot of unwinding together; a lot of group building, team building," one teacher recalled.

Administrators noted trust and risk-taking, higher quality communication, more reflective practice, and an expanded knowledge base as some of the major benefits of study groups. Administrators felt that a major benefit of study groups was the amount of trust that was built among teachers. One stated, "I think the trust amongst each other is higher because they know it is okay to try new things." Trust allowed teachers to take more risks and try new and different things without fear of being penalized if the new directions did not work.

Advantages of WFSGs Over Traditional Professional Development

Whether teachers were enthusiastic about study groups or lukewarm toward them, they still believed study groups were more beneficial than traditional professional development models. Teachers viewed study-group members as more credible and the topics as more relevant and as providing them with more feedback than traditional forms of professional development.

Teachers thought that study groups offered peer learning and enhanced their peer credibility. Teachers spoke frequently about learning new ideas in study groups from their peers and finding their peers more credible than outside experts. Teachers were more likely to try a new strategy if one of their colleagues suggested it than if they heard it from an expert or at a workshop. When a group of teachers was asked why they were more likely to try new things when suggested by a peer, one responded, "These are people we know!"

Teachers in Tigerville also felt that study groups offered them continual and ongoing feedback, which they did not feel was available to them in more traditional professional development models. A teacher lamented, "There is no feedback [in a typical workshop]. Like they always tell us with the students, immediate feedback is best."

Administrators in Tigerville were clearly more satisfied with study groups over more traditional models of professional development in affecting teachers' practices. Administrators maintained that study groups were more beneficial and more effective than teacher workshops, conferences, and one-day inservices. Administrators mentioned ongoing dialogue, teacher self-direction, and relevance as attributes that made study groups superior to traditional forms of professional development.

Structural and Cultural Change

This study also sought to determine the effect of study groups on the structure and culture of the organization. Study groups, in themselves, were a structural change for the Tigerville schools. District administrators, however, perceived many other structural changes as a result of the enactment of WFSGs.

One of the major structural changes administrators noted in Tigerville involved moving from individual teacher initiatives to schoolwide initiatives. Study groups, in their opinion, provided a mechanism for shifting from individual teachers making idiosyncratic instructional decisions in their own classrooms to a schoolwide focus on specific instructional strategies. Teachers, through the study group process, were collaborating in concert to make systemic changes in their schools. This was manifested in schoolwide initiatives in each school building.

Administrators also believed that study groups had created a different culture in their schools. In their opinion, teachers were bonding together, communicating more effectively, collaborating and working together, and looking to continually refine their teaching skills, which had not occurred previous to study groups. One principal stated, "Well it is real easy to say this. I think we are able to communicate on the tough issues. Not that it is always pleasant to do, but I think it is easier to get into those discussions [as a result of study groups]."

Teachers were mostly unaware or unsure of any cultural shifts and felt the culture of their buildings had remained much the same since study groups began. Although some teachers did not explicitly note cultural changes in their buildings, some of them spoke about how study groups had changed the way they worked together. An elementary teacher stated, "It [study groups] kind of keeps you going so that you are not in your room closing your door, doing your own thing. You hear what other people are doing."

Problems With WFSGs

Despite mostly positive attitudes toward WFSGs, some problems and tensions existed regarding these professional learning communities. One of the most talked about concerns, from the teachers' perspective, involved control over the study group process. Data from the teacher survey and interview participants revealed that most teachers felt they did not own the study group process.

From the beginning, teachers, in general, felt study groups were under the control of the administration. Administrators acknowledged that the initial implementation of study groups was completely a top-down decision. The early implementation process caused tension and disagreement about ownership of WFSGs. Most of these issues revolved around topic choice and flexibility and purposes of study groups.

Topic Choice and Flexibility

The main concern of the teaching staff with respect to study groups was the ability to choose topics that interested them and having control over their own learning. A majority of the teaching staff in each building wanted more flexibility and input into choosing study-group topics. Teachers in Tigerville felt strongly about wanting to choose a topic of interest to them. This issue of control impacted the early support or lack of support by teachers in the district for this professional development model.

Purpose of Study Groups

To a lesser extent, differences of opinion between teachers and administrators on the purpose of study groups were apparent. While both groups believed that study groups in Tigerville were student focused, some teachers wanted the purpose to be more teacher focused. Both groups seemed to view these options as an "either-or" rather than study groups' serving dual purposes.

Summary of Perceptions of WFSGs

In many ways participants confirmed that the school and teachers had truly *changed* as a result of study groups. Teachers were meeting together on a regular basis in an environment meant to encourage collective inquiry to improve their professional practices. This was a new way to learn for many teachers in the Tigerville district. Although some changes were evident, the culture at each school seemed to control how each school reacted to the WFSG model.

Each school in the Tigerville district appeared to mold, manipulate, and shape study groups to meet their own individual building needs. At the elementary level, where teachers were already collaborating and sharing, study groups were positively received and accepted. Consequently, elementary teachers perceived little or no change in school culture. At the secondary level, study groups were adapted and changed to fit the already existing culture in their buildings. Rules were bent at the high school, paperwork was reduced, and times were changed to make the study-group model more palatable to teachers. These observations raised a question: Whether study groups truly changed the culture in Tigerville or whether the culture changed the study group model to fit it.

Understanding the Change Process in Tigerville

Change was not easy in Tigerville. As was stated earlier in this chapter, change is just difficult for individuals and organizations (Argyris, 1992; Fullan, 1991; Lewin, 1951; Schein, 1992, 1996). Change involved painful unlearning and difficult relearning (Lewin, 1951). Teachers in Tigerville had to learn to work collaboratively and collectively within a new professional development framework. This was a significant departure from their previous professional development experiences of one-day workshops and cafeteria-style inservices scattered throughout the school year. The WFSG model represented a different way for teachers to learn and so was met with some not unexpected resistance.

Individual Change: Effects on Teachers in Tigerville

Lewin's (1951) theories about individual change can be applied to the effects of WFSGs on teachers in Tigerville. The first step in the change process, according to Lewin, is to "unfreeze" one's current perceptions. WFSGs required teachers to use research to learn about current educational best practices. Disconfirming information (new learning) provided teachers in Tigerville a catalyst for them to "unfreeze" their old perceptions about their own practices.

As Lewin (1951) noted, just providing new information is not enough to change a person's perceptions. A sense of urgency must be present so that if a person does not change, some valued goal will not be achieved. In Tigerville, that valued goal was most likely student achievement and student learning. Teachers and administrators alike cared deeply about their students and student learning.

Therefore, according to Lewin (1951), the next step in the change process involved a fear of new learning or "learning anxiety." One way to reduce fear is to provide psychological safety as one tries out new skills without fear of failure or rejection. In Tigerville, WFSGs provided a sufficiently safe environment for teachers to try out new skills and strategies. Both teachers and administrators spoke eloquently about teachers' sense of security as a benefit of WFSGs.

The final phase in the change process involves "cognitive redefinition." This step occurs as individuals begin to modify and change their assumptions, beliefs, and behaviors. An important restraining force in this step is the cultural norms of the group with which the person associates. As members test out new perceptions on other group members, acceptance or rejection of these perceptions is key in determining whether the new perceptions become ingrained and "refrozen."

In Tigerville, the strong cultural norms of each school faculty played a key role in changes in teachers' instructional practices. Elementary teachers continued to try new strategies and shared these with each other, because their culture of risk-taking and collaborative sharing already existed at this level prior to the introduction of study groups. In addition, it seemed that elementary teachers felt "pressure" to try new things if they heard others in their study group talk about using new strategies. This kind of group norm supported changes in instructional practices rather than inhibiting them. Middle school teachers also had a culture of working together in teams, so working collaboratively and trying new instructional strategies was not as much of a stretch for them.

The culture of the high school, however, was not accustomed to collaboration and sharing prior to study groups. It was challenged and stretched by study groups, which reflected on members' instructional practices and the "unfreezing" and "refreezing" of their own perceptions of teaching and was, at times, painful, unpleasant, and unpopular with them.

Organizational Change: Effects on the Structure and Culture

The Tigerville School District has changed significantly as a result of the introduction of the Whole-Faculty Study Group System. Teachers were no longer working in isolation from one another; instead, they worked together to improve the school as a whole. Changes in the school schedule to accommodate WFSGs were a major structural change that required teachers, administrators, parents, and students to think differently about the structure of the school day and to recognize that teachers needed time to learn.

It is likely that WFSGs in Tigerville over the past six years have modified the deeply held beliefs and assumptions of most teachers in Tigerville. The true test of cultural change will be when the agreed-upon beliefs and assumptions of the teachers in the entire school district have been *unfrozen* from their old assumptions of "how to educate children" and *refrozen* with new assumptions and beliefs about "how to educate all children for a dramatically different future."

Mismatch Between Organizational and Individual Needs

Organizational theorists (Argyris, 1959; Clark & Astuto, 1988) claim that many conflicts in organizations arise because of a mismatch between the needs of the organization and of the individuals in the organization. Organizations sometimes become so concerned about their problems that they neglect the most important unit of the organization, the *individual* (Clark & Astuto, 1988).

Mandates from the new federal No Child Left Behind Act (U.S. Department of Education, 2002) and Tigerville administrators' desire to meet these accountability demands gave rise to a disagreement between teachers and administrators over the choices of study-group topics. Administrators felt compelled to narrow the focus of study-group topics to reading and math, whereas teachers wanted to be able to choose topics that interested them and were relevant to their own classrooms. Most teachers wanted more flexibility and control over study-group topics, while most administrators wanted more focus and less flexibility in study-group topics. This mismatch between the needs of the administration in Tigerville and the professional and personal needs of the teachers created growing tensions between the two parties.

Argyris (1959) argued that organizations should attend to issues of misalignment. If they do not, individuals in the organization may create informal structures against management, negatively affecting organizational cultures.

Implications

As Lewin (1951) posited, change for all individuals is a difficult process. Schools desirous of significant improvements must understand the process others go through in order to accept and learn new perceptions and skills. Schools can help teachers through the process of *unfreezing* their current perceptions, changing those perceptions, and then *refreezing* the new perceptions.

Leaders with a good understanding of the change process can support and facilitate high-quality professional development in their schools. By supporting teachers through each step of the change process—*unfreezing, changing,* and *refreezing*—school administrators can provide a powerful and essential component of meaningful and sustainable changes in their schools.

Facilitating acquisition of new instructional practices in individual teachers alone will not be enough to improve the quality of teaching and learning in America's schools. School leaders also must have a firm understanding of organizational change theory and its implications for their school setting.

Organizational change theorists (Argyris, 1959; Clark & Astuto, 1988; Eaker et al., 2002; Fullan, 2002) concluded that effective organizations have a good understanding of how change affects the entire system. Argyris (1959) argued that effective organizations are those that align both organizational needs and individual employee needs. When individual needs do not match organizational needs, frustration, conflict, and subversion emerge in the organization. Deft leadership resists the temptation to increase controls over the organization and actually creates more freedom and flexibility, and more opportunities for authentic dialogue and input for people within the organization.

Whole-Faculty Study Groups were designed to be a more teacher-driven approach to professional development. In theory, this design seems to include more distributed leadership principles and more shared decision making than most traditional professional development models. Finding common ground and alignment between the needs of school districts and teachers, including their own personal and professional needs, was the key to increasing the capacity of schools to meet the challenges that lie ahead. Beatty (2000) found that the most effective professional development models were ones that created "flow." *Flow* occurred when professional development met teachers' personal needs and professional interests *and* organizational needs. Professional development opportunities in which these goals came together were found to be the most effective, allowing professional growth for both the school and the teachers who worked in them.

SUMMARY

The professional development commitment for all those involved in the schools should be: designing a system that creates structures and cultures that support high levels of student and adult learning. Too often, professional development and school improvement strategies are superficial and leave teachers' knowledge, skills, beliefs, and assumptions virtually untouched. Professional learning community models, such as the Whole-Faculty Study Group System, show great promise for positively affecting teachers' instructional practices and school culture if thought and care are taken during the implementation process. Understanding how the change process influences individuals and organizations will be the key to any successful professional development model.

8

Establishing Student Study Groups

Robin P. Cooper

Gwendolyn Baggett

Student study groups were conceived from the concept of teacher study groups in the Whole-Faculty Study Group (WFSG) System; the objective was to produce effective student leaders to promote democracy inside and outside of the classroom following constructivist leadership practices. Lambert et al. (1995) define constructivist leadership as "the reciprocal processes that enable participants in an educational community to construct meanings that lead toward a common purpose about schooling" (p. viii).

Often complaining about students' lack of motivation, poor self-esteem, and low test scores, the authors, who were teachers, met with students to discuss possible reasons as to why they were not actively participating in their own learning process. Overall, students did not believe that teachers cared enough to allow them to have a voice inside the classroom. As a result, in 1997, student study groups were developed in two classes with sixteen students being identified as student study-group leaders, and sixteen groups were formed. The major focus of student study groups was the placement of students at the center of their education with everyone else serving as supporting members of the team. Students in this process attended professional development sessions and were trained in the areas of instructional and collaborative learning techniques, peer mediation, and conflict resolution. Teachers in the process were facilitators who worked closely with students to develop a rapport built on trust, and where students sought to uncover their own potential without relying on teachers as the sole authority. Using the multiple intelligences model by Howard Gardner (1993) in the Eugene Washington Rhodes Middle School in Philadelphia, Pennsylvania, students were taught how to discover their own talents and help one another in their quest to uncover their talents. The Rhodes Middle School model for student study groups is discussed in detail in the remainder of this chapter.

Background for the Rhodes Middle School Model

The Rhodes Middle School is a large middle school with approximately 1000 students in Grades 5 through 8. The school is located in North Philadelphia, a low-economic urban area where students are entitled to receive free breakfast and lunch as a result of Title 1 funding. The school, at the time, was not achieving very well by local and state requirements, and, as a consequence, teachers and administrators were given an ultimatum by the cluster (region) to actively review successful research models designed to improve academic achievement. Using Comprehensive School Reform Development (CSRD) funds, a committee was assigned the task of choosing one of the models. After many visits to observe models such as Little Red Schoolhouse and Success for All, the ATLAS model was selected (which meant that the WFSG System would automatically be included), due to its focus on the thought processes of individuals as opposed to programs. With the ATLAS program, there was an intensified focus on the development and implementation of WFSGs as opposed to the other models focusing on specific programs to be completed at specific times. With ATLAS, the design was to change people's behavior, build communities, change thought processes, and have teachers and staff think about, "What is happening differently inside of the classroom as a result of being an active member in a study group?" This critical question was designed as the connector between professional development sessions, WFSGs, and the classroom. With mounting pressure to perform to state requirements, Rhodes embraced the ATLAS model, which works with teachers over time to change students' and teachers' behaviors in positive ways and allows for teacher creativity centered on student needs.

Background for Student Study Groups

Schools currently spend a great deal of money providing professional development to teachers for the effective implementation of study groups. Study groups are used as a vehicle to provide collaboration among teachers to view student work and engage in professional dialogue. The guiding question for study groups, according to Murphy and Lick (2005), is, "What are students learning and achieving as a result of what teachers are learning and doing in study groups?" (p. 13). In this process, WFSGs serve as a catalyst for change in teaching practices. Teachers honestly reflect on teaching practices, prepare to change practices that do not work, and focus on progressive processes such as "teaching for understanding" by examining student work using colleagues as critical colearners. The authors felt that it was time to recognize that students have much to say about their learning; the problem was that no one was asking them. While teachers spend time collaborating with one another concerning teaching and learning, their implementation and intervention plans have not fully included students, the very ones who need to be included if success is to occur in a meaningful way. Littky and Grabelle (2004) echoed this sentiment: "our education system should see creating mindful learners as its goal" (p. 10). Curwin and Mendler (1988) remind teachers to "teach in a way that is either interesting or meets students' needs as learners" (p. 41). Students have much to say about their learning; the problem, however, is that no one is asking them.

Goals of Student Study Groups

The Student Study Group Model is a design for educational reform and was adapted from the WFSG System, which focuses on bringing together faculties for specific meeting times to collaborate on classroom practices. Similarly, student study groups seek to bring together students to collaborate on what is needed from students in order for them to be successful learners. Students are grouped together in collaborative learning settings for the purpose of problem solving; communicating; and thinking critically about lessons taught, classroom climate, and personal outside areas of concern. The *primary goal* of student study groups is to teach students strategies designed to make them active participants in their own learning. From this context, students can think critically to solve problems that are important to them. Perkins (2004) writes, "Teaching for understanding can bring knowledge to life by requiring students to manipulate knowledge in various ways" (p. 17). An important *secondary goal* of student study groups is to produce effective leaders who will work with group members on academic and social skills, as well as hone their own leadership skills. A *final goal* involves the role of teachers "facilitating" instead of "dictating" classroom instruction, in order to produce leaders who will learn to apply their own meaning to various situations in order to bridge the gap between the classroom and society (Dewey, 1944). Lambert et al. (1995) agree that "it is important to regard the community as the shop in which thoughts are constructed and deconstructed and about how cognition, perception, imagination, memory must be conceived as themselves and directly, social affairs" (p. viii).

Collaborative Student-Learning Groups

Student study groups are groups where collaborative learning is emphasized to encourage all members to work together using a variety of study-group protocols to reach common goals. All members of the study group are trained to take on group responsibilities such as facilitator, recorder, reporter, and timekeeper. All groups are required to develop norms. All students must abide by classroom and individual small group norms. In addition, members are taught how to communicate effectively with others in the group to avoid unnecessary conflict. These communication techniques are taught in class weekly and then reinforced on a daily basis by teachers during classroom instructional activities.

Group members are selected in a variety of ways, most often through teacher selection, student study-group leaders' recommendations, or by study-group members themselves. Initially, teachers develop heterogeneous groups using student portfolios and hard and soft data. The heterogeneous process is favored to promote diverse learning styles. Each group is encouraged to develop and share members' own expertise within the group. This process fosters respect for all intelligences demonstrated by group members. Members' differences are celebrated. Second, in well-defined study groups where students have actively employed the study-group process for a specific length of time, group leaders have input into the selection of group members assigned to their study group. Their input must focus specifically on what student leaders have observed about group members' academics and social behaviors over time. This is done to keep leaders focused on what is needed to improve the climate of the classroom, which will lead to improving learning behaviors, as opposed to focusing on personality issues such as popularity and gaining access to groups based on that popularity. Lastly, as group members develop critical thinking skills they are allowed to identify specific study groups that they believe can meet their individual needs. Allowing input into the process from teachers, student leaders, and study-group members serves to empower all participants in the process to work actively toward creating a democratic environment (Dewey, 1944).

Student Study-Group Leaders

While all students are needed in order to have successful study groups, an integral part of the process are the student study-group leaders. They act as facilitators of small learning groups. As in the WFSGs, students attend professional development sessions just like teachers. Student study-group leaders meet periodically with other such leaders to be trained in areas of conflict resolution, communication skills, and instructional strategies. Sessions are active, and preparation by teachers is extensive as they plan rigorous activities for leaders designed to have them think through areas of concern that they may encounter, for example, in their classroom, neighborhood, and home. In the classroom, student study-group leaders bring cohesiveness to study groups by keeping everyone on task. They involve everyone in their study group by asking questions concerning the task at hand to ascertain if the objective was understood and if it can be implemented by the study group or by an individual study-group member. Student study-group leaders share their knowledge using various strategies learned from earlier professional development sessions. In addition, student study-group leaders actively encourage members of their groups to stay on task and complete all tasks. They do so by reminding members of the objectives and asking questions to see if objectives are being met. While doing this, the leaders constantly work to reaffirm to group members that it is okay to ask questions. Further, group leaders are trained how to praise group members effectively concerning group work and behaviors. Curwin and Mendler (1988) write, "Praise can help people master basics skills, work harder for certain extrinsic goals, and overcome extreme cases of poor self-concept" (p. 85). By doing so, group leaders are not only building a cohesive unit but also helping to strengthen the self-esteem of group members. Although student study-group leaders serve as mini-facilitators inside the classroom, their job is to empower group members, not to exhibit power over them. When problems do arise, teachers do not provide an easy answer; rather, time is given to the students to discuss the problem and seek appropriate answers to properly resolve concerns.

Student study-group leaders may be chosen using a variety of methods. Teachers may informally assign students to serve as group leaders, or, as highlighted here, group leaders may formally apply for the position by filling out a job application. The application details leadership expectations in terms of the desired characteristics and academic and creative abilities. Interested candidates are required to complete the application along with writing an essay on leadership. Finally, candidates would meet with a team of teachers, who employ the student study-group process, to interview them. Questions on the application and essay include input from classmates, who give their ideas on characteristics that student leaders should possess if they are to lead a group to success. Among leadership characteristics suggested by middle school students were:

Determined	Tactful	Respectful
Dependable	Peaceful	Trustworthy
Enthusiastic	Outgoing	Assertive
Energetic	Encouraging	Motivating
Flexible	Kind	Responsible
Friendly	Cooperative	Collaborative
Humble	Problem Solver	Diplomatic

While it is not necessary for group leaders to possess all of the above characteristics, it is preferred for teachers to model and provide different scenarios designed to help students develop these characteristics over time. By working to hone their interpersonal skills, teachers help students build rapport between themselves and their group members. Further, it is the expectation that teachers will work to develop student characteristics in the hope that students will use them as they transition from the classroom to the real world.

Role of the Teacher

Teachers are crucial to the success of the student study-group process. Initially and regularly, teachers should share with students the importance of being in groups and of students' being respectful of one another. Furthermore, students should be properly trained to use instructional strategies designed to promote not only collaboration during learning activities but also effective use on standardized tests. An example might be conducting a think-pair-share activity that allows students to think about a topic and share thoughts with group members, and then share ideas with the entire class about the topic that encourage a collegial environment. Another example might include having students use graphic organizers like a KWL or a Venn diagram to organize their thoughts to help them arrive at a logical answer. Learning these instructional strategies will help students gain a "repertoire of strategies" for doing well on local and state assessments and in their personal lives.

In addition, it is the teacher's role to build rapport with every student in the classroom, because it is the students who must feel empowered to work within the collaborative study-group structure. If students do not trust their teachers, they will not actively support the process. It is vital to understand that students initially will test their teachers to see if they are truly committed to building a democratic classroom. So, it is imperative for teachers to build trusting rapport with their students. Teachers cannot empower students one day and then take back the empowerment the next day, since empowered students will actively challenge anything or anyone who is not fair to the process. So, teachers must believe in truly developing critical thinkers, empowerment efforts must be consistent over time, and the students must understand the democratic process.

Use of the Dialogue Journal

Since being a leader is not easy for teachers, imagine how difficult it is for students, especially those in middle school where peer pressure is ever present. Group leaders require regular communication with their teachers so they will feel supported. To support students in their group-process struggles, teachers can communicate effectively with group leaders via a dialogue journal. Student dialogue journals serve multiple purposes, such as (a) providing opportunities for students to build an individual rapport with their teachers, (b) sharing vital information concerning group dynamics, and (c) helping teachers informally assess whether strategies taught were clearly understood by students. Further, dialogue journals help teachers determine whether democracy is actually occurring and where students feel comfortable enough to share with teachers their innermost thoughts about their education. Fundamentally, a dialogue journal serves as a two-way, written communication process between a student and the teacher. In addition to regular written communication between students and teachers, group leaders must share insights concerning their groups' progress with their teachers on a weekly basis.

Because group leaders take on greater responsibility in their accepted assignments, it is critical that they feel respected by the teacher. In their journals, group leaders can share both their triumphs in helping classmates show improvements and their frustrations concerning inner group dynamics that cause subtle problems that their teachers may not have noticed. The dialogue-journal process allows teachers more time to observe various groups without betraying the confidence of group leaders who shared important information with the teacher (e.g., possible fight at lunch, group member completing homework but not turning it in, group squabbles, and group leader's frustration at being a leader all of the time). These issues will arise from time to time, and if group leaders trust their teachers, they will verbalize or utilize their dialogue journals to inform the teachers of these issues that can make or break a cooperative learning group.

APPLICATION OF THE RHODES MODEL

As middle-school teachers it was our job not only to instruct but also to understand our students. However, understanding includes focusing on discipline problems, which may leave a limited amount of time for academic instruction. Students frequently do not want to work together, teamwork activities lead to group conflict, and though class work and homework are completed, students do the work reluctantly. When the work is done, it is often done haphazardly. As teachers, we go home exhausted each evening but return each day to pull out a new bag of tricks, only to experience continued failure. We continuously try the same instructional techniques and expect different outcomes, but to no avail. Classroom assessments, for example, paper-and-pencil tests, are given but students still do poorly.

As teachers who attended weekly WFSG professional development sessions in our school reform model, we began to brainstorm about the possibility of creating student study groups. The overall purpose was to: (a) increase academic and collaborative learning by having more time on task, (b) provide meaningful experiences where students are placed at the center of their own learning efforts to develop and strengthen problem-solving skills, and (c) have students develop positive social behaviors with classmates to promote democracy.

STRUCTURING OF THE MODEL

Typically, students did not believe that teachers cared enough to allow them to have a genuine voice in the classroom. As a result, in 1997 two classes employed the study-group process by identifying and training sixteen student study-group leaders and forming sixteen heterogeneous study groups. Group leaders were responsible for between two and four group members. In order to ensure the success of the process, we researched information on study groups and attended study-group professional development sessions. We then met together to determine our actual plan for how we wanted our study groups to operate. We decided against having homogenous groups and instead employed Gardner's (1993) multiple intelligences so as to recognize all of the talents that students bring.

Gardner employs the following seven intelligences: linguistic (poet), logical (scientist), musical (composer), spatial (sculptor), bodily kinesthetic (dancer), interpersonal (teacher), and intrapersonal (individual's accurate view of self). Gardner believes that children come to school with various intelligences and that it is imperative that educators somehow incorporate the multiple intelligences in their daily instruction. By recognizing that children possess certain talents and potential, teachers can help students become motivated through learning. Curwin and Mendler (1988) write that "students who are highly motivated rarely become discipline problems" (p. 41). Using Gardner's theory of multiple intelligences, we allowed students to explore and direct their own learning pathway. Recently, Gardner added an eighth intelligence, natural (humanistic intelligence).

We wanted to have leaders who could (a) serve as group motivators, to encourage students to believe in themselves and the group process, and (b) understand their roles in the educational process. During preparation time, lunchtime, and after school we worked together to carefully plan our program that would empower students to learn.

Initially, because we knew about our students' progress, we had our own ideas of who we wanted to be group leaders. However, since we desired them to own the process, we opted to have students apply by completing a job application specifically designed for study-group leaders. This process led to a diverse selection of study-group leaders with all having the potential and desire to become good leaders and group leaders.

As teachers, our role was to teach students how to utilize the shared inquiry method and facilitate instruction. In lieu of teachers' giving the right answers, students were asked higher order of thinking (HOTS) questions to help them generate answers and then defend their answers with evidence. The process was more important than the end result. During the beginning stages, it was difficult for our teachers to move away from traditional modes of teaching, such as chalk and talk, teacher-directed lessons, giving worksheets, and various activities and assessments.

As the program progressed, we began to relinquish control by employing more student-centered approaches to teaching and learning. For example, we used the multiple intelligences to promote active participation and positive self-esteem.

Benefits of the Model

There are many benefits to using the Rhodes student study-group model; that is, using an intensive collaborative learning structure in a student study-group process. First, students learn how to communicate and collaborate effectively with one another with in-class support given by the teacher. The teacher explains and models the rules for being in small groups and how students are supposed to function in them and sets specific expectations. Second, the teacher works to replace the myth of "teacher as authority" with "teacher as a partner in the learning process." The teacher acts as a guide, working to help students discover learning in a variety of ways. Answers are no longer the most important thing; the focus, instead, is on how students arrive at the answers. Third, based on training and daily interactions with others, students learn how to responsibly resolve conflicts with peers by properly utilizing their communication and critical thinking skills. Fourth, students at the Rhodes Middle School involved in the student study-group program have shown an improvement in speaking and writing skills, as evidenced by informal assessments such as teacher-made tests, and formal assessments such as the Pennsylvania State Systems Assessment (PSSA) writing assessments. In addition, students made slow, steady improvements on the PSSA in the areas of reading and mathematics when compared to same-grade students who did not employ the study-group process.

Limitations of the Model

Although the benefits far outweigh the limitations, there are a few limitations that teachers should be aware of before instituting this process. One limitation is that it takes a substantial period of time for teachers to work together to successfully employ the student study-group process and adequately train student leaders so that they are able to use critical thinking skills in a variety of situations. If teachers are looking to this process as a quick fix, then they will be disappointed. It takes serious time to implement a truly student-centered process. The objective is to build a "community of critical thinkers," leaders who are able to apply learning to new situations and not just in a classroom with a teacher. As a result, over time, learning will occur, students will learn to be leaders, and improvements will occur.

Another limitation is that the teachers may find it difficult to share the management of their class activities and instruction. Once students are empowered to speak for themselves concerning their education, they may exert their independence at the most inopportune time, which may cause frustrations for the teachers. For instance, this occurred when the authors used student study-group leaders, as an excerpt from Cooper's class clearly illustrates:

> My group leaders were trained on a weekly basis and group members understood their roles within the groups. My students and I discussed all aspects of

their learning in a language that eighth-grade students could understand. The process worked well until one day, exasperated by one of my group leaders continuous decline in behavior, I removed her from her position as study-group leader. Jeanine pouted and stated, "So what, I don't care!" She carried her "don't care" attitude with her for the next couple of days and I reveled in the fact that I knew that she missed working with "her group" to help them to improve upon goals that they set as a group. On the third day, Jeanine came to me and stated that she wanted her position back. I told her that I did not think that it was a good idea. She walked back to her seat and sat down. I smirked feeling confident that I was teaching Jeanine a hard lesson. After lunch, Jeanine came to me with a petition signed by her classmates requesting for her to be placed back in her position pending a speech and discussion by the class. I was a little taken aback by what I felt was a challenge to my authority. I put the petition on the desk. Jeanine was not to be deterred. She asked, "Ms. Cooper, aren't you going to read the petition?" I responded, "Jeanine, sit down." She sat and I immediately began to vacillate between my feeling of loss of authority and my feeling guilty for being angry at Jeanine for using her critical thinking skills to petition the class to allow for her to be heard by her peers. As I struggled with these feelings, Jeanine sat down and continued to complete her work; however, I noticed that there was a hush over the room as one student, Antwoine whispered, "See, I told you not to take that petition to Ms. Cooper. Save that democratic stuff for when you get home.

"Now, we are all in trouble." Everyone sat quietly and continued to complete their work. I slowly read all of the signatures on the petition and I called Jeanine up to my desk. I informed Jeanine that I would allow her to give her argument to her peers as long as I was able to give a rebuttal after she was done. Jeanine was excited and she agreed to the terms. I still felt in control because I knew once the class heard my sound rebuttal they would agree that it was best for Jeanine to step down from her position. Jeanine eloquently spoke to her classmates and informed them that everyone in her study group respected her and they worked well as a team, turning in homework, participating in all class discussions and showing improvements on assessments. She informed them that she had been declining in her overall behavior and that as a group leader, she set a poor example and she was sorry. She then turned the floor over to me. I was ready. I informed the class that Jeanine and her group had shown overall improvements but over a course of weeks, Jeanine had run-ins in the lunchroom and classroom. I ended by asking for her peers not to return her to the esteemed position as student study-group leader. The vote was placed on the floor. It was unanimous that Jeanine be returned to her position. Briefly I was deflated, but upon reflecting on the situation, Jeanine feeling a part of a democratic classroom put the teachings that I had employed to work for her. She felt empowered to work within the confines of the democratic classroom and I had to put what I had been teaching to work. I had to utilize a fair process, one that shows students that their ability to extend meaning as it relates to them was something that was not just taught but a way of living. Jeanine won but I won as well because my students actually were becoming effective problem solvers inside and outside of the classroom.

CONCLUSION

Student study groups emphasize collaborative learning and seek to encourage all members to work together using a variety of study-group protocols to reach common goals. Study-group leaders are integral to the study-group process because they work to motivate their groups to do the best work possible. Group members are taught in the areas of conflict resolution, communication, and problem solving. Becoming a classroom that employs the student study-group process takes time, energy, and commitment because teachers must spend time developing collaborative-learning structures inside and outside the classroom. Teachers must prepare lessons that promote opportunities for students to openly debate and discuss subject matter as it relates to students' personal experiences. In addition, students must be taught how to provide evidence for answers given, how to agree to disagree, and how to extend meaning to new situations. This type of teaching will not necessarily help students for particular subject purposes, but it will prepare them in how to handle new situations in school and life.

Initially, it takes a lot of hard work to put the processes in place for such a process to work. However, once teachers and students become familiar with crucial aspects of the student study-group process, the classroom operation will run more smoothly because children will take ownership of not only their behavior but their academics as well.

9

Implementing Study Groups for Principals

Emily Weiskopf

To state that the role of the principal has changed in the past five years would be an understatement. Going from managing schools to leading reform has placed both seasoned and beginning principals on a major learning track. Besides dealing with the regular daily problems and demands, we are now challenging leaders to develop a context of a professional learning community in which continual, rigorous learning exists for both teachers and students. Yet, who is responsible for creating this context for principals? How do we ensure that principals have the knowledge, tools, and experiences that allow principals to facilitate the change in the culture of schools from that of isolation to one of collaboration?

It was these burning questions that allowed one Midwestern school district to create a collaborative culture among district administrators by forming Principal Whole-Faculty Study Groups. When principals experienced a type of professional development system that they had been leading for several years in their own buildings, they began to understand the power of learning in the workplace, engaging in collective inquiry, and learning from one another.

THE STARTING POINT

In our work with school leaders, we often ask them to describe the biggest problem they face in trying to raise student achievement. Mediocre instruction—the

71

ability to provide reliable, consistent high quality teaching in every classroom—surfaces quickly on their list of frustrations. (Platt, Tripp, Ogden, & Fraser, 2000, p. 1)

When facing new challenges or implementing a new idea, common ground is essential to begin "the work" of improving schools. Mediocre teaching is common ground for all school leaders. The issues around mediocre teaching are well known and the pressure to improve these teachers is prevalent in all schools. It was this notion that "mediocre teachers must be confronted" that began our implementation of school leadership study groups.

FORMING STUDY GROUPS FOR PRINCIPALS

Whole-Faculty Study Groups (WFSGs) in schools was not a new idea for us. In fact, almost every school in our district is implementing this school-based professional development system. Yet, the idea of forty-three elementary principals forming into study groups was uncharted territory. The district was in the midst of a major reform initiative, both with school improvement plans and with professional development. Principals were being held more accountable than ever before for creating a "learning school." The pace was quick and the work was challenging. The notion of setting up study groups with principals really evolved from two premises. One was a reoccurring plea for "time to talk" at principals' meetings. The leaders felt that there was not enough time built into their meetings to discuss prevalent issues that were common among the group. The other was a need to experience what was expected in their schools. So, the timing was right to implement a familiar structure in which productive conversations could begin.

THE SETTING

Springfield Public Schools is a large district with approximately 25,000 students. The infrastructure of administration in a large district is always interesting and typically complex. The district is divided into three zones with an associate superintendent for each zone. Two district administrative meetings were held each month. Associate superintendents led zone meetings and together they led Job-Alike meetings. With the new accountability plan in our district, all meetings now placed heavy emphasis on quality teaching and improved student achievement.

STARTING WHOLE-FACULTY STUDY GROUPS FOR PRINCIPALS

At first glance, implementation of study groups for principals would seem like an easy task. In a large district, however, it was important to bring district administrators on board to ensure success. The Director of Staff Development was the originator of the principal study-group idea. Being a member of the superintendent's cabinet, she had the standing to present the idea and gain approval. As with any new initiative, there is always the question of time.

Setting the Time

We began by having a conversation about time for study-group meetings. This conversation takes place at any level when beginning WFSGs. As with any strong professional development plan, we knew it would be important to build in time during the day for the groups to meet. Each month, the principals come together to a Job-Alike meeting with the three associate superintendents. The associate superintendents agreed to give up the first forty-five minutes of the Job-Alike meeting for principals to meet in study groups. An hour would have been more ideal, yet forty-five minutes was a place to begin. It was important to discuss when the forty-five minute time allotment would come within the meeting. We began to have a conversation about the importance of modeling the placement of professional development high on the priority list. Therefore, we felt it necessary to begin each Job-Alike meeting with the WFSGs.

Responding to Logs

Once time was established and set, there were other details that needed to be resolved. The biggest of these was who would be responding to the logs of the study groups of principals. The associate superintendents, along with the director of professional development, felt that it would be logical for the Instructional Specialists for School Improvement to respond to the principals' logs. As an Instructional Specialist, I felt this presented a challenge. Although my instructional knowledge base had always been "ahead of the curve," I had never actually been a building principal. I knew it would be best to tread carefully when responding to logs that principals were writing. My first task became: to review the structure of WFSGs and form groups.

Forming Study Groups

The first meeting with the principals consisted of presenting a review of the "basic steps" in developing study groups. We reviewed the fifteen guidelines and the five guiding principles. The essential question, "How can we effectively confront mediocre teaching?" was given to the leaders. We explained that this would be the basis for all of our work together this year. Groups were then formed with members from each zone being represented to create a diverse look at addressing mediocre teaching. Each principal was given the book, *The Skillful Leader: Confronting Mediocre Teaching*, by Platt, Tripp, Ogden, and Fraser (2000) to use as a starting point for new knowledge.

Planning for Action

Once groups were formed, the groups were asked to begin working on their action plans for their work together. I assumed that since many of the principals had been responding to action plans and logs for a few years that they would have a good sense of developing an action plan. The action plans were sent to me and my colleague Becky Wells for our review and response. I realized that I had made an incorrect assumption about leaders' understanding the parts of the action plan. The most difficult section was the performance goals. For teachers, this section is clear.

However, what would the expectation be for leaders? What would accountability for their work look like? When responding, we carefully redirected some thinking in order to ensure that the groups were on the right track. Our typical response was,

> As far as your action plan goes, it looks like there is still discussion about performance goals. Continue to mull the idea of performance goals over and add them to your action plan. You will still need to also provide some information about how we plan according to data. What data do we have that supports that mediocre teaching is something we need to confront?

It was critical that I not tell them what the performance goals would look like but that they begin to have conversations about how their work together would impact teacher quality and result in improved student achievement.

LOOKING OUT, LOOKING IN

As with any collaborative work, the thought of changing one's own practice seems hard to grapple with. The same is true for WFSGs with leaders. Most groups began discussing the current evaluation system and how it did not address the needs of mediocre teachers.

Looking at Mediocre Teachers

The logs stated concerns such as, "How can we establish consistency in our Performance-Based Teacher Evaluation (PBTE) process—e.g., teachers expecting a 'needs improvement' on evaluations—we could add a progressing category to take the negativity out of the process." The other main concern with the current evaluation system was that many mediocre teachers had satisfactory evaluations from past schools. When responding to these concerns, I felt it important to recognize that these are valid concerns on study-group members' part. However, developing a new PBTE system was not going to be accomplished this year. I tried to state clearly that WFSGs are a way to begin to change current practice. I provided feedback on investigating other avenues for improving teacher performance, rather than just evaluations, and reiterated that we must work with the current system. And, I challenged groups to think outside the box and expand the possibilities for improving mediocre teaching.

Looking at Interviewing Practices

The study groups seemed to gain momentum by midyear and began to look at current structures and practices in place that they could improve upon. One specific practice was interviewing. This stemmed from a discussion of two ways to improve a school; improve the teachers you have or hire better ones. One group began to develop new interview questions to ensure quality teachers were being hired. This document was shared with the other groups. From that sharing, two other principals developed a rubric for scoring an interviewee's answers. The development of the rubric sessions caused the two principals to take a hard look at what quality teaching looked like. This was then shared with other groups, and the mold was broken. We now had leaders *working collectively* to improve their practices.

CHANGING EVALUATION CONFERENCES

One of the major results of the work of the study groups was how they conferenced with teachers before and after evaluations. It became apparent, through reading and discussing, what "quality instruction" looked like versus "mediocre instruction," in which all teachers had some room to grow. But, with the current evaluation process in place, it seemed that growth was difficult to detect. One idea that arose from the logs and feedback was to ask each teacher before an evaluation, "What will I see that's different in your teaching this year as a result of your study group's work over the last year?" A simple question, yet one that provoked serious thought on the part of the teacher being evaluated. This question in itself put teachers automatically in the mindset that they were to be constantly improving their practice in the classroom as a result of their professional learning experiences. This question also was a starting point for some quality discussions about whether or not the work of teacher study groups was improving practice. Conferencing with teachers became information gathering sessions for leaders to assess the strengths, weaknesses, and supports needed to improve teacher practices.

OLD INFORMATION BECOMES NEW NEWS

Principals have known for years that when teachers share practices, model lessons, and teach with each other in the classroom, instructional practice improves. What leaders came to know through their work with WFSGs was that the same holds true for them—that sharing improves practice. This became apparent through conversations around the classroom walk-through process.

Classroom walk-through training to improve instructional practice had been done in our district the previous year. Every principal participated but had concerns about the process being nonevaluative. Many discussions arose in meetings about what the expectations were for the implementation of the walk-through process and how it could be used consistently throughout all schools. Many principals found it difficult to make time for the classroom visits and some didn't see the value. As a result, it was discovered that the walk-through process was being used sporadically and haphazardly throughout the district.

Once study groups moved through the stage of looking outward at the evaluation process and began to look inward at their own practice, the walk-through discussion surfaced again. Groups began to see this process as a way to monitor and address the needs of mediocre teachers. There seemed to be a realization that a walk-through now had a place in instructional leadership for principals. The reflective questions that followed the walk-through discussions helped leaders understand that by asking reflective questions about teaching and learning in a nonthreatening way, they were meeting the need to "grow" master teachers in a much more effective way than through the current evaluative process.

A TIME TO REFLECT, A TIME TO CELEBRATE

Max Depree, CEO of Herman Miller, Inc., says that the first responsibility of a leader is to define reality. Depree goes on to say that in between, the leader is the servant, and that the last responsibility is to say "thank you."

Standards-Based Education

The current reality is that with the standards-based education movement, teachers are being held accountable for their teaching practices as well as student learning in their classrooms. There is a gap widening between those teachers who have "mastered" standards-based teaching and those who are still struggling as mediocre teachers. The need for leaders to address this issue is apparent not only in Springfield, Missouri, but all over the United States.

Servant Leadership

Servant leadership deals with one truly "being there" for others. As an instructional specialist, it was my job to demonstrate being a servant leader and make sure that the study groups of principals had timely and effective feedback and the resources they needed to study such a critical need for principals. If groups asked for additional resources, the district administration found the funds. I learned more about servant leadership in this year of responding to logs and facilitating the study groups of principals than I had in many years of being an instructional leader.

The Reflection

In May, it was time to say "thank you" to all the leaders who had engaged in this work together. We reviewed our work by addressing the following three questions:

What was the most significant piece of learning for you this year?

What difference has it made in your leadership?

What will you do differently next year as a result of your new learning and implementation experiences this year?

We also looked at the WFSG rubric to see where we were with implementation. Groups set goals for the next year and began to think about essential questions for further study.

Small Celebrations

Being the first year for implementation, it was important to notice the "little things" that began to change in the context of the district meetings. Yet, the culture was changing. Study groups began to show up early to meetings so that they could have more time to collaborate. Groups began to communicate in between study-group meetings through e-mail and phone calls to gain insight or advice from their newfound confidants. At the end of the year together, many study groups asked to stay together, which showed a great sense of collegiality toward one another. Groups also began bringing items to the Job-Alike meetings to share with the other principals and with the associate superintendents.

A principal's job is exciting, surprising, and challenging. It will never be redundant or routine. By celebrating through collaborating and networking with each other, the work becomes invigorating.

COMMON THEMES FOR REPLICATION

Two major items of learning occurred while working with the study groups of principals. The first was that *the frequency of meetings truly mattered* when it came to groups' doing genuinely productive work. The groups that met once a month, only at the time provided for them at the Job-Alike meetings, spent most of their time discussing outside factors over which they had no control. They may have shared stories but never really engaged in the rigorous work of improving their knowledge for helping mediocre teachers grow. The groups that met twice a month spent the first few months discussing factors that were beyond their control, but once they became comfortable with each other, they began to look within and discuss their leadership skills for working with mediocre teachers.

The second major learning was really just a reinforcement of something already known. That is, *we must experience a process to truly see its value.* The principals had been the facilitators of study groups in their own buildings for a few years, yet going through the process themselves was instrumental in leaders' seeing the importance of collaborative teams as a way to enhance professional practice.

CONCLUSION

To create a culture that fosters continual growth in teachers, it is imperative to create this same culture for the leaders of these teachers. Principal WFSGs provided an opportunity for Springfield Public School principals to grapple with the important instructional leadership challenges. This system still exists today, surviving both district leadership change and infrastructure change. The work evolves each year. New challenges arise as to how to lead the groups, how to ensure that principals find value in them, and how to create a rigorous learning community that exists at all levels of the district. Yet, the vision remains constant, the focus is still clear, and the climate of continuous improvement keeps leaders energized and focused on the job of leading learners.

PART IV

Key Success Elements

School improvement, even when you have the availability of a successful process such as the Whole-Faculty Study Group System, is not an easy task. This challenge involves myriad factors that must be dealt with effectively for success to have a chance to emerge from the process, including many people and their varying perspectives and existing mental models, the climate and culture of the institution and district, the adequacy of relevant data and their applicable use, the lack of understanding of study groups and how to implement them to gain commitment for and build learning communities, and limited experience with the "action research" approach as a powerful tool to create new meaning and results.

This section of the Fieldbook, *Key Success Elements,* presents six chapters that deal directly with and give important insights into the key issues indicated above. In particular, the chapters: (a) provide a comprehensive rubric for understanding and generating professional learning communities; (b) show how to build commitment for effective study groups and create and sustain learning communities; (c) use study groups and the WFSG process to bring about necessary and meaningful changes in the school culture; and (d) introduce in detail the process of data-based decision making and its application to enhance student achievement.

10

The Whole-Faculty Study Groups Rubric

Defining Context, Process, and Content

Carlene U. Murphy

Would you recognize a high performing study group if you saw one? Do you know the difference between a professional learning community (PLC) that "meets to satisfy an expectation that teachers collaborate" and one that "holds itself accountable for having a measurable impact on student learning"? If your answer is "No" to either question, this chapter will help you turn "No" into "Yes."

In the fall of 2005, I conducted a Whole-Faculty Study Group (WFSG) Basic Training Institute for a district in a state where the state department of education strongly recommended that all schools have faculties in PLCs. This recommendation, since 2002, had been communicated across the state by district-level, professional-development coordinators. In that district, with twenty-six schools, I met with all principals, assistant principals, instructional coaches, and district instructional support staff. Within the first hour of the first day, I learned that all schools had professional learning communities in place. Administrators knew the rationale and theory behind the concept, as they had been studying the PLC literature during the previous school year. I quickly discovered, though, that there were no clear structures, specific guidelines, and accountability systems in place for the PLCs. School leaders had the impression that if teachers were meeting and talking to each other, they were collaborating and fulfilling the expectations for a PLC. Setting the Institute agenda aside for the morning, I asked the school leaders to turn to the WFSG Rubric in the training notebook. Next, I asked them to read all the descriptors under the heading "Advanced Implementation." By reading the descriptors of specific behaviors, expectations for collaborative groups became clearer. By mid-morning, as a result of the small-group and whole-group discussions of the behaviors in the WFSG Rubric, leaders understood what student-focused, professional-learning communities must do to be effective.

This chapter discusses the development and implementation of the WFSG Rubric; this rubric is given at the end of the chapter.

NEED FOR A RUBRIC

Shortly after I started working with ATLAS Communities in 1997, its director, Linda Gerstle, asked me: What does a high performing Whole-Faculty Study Group (WFSG) look like? That question and Linda's persistence in continuing to ask the question led me to, what was initially, a personal, brainstorming exercise. I began thinking about opposites in relation to what I have seen groups doing and how I have seen them working in schools of all kinds. I could immediately picture a specific study group at a particular school that was not functioning well. At the same time, I had a mental picture of a study group that was functioning extremely well and doing high quality work focused on student results. What factors made the difference? My initial brainstorming was totally unorganized. I simply listed for myself whatever jumped into my mind. As I looked at my list, it was obvious that I could easily organize my list into the three components of the WFSG framework: Context, Process, and Content. Since these were consistent with prior descriptions of WFSGs, I had confirmed that I could organize an assessment tool that could be divided into those three parts: Context, Process, and Content.

Context—Process—Content

Georgia Sparks (1983) introduced the context/process/content schema as a way of organizing research findings. Her schema was used by the National Staff Development Council (NSDC) as the organizer for NSDC's Staff Development Standards (2001). Murphy and Lick (1998, 2001, 2005) used the concepts of context, process, and content to build the framework for describing the WFSG System. Because the components have different characteristics, distinct behaviors are aligned with each component. These components are equally important and create a seamless whole; in reality, however, the components are inseparable.

PART I OF THE RUBRIC: CONTEXT

The *context component* of the WFSG Rubric describes the range of behaviors that impact the context of the school and the study group itself. *Context* addresses the organization, system, or culture in which the study groups exist. It is the organizational or cultural factors that facilitate or impede progress toward the organization's intended results. The context includes how the organization "feels" to the personnel, as well as the norms that govern personnel. It is often the informal structure of how things get done. The context will largely determine how psychologically safe individuals feel, how willing they are to take risks, what behaviors are rewarded and punished, and whether it is standard to work in isolation or with peers. The context of an organization is typically the first line of concern for leaders, sponsors, and change agents.

PART II OF THE RUBRIC: PROCESS

The *process component* of the WFSG Rubric describes the range of behaviors that apply to the procedural guidelines and to the functioning of groups. *Process* refers to "how" work gets done and how individuals and groups function. It describes the means for the acquisition of new knowledge and skills. A process is a way of doing something. It is how change happens and continues to develop over the course of time. A process generally infers that there are steps or procedures that one goes through in the course of accomplishing a goal. Most of the 15 WFSG Procedural Guidelines (Murphy & Lick, 1998, 2001, 2005) are included in the Process part of the WFSG Rubric.

PART III OF THE RUBRIC: CONTENT

The *content component* of the WFSG Rubric describes the range of behaviors that apply to what study groups do when members meet. *Content* refers to the actual skills and knowledge educators want to possess or acquire through staff development or some other means. In WFSGs, the search for content begins with identifying student instructional needs. The decision-making cycle (DMC) is a step-by-step set of procedures for establishing the student needs that study groups will address. The student needs lead members to what the groups will do. The content of WFSGs is what study groups do to become more knowledgeable and skillful. It is the substance of the WFSG process. For teachers, it is teaching students how to read and the history, English, science, and mathematics that they teach. It is also how to teach for understanding and what brain research tells us about how to meet the needs of students. It is instructional strategies and skills and how to plan and assess instruction. We often refer to content knowledge or what one knows about a subject. When we read a book, the content is the text, what we learn. We could think of the content as the ingredients of a process, what is in the process, what the process holds. The content of WFSGs usually involves paying attention to expert voices and referring to resources. The expert voice may be in the form of a consultant who visits a study group or members going to a consultant via enrolling in a course or workshop. Expert voice may also come from viewing a video or reading excerpts from a book or an article. Resources are primarily materials from training sessions that teachers have attended and from instructional programs being implemented at a school.

RUBRIC FORMAT

Once we knew how we would organize an assessment tool, the format had to be decided. My colleagues and I determined that we would borrow from what teachers were doing with their students. Teachers and students use rubrics in classrooms to identify exact behaviors that describe levels of student work, especially in writing assignments. A rubric is a scoring tool that lists the criteria for a piece of work; it also articulates gradations of quality for each criterion, from excellent to poor.

Another possibility was to use a Likert scale. On such a scale, one can describe an optimum behavior and have users of the tool suggest, on a scale from one to five, the degree to which the behavior is present. We believed that this option might be too inconsistent from user to user.

As I saw study groups developing rubrics for assessing the work of students, and students using rubrics to assess their own work, it seemed that a rubric would fit our needs and that teachers were already familiar with the use of such a tool. Therefore, just as students assess their own work, we wanted members of study groups to assess themselves using a set of descriptors, a rubric.

Other Considerations in Developing a Rubric

As my colleagues and I proceeded to work on the rubric, another important body of research was ever present in our thinking, the Concerns-Based Adoption Model ([CBAM]; Hall & Hord, 2001). Introduced to CBAM in 1981, I have used the concepts of CBAM to help me work more effectively with individuals and innovations for more than twenty-five years. CBAM uses innovation configurations to chart the levels of use of innovations by individuals. Individuals go from nonuse to collaborative use of a specific innovation. A rubric is similar to an innovation configuration. Both identify and describe, in operation, the major components of a new practice when the innovation is in use. Both represent the patterns of innovation use, usually on a scale using specific descriptors of behavior. The WFSG model is a major innovation in schools. Actually, it is a bundle of innovations. The scale on the WFSG rubric is as follows: *not yet, beginning implementation, developing implementation,* and *advanced implementation.*

The stages of group development also informed the creation of the WFSG Rubric, especially in describing a range of behaviors. Murphy and Lick (1998, 2001, 2005) devoted part of a chapter to the growth stages of groups.

Another piece of research that contributed to the development of the rubric was what we know about what makes a learning team synergistic. A chapter in Murphy and Lick (1998, 2001, 2005) is devoted to how study groups become synergistic, self-directed, learning teams.

USING THE RUBRIC

All faculty members at a school are given a copy of the WFSG Rubric. Usually in January, one study-group meeting is spent discussing the rubric. Before a designated study-group meeting, members are asked to check the behavior in each set of descriptors that most accurately describes the group. When the group meets, members share their placements and discuss differences in perceptions. Groups may decide to consider only one component (Context, Process, or Content) of the WFSG Rubric at a time. Groups are also asked to discuss what the group needs to do to "move up" on the descriptors of a given behavior. The rubric is *not* used as an administrative-evaluation tool. Faculties have been creative in finding interesting and fun ways to complete the rubric and share placements on the rubric.

The rubric is also used to compile how the whole school is doing in the implementation of WFSG. Some faculties have done charts to indicate where study groups are on each of the behaviors described on the rubric. Schools have enlarged each page of the rubric to fit it on sheets of paper as large as chart paper. Each study group is given a different colored dot. One study group may have blue dots, another red, another yellow, and so forth. A representative from a group places the dots on those descriptors that best describe that group's behavior. When all the groups have finished, everyone can see the progress of each study group. If several study groups are "stuck" on non-productive behaviors or on behaviors that are not indicative of high performing teams, the principal can ask the WFSG consultant or other resource persons to provide support or technical assistance in those specific areas. The rubric may also guide the principal in determining what types of training the faculty needs. If groups are not using protocols to look at student work, the faculty may need more training in how to use protocols.

Study groups should meet at least four times before making any attempt to complete parts of the rubric. The amount of time members of study groups spend working together directly impacts their progress toward attaining "Advanced Implementation" on the behaviors. A group that meets weekly is likely to be "more advanced" on the behaviors than a group that meets every other week or monthly.

Another factor that impacts a group's movement along the rubric is changes in the group's membership. If a member transfers to another school or leaves the school for any other reason, it may take the group back to an earlier point in its development. If a member is added due to an increase in student enrollment, the dynamics of the group change. If the group decides that it wants to revise its action plan or develop a new plan, several behaviors will be affected. When school conditions change, for example, time of meetings, or when major interruptions occur, groups may experience a "recycling" effect. Another factor that impacts how a group places itself on the rubric is how long the group has been together. For example, some groups remain intact for two or more years.

Even though the rubric appears linear, it isn't. As already described, groups often have to "regroup" or, essentially, start over. A group may place itself in the "advanced" column on a given behavior in November and in the "developing" column in March, depending on circumstances. Faculties that complete the rubric in January may see changes in both directions when the rubric is reexamined in May.

SUMMARY

The WFSG Rubric was used with a faculty for the first time in 2001. Since that time, it continues to evolve into a usable, meaningful tool for groups to answer their own question: Are we doing this right?

Teachers often tell us that after they have experienced several study-group meetings and go through the Rubric with their study-group colleagues, they have a much deeper understanding of WFSGs. With the experience of being in a study group, they will derive more meaning from the Rubric than when they reviewed it during the initial training or introduction to WFSGs. Going through the behaviors as a study group is a learning experience. The rubric (Table 10.1) actually shows the teachers what it takes to have a synergistic study group that has the power to impact student learning. The rubric has become a critical piece of information for faculties.

Table 10.1 Whole-Faculty Study Groups Rubric

Context	Not Yet	Beginning Implementation	Developing Implementation	Advanced Implementation
Forming WFSG	• WFSG Decision-Making Cycle not followed to identify student needs or to form groups.	• Steps 1–3 of DMC were followed, but groups are formed based on teacher needs, availability, existing groups, or personal friendships.	• Steps 1–4 on DMC followed to identify student needs and to form study groups.	• Study groups are formed each year around student learning needs using Steps 1–4 of the DMC.
Principal Feedback	• Members disregard, resent, or do not receive feedback from the principal.	• Members review principal's feedback with no action.	• Members discuss feedback, making attempts to comply with principal's suggestions.	• Members often refer to principal's helpfulness and seek additional input.
Feedback From Others	• Members do not utilize feedback given to the group by anyone external to the group, e.g., Instructional Council.	• Members pose few questions for feedback and are unsure what to do with the feedback received.	• Members appreciate the feedback they receive, sometimes acting on it, sometimes not.	• Members engage in a rich dialogue with those giving them feedback, evaluating all input for its value and usability.
Communication	• Study Group Action Plans (SGAP) and Logs are not posted or have a number of logs missing.	• SGAP and Logs are posted but not immediately upon completion; members often have to be reminded.	• SGAP and its revisions during the school year and all of the group's logs are posted in a timely manner.	• Items promptly posted; members show evidence of reviewing and using the feedback from other groups.
Collaboration	• Members show no awareness of and no interest in what other study groups are doing.	• Members indicate some interest in learning about what others are doing.	• There is evidence in logs that the study group is discussing the work of other groups.	• Members frequently seek out and use work from other study groups at the school.

Instructional Council	• There is no Instructional Council (IC) for members to attend.	• Same member of study group attends every meeting of the IC.	• Members rotate attending IC but little, if any, time is spent at the next study group meetings sharing what took place.	• Members rotate attending the IC, discuss and use information from IC, and tie what the SG is doing to what other groups are doing.
Communication Networks	• The only way groups know what other groups are doing is by word of mouth.	• Action Plans and Logs are posted.	• In addition to reports from IC meetings and posting plans and logs, little else is done to highlight work of groups.	• In addition to IC and posting materials, groups make presentations at a variety of types of meetings, items are in the school newsletter, and celebrations are held.
Connections	• Members do not connect their work to others in the group and to whole school improvement.	• Members connect to each other but not to whole school improvement.	• Members talk about whole school but no evidence of tying their work to SIP.	• Members continually refer to SIP and their role in meeting schoolwide goals.
Data-Based Decisions	• Members are uncomfortable with routinely examining data and prefer reviewing data in faculty meetings using computer printouts supplied by the district of which they have little understanding or interest.	• Members are transitioning from having state test data presented in grade level or department meetings to using classroom assessment data in study group meetings.	• Members are becoming more comfortable in study group meetings with making data-based decisions, looking at results together, and taking ownership of how each other's students perform on a range of assessments.	• In study group meetings and other settings, staff value collaboratively using qualitative and quantitative data from several sources for diagnosing their students' instructional needs, setting improvement targets, evaluating effectiveness of instructional strategies, and monitoring progress toward targets.

CONTEXT: The organization or culture in which the study groups exist.

(Continued)

88

Table 10.1 (Continued)

Process	Not Yet	Beginning Implementation	Developing Implementation	Advanced Implementation
Leadership	• The same person leads the group each time it meets.	• Leadership is rotated.	• Leadership is rotated, and group members feel comfortable with this.	• Each member willingly takes his or her turn leading the group.
Norms	• The group has not agreed on a set of norms.	• Norms are written but not honored.	• Group norms are written and mostly honored.	• All feel responsible for the success of the group and hold each other accountable to the group's norms.
Action Plan	• The Action Plan is not complete, and/or recommended revisions have not been made.	• The Action Plan is complete. Occasionally the group reviews it and makes minor revisions.	• The Action Plan is complete and is revised, adding and deleting as work progresses.	• The Action Plan is complete and often referred to during meetings, is a living document, and is kept in front of the group at all times.
Logs	• Logs are not turned in, not complete, or do not accurately describe what the group did.	• Logs are turned in, but group members do not use them as a point of reference for future work.	• Logs are helpful reminders of the work of the group.	• Logs tell a rich story of dialogue and action around student learning.
Reflection	• The group does not show evidence of reflecting on student work or reflecting on their own learning and teaching.	• Reflection on learning and teaching is practiced as debriefing.	• Members look at student work but without its generating reflection on practice.	• Looking at student work is the basis of reflection on learning and teaching and guides actions.
Interaction	• Members are confused and feel alienated because of misunderstandings.	• Members are beginning to trust each other and to build credibility with each other.	• Members are communicating effectively with each other and actively listening to each other but continue to be too judgmental.	• Members respect and appreciate differences, empathize with each other, and consider all input.

Synergy	• Members feel they have nothing of value to contribute and what they have to offer will have no bearing on the final outcome.	• Members feel valued but are not sure they can depend on other members.	• Members feel empowered but continue to hold back and do not openly and fully share their skills, knowledge, and ideas.	• Members feel they have something to contribute and what they offer will have a bearing on the final outcome. They are genuinely cooperative and mutually dependent.
Group Size	• Group size is not within guideline of 3 to 5 in a group.	• Group size is 5 or less but one member dominates.	• Group size is 5 or less but several members are not fully engaged.	• Group size is 5 or less and all members are equally and fully engaged.
Time	• The group meets once a month or for about one or two hours a month.	• The group meets for an hour every other week or for about two hours a month.	• The group meets two or three times a month for a total of three to four hours a month.	• The group meets weekly for at least an hour or for four hours a month.
Equality	• There is a hierarchy within the group.	• Some members have more influence than others.	• Members espouse equality but it is not always evident in practice.	• Equality is evident in all behaviors and actions.
Assessment of Results	• The group uses annual district and state assessments to measure changes in student performance on their student learning needs.	• Some members use a classroom assessment to assess student results at the end of the year on the study group's targeted student learning needs.	• The group uses a common classroom assessment to collect baseline data and assess student results at the end of the year on the group's chosen student learning needs.	• The study group uses a common classroom assessment to collect baseline data, monitor student progress every 6–12 weeks, and assess results at the end of the year on the study group's chosen student learning needs.
Shared Responsibility	• Members act as if the study group is a committee with one person primarily responsible for the work.	• Members claim to be equally responsible but still depend on 1 or 2 members.	• All members take responsibility but do not always follow through.	• All members do what they agree to do.

(Continued)

Table 10.1 (Continued)

Process	Not Yet	Beginning Implementation	Developing Implementation	Advanced Implementation
Mechanics	• Members are trying to figure out what a study group does, focusing on the mechanics of group work.	• Members have established a routine for their meetings, but remain overly conscious of "are we doing this right."	• Members are focused on their work with little energy being spent on logistics and more attention being given to the impact the work is having on students.	• Members function in such a way that the operational system is invisible; all of the group's energy is focused on the task; the work is stimulating and impacting their students' learning.
Willingness	• Members do not show evidence of their willingness to be vulnerable within the group.	• Members are hesitant but will share what is not working.	• Members accept suggestions and share the results of the revisions.	• Members are genuinely open with one another about their strengths and weaknesses and willing to give to each other whatever support is needed.
Commitment	• Members rarely, if ever, buy into and commit to decisions	• Members feign agreement during meetings.	• Members are cautious yet show willingness to confront and be confronted on expected behaviors and actions.	• Members openly remind each other of behaviors and actions that aren't consistent with agreed-upon behaviors and receive reminders without resentment.
Openness	• Members seem to have no interest in observing in each other's classrooms.	• Members have invited other members to observe in their classrooms, but no action taken.	• Members are observing in each other's classrooms but not debriefing within the group.	• Members routinely observe in each other's classrooms and pre- and post-conference within the group.

PROCESS: The means for the acquisition of new knowledge and skills; how change happens; how study groups function.

Content	Not Yet	Beginning Implementation	Developing Implementation	Advanced Implementation
Students	• Members are focused on teacher needs, not on student.	• While student needs guide the group's work, considerable time is spent on hearing opinions of group members that are not grounded in data.	• Members use classroom data to understand student learning needs and research strategies to try, spending little energy rehashing opinions.	• Members are focused on the learning needs of the students in their classrooms and engage in cycles of action research in their group.
Action Research	• Members spend many meetings examining standardized tests and trying to establish a baseline for current work.	• Members give prompt attention to current assessments in establishing a baseline but get stalled on researching strategies for addressing needs.	• Members develop lessons using new strategies and materials but do not show evidence of using the lessons in their classrooms.	• Members establish baseline and targets, identify best practices, develop lessons, use lessons in classrooms, and reflect on results within repeated cycles of inquiry (one cycle equals about four weeks).
Actions	• Logs reflect little, if any, differences in types of actions taken from one meeting to the next, indicating members spend most of their time talking about behaviors of students.	• Planning to take action is the primary work of the study group.	• Members actively practice or demonstrate strategies routinely, teaching each other what works.	• All members are active in planning, teaching each other, and examining student results from all the members' classes.
Implementation	• Members are not open to doing anything different in their classrooms.	• Members identify and discuss strategies they think will work in their classrooms but show no evidence of using the strategies.	• Members design lessons to teach and share results of what happened when the lessons were taught.	• Members incorporate new content and strategies into their repertoire for continued use and revise curriculum units accordingly.

(Continued)

Table 10.1 (Continued)

Content	Not Yet	Beginning Implementation	Developing Implementation	Advanced Implementation
Depth	• Members address only what is in their comfort zone and what is of interest to them.	• Members identify key issues related to student learning needs and their teaching, but only skim the surface.	• Members work together to learn and experiment with best practices, actively engaging their students in work emanating from their study group.	• Members examine key issues deeply and challenge each other's assumptions, evaluating all input for its value and usability.
Student Work	• Members seldom bring student work to examine collaboratively using a protocol.	• Members share examples of their best students' work from a culminating lesson, meaning there is no obvious intention to reteach the material.	• Members share examples of a range of student work and discuss how to improve it always using the same protocol.	• Looking at student work together using protocols is the heart of group work. It is used routinely on varying levels and content, and leads to further changes in teachers' practice.
Expert Voices	• Members rely on what they already know.	• Members bring some types of literature into the meetings, discussing material only superficially.	• External content "experts" are invited to group meetings, books are used as resources, and videos are viewed. But members do not hold each other accountable for using the expert knowledge.	• Members actively seek multiple sources to push themselves to higher levels of understanding of academic content and effective pedagogy.
Instructional Focus	• Logs indicate that members spend a lot of time on administrative and managerial issues.	• Members focus on designing instructional projects for others to implement.	• Focus is on improving members' teaching but not on improving their students' learning in their classes this school year.	• Members have internalized: "What do students we are teaching now need us to do?"
Coherence	• Members do not use materials and strategies from any of the school's current instructional initiatives.	• Members refer to new programs at the school, but there is no deliberate effort to connect the initiatives to the study group's work.	• Members investigate strategies for connecting the group's work to new instructional programs at the school.	• Members incorporate materials and strategies from several initiatives and existing programs into the group's work for coherence and

Content	Not Yet	Beginning Implementation	Developing Implementation	Advanced Implementation
Joint Work	• Members share lessons they developed in the past and tell about their classrooms.	• Members develop lessons separately and sometimes share what they are going to do or have done.	• Members develop lessons separately but with input from the group and share classroom results.	• Members routinely do joint work, meaning that the group works as one in the development of lesson components and use each other's results in modifying their work.
Valuing the Work	• Members complain about study groups being a waste of time and that what they are to do is not clear.	• Members indicate that study-group work seems more like busy work than real work.	• Members are trying to "do the work they have to do anyway," but find that expectation hard to actualize (do).	• Members value their work and indicate that study group work is meaningful and saves them individual preparation time.
Consequence	• Members are not focused on improving student performance in specific learning needs for their current students.	• Members are easily distracted and express doubt that results are possible.	• Members refer to data and express concern and desire to attain results.	• Members are confident that the work of the group will impact student learning and hold themselves accountable for attaining results.
Experimentation	• Members seem to have no interest in trying new strategies and materials.	• Members are hesitant to try new strategies and materials.	• Members develop lessons that incorporate new strategies and materials in classrooms.	• Members share results from using new strategies and materials in classrooms.

CONTENT: The actual skills and knowledge educators want to possess or acquire; what study groups do to become more skillful and knowledgeable.

Murphy, C. U., and Lick, D. W. (2005). *Whole-Faculty Study Groups: Professional Learning Communities That Target Student Learning*. Thousand Oaks, CA: Corwin Press.

® Registered Trademark to C. Murphy, 2005

11

Building Commitment

Kenneth Sherman

Kim Reynolds-Manglitz

Building and sustaining commitment is key to a successful Whole-Faculty Study Group (WFSG) System in any school. You can't start a WFSG process without commitment, and you can't maintain your WFSG process without nurturing and sustaining your commitment every day.

SOME EARLY SLIPS

Eight years before we embarked on the WFSG plan (when Dr. Sherman first became principal at Clarke Middle School) a group of teachers worked together to develop our own homegrown, shared decision-making and governance process. We were sincere in our efforts, but we were naïve about many things. One of our fatal flaws was to build into the plan an opportunity for faculty to "opt out" of the responsibility for school improvement and shared decisions, as long as those who decided not to participate promised to support—and not subvert—what the rest of the staff came up with. As we write these words, they sound awfully foolish. It's like putting a delicious (at least in the cook's opinion) five-course dinner in front of someone, and then telling that person they are not to take a bite, or—if they do take a nibble—not to criticize the chef!

As a result, we had some very involved staff members, but there were others who sat back and watched—and could not resist taking a bite, that is, commenting on the process. It became rather divisive and inefficient. We also devolved into a focus on lots of "administrivia"—who parked where in the teachers' lot, whether students could chew gum or eat candy in school, what time a school dance or football game should begin, and lots of other tinkering that deflected our attention from serious, core issues.

WHOLE-FACULTY STUDY GROUPS

Why were we attracted to WFSGs? They provided an intentional and potentially effective approach to giving serious attention to the core academic issues facing our school. They allowed us to refocus our efforts on what was most important—student achievement—and they provided several key commitments that were not part of previous school improvement and governance efforts, including:

- A commitment by *all* faculty to participate actively in school improvement, professional learning, and shared decision making
- A commitment to look honestly at the achievement of all of our students
- A commitment to look genuinely at our instructional practices, to determine how student achievement has impacted those efforts
- A commitment to work together on school improvement, focusing on how we can change and improve to serve student needs
- A commitment to make professional learning and growth part of our daily work
- A commitment to hold each other accountable, by adhering to norms and standards (including such "basics" as common meeting times and routines and standardized action plans and meeting logs)

As we began to talk with staff about how WFSGs might reenergize and refocus our efforts, there was a lot of excitement, and also a fair amount of skepticism, as you might expect. We knew we had to take our time—change is not easy, and rapid change is almost impossible—and do our "homework" first, which included attending the national WFSG conference, speaking with other schools that had implemented WFSGs, and reading. The entire process, from raising the idea and doing our research to collecting and sharing data to setting up our study groups, took eight months. We strongly recommend building in enough time on the front end to plan and build commitment, to ensure that the WFSG program will take root and succeed.

LAYING THE FOUNDATION FOR WFSGS

Armed with our research, we met with all staff. Rather than simply taking a vote on, "How many of you would like to meet more often, please raise your hands," we worked on reaching consensus on our issues and needs. Together, we asked:

- What issues does our school face? (Most important: the need for *all* of our students to meet and exceed learning standards)
- Should all faculty members be involved in solving school problems and raising achievement? (The answer was "yes.")

- Should student achievement needs drive our professional learning activities and school improvement plan? (Again, "yes.")
- Would we be willing to work on these issues in small study groups if we could carve out and protect time for faculty members to get together? (A resounding "yes.") We ultimately decided on a plan to "bank" enough extra minutes of instructional time every day to allow us to release students two hours early a dozen times during the school year. The remainder of our WFSG meetings would take place during teacher planning days.

We moved slowly but steadily. We allowed staff time (a few weeks) to meet as teams and grades, and we provided several discussion opportunities, electronic and face-to-face, for everyone to ask questions and raise concerns. One issue about which we were very clear was that this new effort was not going to be "the flavor of the month." Rather, we were making a long-term commitment to use the WFSG model as a framework for pulling our many school improvement efforts together. It was to become our "lifeblood," a way of monitoring our teaching efforts and student achievement outcomes. Once we reached consensus as a staff that we were ready to move forward and establish a WFSG program in our school, we spent the next few months publicizing our efforts and building broader support.

IMPLEMENTING WFSGs

Critical to the effective implementation of WFSGs were: integrating WFSGs with existing structures and initiatives, cultivating support, and dealing with logistics, as discussed below.

Integrating WFSGs With Existing Structures and Initiatives

The timing of our WFSG start-up effort was fortuitous because it coincided with a districtwide push for all schools to rewrite their School Improvement Plans (SIPs). As a district, we realized that our improvement plans were too broad and too vague. They had to be pared down, based on specific student achievement data, and refocused on student achievement goals and targets. Integrating the WFSG process directly into our new SIP was a key step. We wanted to use WFSGs to streamline our process and tie everything together. We worked to avoid, at all costs, the perception that this was an additional or contradictory layer that would add to our workload without any payoff.

Thus, we made our adoption of the WFSG System an actual component of our school improvement planning, rather than leaving it as something we assumed would happen. We detailed in our SIP specific ways in which we would revise our daily schedule to "bank" time for early release days, to allow staff to meet on contracted time. We also spelled out the specific steps that we would take in terms of data collection and school governance to support and incorporate our WFSG program. For example, we combined the WFSG Instructional Council with our state-mandated School Council, thus including parents, community members, and staff in school improvement discussions and decisions. It was also important that we integrate the WFSG process into other existing structures, such as teacher observations and evaluations, professional goal setting, curriculum renewal, and school-wide professional learning activities. As teachers wrote their individual professional development goals and plans, a vital component for implementing and evaluating their efforts was the study-group process.

Cultivating Support

Of primary importance, before we could move forward at all, was gaining the support and trust of parents and the local community. Parents, especially, had to know why their children were being sent home early twelve times during the school year, and they must understand how this would help us be a better school. Over a period of several months, we met with parents and community members at PTO and School Council meetings and a variety of other forums. We also sent out letters and e-mails to communicate our plans and explain our rationale ("We want to be better teachers for your children"). Overwhelmingly, they were impressed that we were setting aside time for staff to examine and improve their instructional efforts, and they have continued to be supportive of our work. This is an ongoing effort, not only because we have new families joining us each year, but also because we must keep all families in the loop and let them see our progress. In the middle of our first year, we sent out a WFSG newsletter with an update from the focus team and each of our ten study teams. We also included a list of emerging ideas and school improvement initiatives that were taking place or being planned, so they could see that our work had real impact and was not merely theoretical.

It was equally important to cultivate support from the Superintendent and other key district-level personnel. We knew that our plan, especially our early release idea, would take some coordination and might be questioned. We worked with district-level instructional and professional development leaders and—this was critical—personnel involved with the logistics of pupil transportation and after-school activities. We opened our process to anyone who wanted to visit—and many did—to see what we were doing, and we sent out e-mails and newsletters to these folks, too.

Dealing With Specific Logistics

Creating a WFSG process was a logistical challenge as much as a philosophical and educational one. We've already talked about the need to build support and keep everyone in the loop. All of the other nuts and bolts, in addition, had to be in place for this to work. To begin, we required a clear plan for continuously collecting data, identifying student achievement needs, and monitoring our progress. It fell to our "focus team," which is discussed in the next section, to be the coordinating and data collection vehicle for our WFSG process. We started with the entire staff, using the WFSG Decision-Making Cycle to identify needs and form our groups.

Next, it was important to us that our study groups be no larger than six teachers, cross-graded and cross-content area, to the greatest extent possible. We established a yearlong schedule for WFSG meetings, using early release days and districtwide planning days. This schedule was published at the beginning of the year and could not be changed. We didn't want to fall into the trap of telling folks, "If you can't meet today, that's OK, just meet tomorrow." Teachers understood that all other business, including such things as grading papers, meeting with students, and going to outside appointments, had to be laid aside; the WFSG meetings were that important. When teachers saw how helpful and positive the study-group meetings could be, there was no need to "sell" them on these commitments; they looked forward to meetings with excitement and energy.

Teachers required guidance and support in how to be study-group members. We provided professional learning and informal sessions throughout the year on the WFSG process, group skills, and data collection and interpretation. We also had to establish and reinforce continually schoolwide WFSG norms and expectations. We agreed on a set format and focus for meetings, and we developed specific forms (action plans and logs), procedures, and due dates for sharing progress with the rest of the school. Again, the idea was not just to "do our own thing"; as former children of the sixties, this was not always an easy change, but it made us much more effective and productive.

Finally, no matter how much support and commitment you build in at the beginning, the success of your WFSG effort will depend in large part on how well you continue to support, encourage, cheerlead, and guide the process. It cannot be stated too strongly how vital it is that the principal and other school administrators provide and demonstrate commitment and support. WFSG work is rewarding, but like anything worthwhile, it takes work and time, and teachers already have very full plates. To the extent that the WFSG process is integrated into all the other facets of school planning and life, it will feel less like "extra" work, but teachers must give their full effort to make the program meaningful.

WFSG FOCUS TEAM

As we mentioned above, to support the efforts of our teachers, we created a "focus team," borrowing the term from Murphy and Lick's (2005) WFSG book; it comprised the principal, assistant principal, instructional lead teacher, and counselor. We extended the role of the focus team beyond getting the WFSG information to staff and getting the process started. We added the critically important task of not only building commitment but also *sustaining it*. The focus team oversees the entire WFSG process, coordinates everyone's efforts, and keeps us all moving forward. Our focus team takes the lead in identifying and collecting data to be used in the Decision-Making Cycle and in ongoing assessments. Once the process is up and running and WFSGs are meeting regularly, our most essential task is to keep all of the study groups on course; we respond in writing, in a structured and timely way, to the action plans and meeting logs from all of the study groups. In our responses, we provide feedback and suggestions for the rest of the faculty to consider for future meetings. We make recommendations and may provide resources, research ideas, and helpful contacts (e.g., outside "experts," guest speakers, and staff from other schools).

As important as anything else, the focus team is the vehicle or clearinghouse for all WFSG-related communications. We act as a conduit of information between and among the other study groups. Teams are often working on similar issues and problems, but may not always be aware of what the other groups are doing. We work to coordinate the efforts of all the teams and to promote team-to-team communication, using e-mail, electronic postings on the school server, and hard copies. This year, we plan to set up a WFSG bulletin board with photos and updates to share information and celebrate our efforts. It is also our role to communicate beyond the school, sharing information at meetings and presentations, and via e-mail and newsletters with parents, community members, and district leaders.

Throughout the year we are called upon to schedule full-faculty meetings and other WFSG-related events; to provide training for teachers in how to work in teams, how to use protocols to look at student work, and how to look at and interpret data; and to collect and prioritize emerging ideas, share them with staff, and incorporate them into the School Improvement Plan. Beyond all of these pieces, we always work to cheerlead efforts, share successes, maintain momentum, boost morale, and advocate for the WFSG process with staff, district, and community.

CONCLUSION

We knew we were on track and really moving ahead in our first year when our various study groups began to communicate more directly with each other. One of our active groups was our HOTS team—our Higher Order Thinking Skills study group. They had a lot of great ideas almost from day one, but had trouble developing a clear focus. At some point, they came up with the terrific idea of doing "HOTS makeovers," borrowing from the extreme makeover craze that is so popular on TV. They began inviting members of other study groups to meet with them, and would work with their invited guests to make-over their lesson plans to incorporate higher order thinking. The HOTS team was thrilled to be able to directly influence others and help them with their teaching, and the recipients left the makeover sessions loaded with great ideas and enthusiasm.

As we write this, we are embarking on our second full year of WFSGs. We are excited about the initial progress we have made, but we know we have much work to do and that we need to continue to promote, refine, and nurture the process. We also recognize that some critically important areas, such as parental involvement and student discipline, do not fall within the realm of the WFSG process. Part of sustaining faculty commitment also involves reassuring our folks that these other areas, which certainly have a major impact on teaching and learning, will be addressed in other appropriate forums during the year. We know that we haven't yet found a panacea for all of our needs and concerns, but WFSGs have been a major step in the right direction for us. They provide a structured, accountable way of involving everyone in continuous school improvement. Our job now is to sustain and grow our efforts.

12

Using Study Groups for Cultural Change in Schools

Michael L. Rothman

Ronald D. Walker

John Dewey (1916) has described education as the socializing force by which a society sustains and renews itself in each generation. This force can help us maintain social continuity, with each generation passing on skills, knowledge, and attitudes to the next generation. In the realm of education, some critics maintain that this social continuity borders on inertia, evident in the outmoded structure and systems of many of our public schools. On the other hand, this "socializing force" can also spur innovation. Change in society as a whole can be brought about through the intentional and thoughtful modifications that we first bring about in our schools. To change schools is thus not only to change the world for a group of children, it is potentially to change the world. If we wish to see changes in society at large, we do well to first determine how we can make those changes in our public schools. Cultural change in schools is no less difficult than it is in society as a whole.

In this chapter, we identify three different ways in which the philosophy and methods underlying the Whole-Faculty Study Group System (see Murphy & Lick,

2005) serve as the basis for cultural change in schools and, by extension, in society as a whole. First, we look at how ATLAS Pathways have brought together districtwide groups of education stakeholders—from school faculty to district administrators to parents, students, and community members—to achieve thoughtful and effective community-directed change. Second, we look at how the safe, supportive environment of the study group can be extended into forums for educators to explore issues of cultural identity and its effect on students in a diverse society. Third, we look at how the Project for School Innovation's Model School Study Groups leverages the study-group model in the Whole-Faculty Study Group System to document and share knowledge about education practice within and among study groups.

ACHIEVING DEMOCRATIC CHANGE

Without intervention, schools tend not to change. This diagnosis is not intended to single out schools. Indeed, this simple fact is true of any institution. Without pressure or reason to rethink what they do, the members of the staff and leadership will continue to act and think as they have in the past. New hires are most likely to recreate what old hires did before them. Culture is an important and valuable feature of institutions: It provides for continuity and stability over time. On the other hand, it can also engender inertia and stagnancy. Practices that may have arisen through accident or chance become a matter of custom and habit; policies remain in force long after their purposes have become forgotten or obsolete.

To bring about change in ossified institutions is nothing short of a colossal task. In public schools, the pressure for that change often comes from the outside. The government declares that it is time that no child be left behind, and a school's staff members are forced to rethink how they teach. A new district superintendent declares that every third grader must be able to read, and schools must respond accordingly.

But there is a problem with such change by fiat. A broad range of research (Bryk & Schneider, 2002; Darling-Hammond, 1992; Fullan, 1995; Wilms, 2003) finds that for change in schools to take root, the educators responsible for carrying out that change must have a genuine belief and trust in the process. Research, along with common sense, tells us that people tend to resist decisions that are imposed upon them and to embrace decisions in which they have been engaged and had their opinions heard. Yet such change "of the people, by the people, and for the people" will tend toward the same inertia and stagnancy we alluded to earlier if there is no impetus for the people to rethink their habits. Those interested in achieving change are faced, then, with a conundrum: offer new ideas that will never take root in institutions or engender democratic involvement that tends toward inertia.

STRATEGY FOR DEMOCRATIC CHANGE: ATLAS PATHWAYS

There is, of course, a third option. As a mechanism for achieving democratic involvement while overcoming inertia, the study-group model offers a unique pathway to change. Whole-Faculty Study Groups (WFSGs) have generally been used to engage school faculty in reflective discussion of the practice of education. These discussions allow faculty to reflect thoughtfully on what they do, giving them the space and opportunity to generate new ideas and new suggestions while maintaining their genuine sense that the suggestions are their own. Within WFSGs, *all* faculty members in an institution have an opportunity to rethink what they are doing and, through the same process, to embrace the changes that arise from that rethinking.

In ATLAS Communities (schools being professionally supported by the "ATLAS Communities" organization, which is a national, nonprofit, consulting entity that strives to improve schools from kindergarten through high school), the WFSG System is mirrored and reinforced through the whole-district Pathways. ATLAS Pathways convene stakeholders across a district to engage in thoughtful discussion about what it will take to help all children succeed. This yields policy and structural change driven by the teachers, support personnel, administrators, parents, and, in some cases, students, who all hold a stake and a role in the institution of public education. In general, Pathways meetings occur once a month and include representatives from each school in a district, including faculty, principals, administrators, and parents, along with district administrators. Stakeholders in Pathways meetings examine data on student achievement—which No Child Left Behind is making increasingly available—and use it to focus on issues of shared interest. At times, Pathways meetings lead to issues of concern to one particular school. For instance, low parental involvement in a middle school may be the cause for feeder elementary schools to explore how they can build a tradition of parental involvement in the lower grades. At other times, Pathways meetings lead to issues of concern across the district. For example, data on student achievement may reveal that strong student test scores in the primary grades worsen in later grades. Schools can then work together to arrive at strategies and policies to address these patterns.

The power of the Pathways approach lies not only in its ability to bring stakeholders in a district together to achieve change, but also in the way that Pathways can both authorize and protect the study-group model within and across schools. A district without the Pathways model is similar to a school without study groups: Staff have little time to reflect on what they are doing and why, and even less time to do so collaboratively with others outside of their own school. A district with the Pathways model, on the other hand, is one in which district leaders become accustomed to reflection on practice and experience firsthand the power of collaborative policy making. When district leadership values collaboration and reflection on practice, teaching staff are more likely to recognize the value of collaboration and reflection as well, serving as an important part of the foundation for a district building a culture of thoughtful change.

VALUING CULTURAL DIVERSITY

Pull together any group of children and adults and they will bring with them a mix of different backgrounds, experiences, and identities. The richness that arises from this diversity is an asset to all involved, expanding their minds and awareness and helping them to better understand themselves and others, what Benjamin Barber (1998) calls the "social imagination." As a nation of immigrants, the United States has grown from and thrives on the diverse experience, perspectives, and talents of its people.

But there is a sadder side of diversity with which all Americans are familiar. For example, the differences between white and nonwhite, native and immigrant, English speakers and English learners are impossible to avoid in our education system. Discussion of the "achievement gap" between white and nonwhite students, for instance, has tended in recent years to focus on test scores and academic achievement. With No Child Left Behind, test scores are now disaggregated into nineteen subgroups, categories such as race and English-speaking ability, that cast an even stronger spotlight than ever before on the ways in which diversity has translated into academic gaps in this country. Curiously, discussion of these gaps rarely probes the cultural, experiential, socioeconomic, and other differences that distinguish different groups. Educators are encouraged to treat the issue as if it were one solely of academic achievement. In fact, the issue of the achievement gap is far more complex than one of studying for tests. Even the concept of "subgroups" reflects an assumption that there is one "group" that we are trying to bring together, when, in fact, there are real and meaningful differences between different groups that we can and should value and appreciate.

This is not a popular argument in educational circles today. Some view any discussion that delves into the complexities of class, race, and linguistic differences between students to be a cover for racism and discrimination. However, we fear that quite the opposite may be true. By ignoring the rich diversity that different children and adults bring to our schools, and focusing solely on the uniform standards we want them all to meet, we risk ignoring the fact that it is not only tests but the very identity of our children that is at stake. What does it mean to be a black boy in an urban school today? What does it mean to immigrate to the United States at age fifteen in order to work in a low-wage job while learning English in high school? What does it mean for a child with cerebral palsy to develop socially and academically? The answers to these questions touch on issues of social identity and cultural norms that are far more complex than studying for a high-stakes test.

Strategy for Valuing Cultural Diversity: Community Forums

We, as educators, will never begin to reach those answers if we do not first start asking the right questions. The study-group environment is ideal for such a discussion. Study groups offer a safe and trusting environment in which participants can share concerns, offer ideas, and reveal vulnerabilities. Typically, this discussion focuses on academic issues, with discipline and classroom management sometimes addressed as well. Both of the authors have engaged in efforts that applied this model to probe more deeply into issues that we believed formed part of the cause of the achievement gap and were too often "swept under the rug" for fear of what might be found if we looked too closely.

One example comes from twenty years ago. When Ron Walker was hired as principal of an urban elementary school in Cambridge, Massachusetts, he was asked, during his interview, how he would "deal with the problems of black boys." Ron, an African American man himself, was surprised by the question. Knowing that it was asked with the best of intentions, he wondered how much the staff or administration of the school had done to *understand* the problems of black boys before trying to "deal with" them. He then treated this as an opportunity for a teachable moment, organizing a community forum for parents, educators, and students to discuss the issue openly and frankly. He invited a panel of African American students to discuss what it meant and how it felt for them to be viewed as "black boys."

Such an experience can be an opportunity for study groups as well. The safe, supportive environment of the study group can be the ideal venue to develop a sense of community awareness about issues that are too often left unaddressed. For example, teachers in study groups could read *Young, Gifted, and Black* by Theresa Perry, Asa Hilliard, and Claude Steele (2004) as a starting point for discussion. They could then follow the typical pattern of study-group discussion, using internal and external data to assess and reassess what they have been doing in relation to the issue. At Ron's school, the data showed a trend for African American males increasingly being referred to special education starting in third grade. Teachers asked what was happening in the earlier grades to lead to this trend. They could then look at their own instruction, teaching strategies, and materials to determine how they might respond to this trend and better address differences among their students. This is, of course, one of the many paths a study group could have taken, all from the same source: an issue of cultural diversity, disaggregated data on student performance, and an openness to collaborative exploration in search of a response.

BUILDING A KNOWLEDGE BASE

In WFSGs, educators have a chance to reflect collaboratively on practice. In so doing, they grapple with issues of teaching and learning and, more often than not, arrive at insights that are well worth sharing. This is, of course, a fundamental premise of the study-group process: Through structured and thoughtful reflection, professionals are better able to understand, articulate, and explain practices. The very process of describing what we do helps us to better understand what we actually do. In describing what we do, we often find that there are nuggets of wisdom, particular strategies or instructional practices, that resonate with other educators and whose effectiveness—evidenced in the story of one student's success or an entire group's test scores—make them worth sharing. In the intimate environment of the study group, where a small, familiar group of faculty gets together regularly with one another, such insights become more common and more compelling with each meeting.

However, a strength of study groups may also be a shortcoming. The intimacy of a small group yields tremendous insights, but it also means that those insights reach only a small number of people. Many study groups will bring student work, test data, or even outside reading by published authors to inform their discussions. In general, however, there is little access to the knowledge generated by other study groups. Considering the value that this information bears for participants in study groups, it seems a shame to not be able to share it. In response to this, James Hiebert, Ronald Gallimore, and James Stigler (2002) have suggested the need for a knowledge base in collecting information on education practice that is accessible and useful for professional educators. Many in education have interpreted this to mean books and videos. While these are an important start, they cannot be the only materials to serve as a knowledge base. Too often, when action research is documented in books, these books become static, theoretical documents that hardly capture the deep and resonating insights that arise out of study-group conversations. Instead, a model is called for that allows educators to engage in the thoughtful reflection that is at the core of the study-group model, while also sharing and learning from the effective practices that are discussed in study groups.

STRATEGY FOR BUILDING A KNOWLEDGE BASE: THE PSI MODEL

The process described above is exactly what we began doing at the Project for School Innovation (PSI) four years ago with our Model School Study Groups (MSSGs). In MSSGs, educators are asked not to delve into new subjects that they are struggling with, but rather to look at old subjects that they have succeeded at so effectively that they took them for granted. An MSSG starts with the identification of a model school—a school that can demonstrate clear success in improving student performance and achieving community satisfaction. Once a model school is identified, surveys and interviews are conducted throughout the school community to identify specific effective practices that are viewed by educators as correlated to the success of the school. Once this is done, a small group of four to eight educators is brought together in a study group to explore one particular, effective practice identified at the school. Participants explore the specific steps of the practice, the challenges of implementing it, advice they would give to colleagues, the impact, and evidence of positive impact. As these discussions continue, they are documented in three formats: chronological step-by-step descriptions of how to set up and implement components of the practice, tips and suggestions based on educators' experience, and narrative stories that describe the practices in action. These are collected in a document that provides a practical teacher-training curriculum. At the same time, the study-group experience helps a group of educators to become "experts" in a particular practice, and thereafter able to serve as mentors and coaches to their colleagues, using the how-to guide as a training curriculum. These MSSGs can then be followed by other study groups that can draw upon the curriculum and coaches and the knowledge they generated within their group.

For example, Roxbury Preparatory Charter School in inner-city Boston has had the strongest scores of any predominantly African American middle school in Massachusetts on the state's Comprehensive Assessment System (MCAS) mathematics examination. The school was one of eight recognized nationally for its success. Through the MSSG, six teachers at the school developed a book titled *Calculated Success* (2003), in which they provided instructions on how to develop curriculum alignment templates and teach procedure and problem-solving classes. The teachers have since used the book to provide coaching to help colleagues at two different schools to develop study groups in which they regularly explore how they teach mathematics while implementing teaching strategies learned from the Roxbury Preparatory Charter School.

Summary and Recommendations

In summary, we believe strongly that study groups can be part of cultural change—not just in our schools, but in society as a whole. We have tried to show here how we have seen that begin to happen, through ATLAS Pathways that bring districtwide conversations of change; through community forums that open the door for issues of cultural diversity in education; and through PSI Model School Study Groups that capture the knowledge that is shared in study groups so that it can be spread to more schools, more teachers, and more children.

Given these experiences, we offer five recommendations for others setting out on a similar course:

First, create the opportunity for districtwide reflection on educational needs. We have found that this is best begun through surveys, interviews, and focus groups. These are low-pressure ways for multiple stakeholders—from administrators to educators to parents—to offer their input and ideas and begin a districtwide conversation.

Second, prioritize what educational needs are best addressed at the district level. Simply because stakeholders across the district have identified particular issues does not mean all of these issues need to be addressed across the district. By brainstorming and prioritizing topics, you can focus your districtwide pathways on the efforts that are most appropriate at the district level.

Third, incorporate leadership development into study groups. By helping some study-group participants build communication, planning, and coaching skills, you can help these teachers become professional development coaches to their colleagues and leaders of change in your schools and across your districts.

Fourth, incorporate documentation into study groups. By budgeting a small amount of extra pay for new teachers, student teachers, or interns to document study-group discussions, you not only give these young educators a meaningful experience, but you also capture the ideas and knowledge that often get lost the moment discussion ends.

Fifth, and finally, incorporate cultural competency into the design of study groups. Whenever there is the potential for a topic to touch upon issues of students' identity or community issues, teachers should be prepared to discuss how these identity issues interact with education.

CONCLUSION

We began this chapter by pointing out John Dewey's reflection on the role of education in recreating society. Dewey was not only an educational philosopher, he was also a political philosopher and a strong advocate of democracy. Democracy, in Dewey's (1927) view, was "community life itself." The very act of people gathering to reflect upon a shared future constitutes democracy in its purest form. In study groups, we see this notion put into practice every day. By engaging in safe, structured, and reflective discourse, educators can begin to change their own schools, recognize the complex issues that affect their students' lives, and develop a body of knowledge to inform future change in education. The power of collaborative reflection cannot be overestimated, nor can the necessity for well-developed and well-conceived structures to support and maintain it. Unfortunately, schools continue to be under-funded and under-supported in this respect, and despite our understanding of the need for this discourse, too much of public education continues to be a race against time with educators hardly afforded the opportunity to take a break, let alone reflect constructively and thoughtfully on the future of their schools and our society. If we do not find ways for them to do this, we not only risk the integrity and quality of our schools, we risk the integrity and quality of our future.

13

Changing School Culture

Jill Potts

Jeff Zoul

This is a story about the impact that Whole-Faculty Study Groups had on the school we were assigned to lead in the 2002–2003 school year. As the new administrators at Coal Mountain Elementary, we faced some challenges in moving the school in a new direction. We knew that the school had significant potential for improving, yet the existing culture did not support a climate of change. We learned that the underlying strengths of the school offered untapped resources for building an exemplary professional learning community.

Our challenge was to mine this potential without sacrificing the fundamental elements of community and tradition that had defined this school for many years. We needed to find a way to unite a faculty of caring, experienced teachers in order to work toward goals for student achievement. Our story outlines the first year of our leadership at Coal Mountain Elementary School and chronicles the changes that came about as a result of implementing the Whole-Faculty Study Group System.

Our narrative includes a description of the school community and the prevailing views of the staff prior to our arrival. We chronicle the strengths we discovered along with the needs we uncovered that kept this school from realizing its full potential. We recount the steps taken to implement Whole-Faculty Study Groups and describe the challenges and the successes that resulted from our efforts. This is the story about how Whole-Faculty Study Groups positively impacted the school culture at Coal Mountain Elementary.

THE SETTING

Imagine that you are a new principal in an elementary school where the expectation for teacher collaboration is nonexistent, and that you have hired a new assistant principal to help you lead this school. Both of you believe that teacher collaboration is the key to school improvement. Faculty members of the school have survived for more than twenty years without support for teacher collaboration, with no expectations for it, and with no formal process to direct collaboration to meet student achievement goals.

This elementary school is in a close-knit community composed of families who have lived in the area for two or more generations. Most of the teachers in the school live in the community, and many of the teachers in the school taught the parents of their current students. The community was once rural, with traces of Appalachian heritage still evident today.

The larger community around the elementary school has undergone a dramatic change in the last decade. Farms and pastures are giving way to housing developments and industry. What was recently rural is now suburban. New residents are filling new subdivisions and clogging the small roads; shopping centers and businesses now occupy formerly pastoral settings. The old is being replaced by the new, and these changes are felt most acutely in the school. The elementary school operates in much the same fashion as it did for years, a holdout in the fast-paced world that is encroaching on the time-honored traditions and values of the community.

The situation described above is real. In the spring of 2003 we were named as the new administrators at just such a school, Coal Mountain Elementary. We came from schools that were within the same school system, but our former schools were both located in another part of the county. Among the many goals we had for Coal Mountain, our foremost was to positively impact the school culture by fostering teacher collaboration. We were not willing to accept the status quo of teachers' working in isolation and teaching the same lessons they had always taught. We were prepared to move forward with a plan that emphasized teacher collaboration and focused on student learning. Fortunately, we inherited a solid team of teacher leaders who were also ready for change.

THE DISCOVERY

Coal Mountain had had two principals prior to our arrival: the principal who opened the school in 1981 and remained in that position for twenty years, and another principal who served for two years. Many of the original faculty members were still on staff. The test scores of the students were average in the state, below average among local district schools. In spite of the changes in the community, Coal Mountain seemed to be static and impervious to the transformations that were happening around it.

What the Data Showed

The expectation for student achievement at Coal Mountain appeared to be low. In the academic year ending in 2003, the school retained twenty-five students and had one fourth of the student population in the Student Support Team (SST) process for academic and behavioral concerns. We heard that Coal Mountain had many student discipline issues and high student absenteeism. At the same time, the belief statements of the school posted in the lobby announced that the school had "reasonable" expectations for student achievement.

In researching student achievement data, we learned that the demographic data did not support low student achievement. Somewhat surprisingly, the free and reduced lunch population was about average compared to the other schools in the system. The ESOL (English for Speakers of Other Languages) and the special education populations were also comparable to other schools. Yet, the percentage of students enrolled in the gifted program was 5%, less than half that of any other school in the system.

What the Faculty Said

What was going on at Coal Mountain? Before assuming our duties in July 2003, as an administrative team we interviewed each staff member individually. We asked each teacher and paraprofessional three questions: Where do you see Coal Mountain? How can Coal Mountain be improved? How can the school's leaders support improvement?

Much information was gleaned from these interviews. We learned that almost one fourth of the staff had been at the school since it opened in 1981. About half had been at the school for ten years or more. Ironically, some teachers still thought that Coal Mountain was among the highest achieving schools in the system, which it was—fifteen years ago. Several of the staff members shared that it was unrealistic to expect "these students" to achieve at the same levels as students in other schools in the system.

Newer teachers discussed the difficulty they experienced in adjusting to the established culture of the school, and they remarked that Coal Mountain had untapped potential. They also commented on the lack of opportunities for professional discourse and staff development. Those who came from other schools recognized that few structures existed for school improvement and shared school governance at Coal Mountain.

Almost all teachers, when asked about administrative support, discussed student discipline issues. "We need more support from administrators in dealing with student discipline," was a common refrain. During several visits to the school that spring, it was apparent that discipline was, indeed, an issue. Students sent to the office for discipline were lined up in the hall of the administrative area, sitting at desks facing the wall. The fact that more than 200 students were currently in the Student Support Team (SST) process for behavioral and academic issues was another concern. Reflecting on the staff members' responses in their interviews, it became apparent that the issues concerning them had less to do with the students and more to do with the loss of efficacy and empowerment of the teachers. The lack of a central focus was manifested in excessive student discipline and SST referrals.

Teachers counted among the strengths of the school the closeness of the staff members, although several mentioned that morale was decreasing and the sense of family was less now than had existed in previous years. Unlike the staff at other schools where we had served, the teachers at Coal Mountain were an integral part of the community. However, the realization struck that the sense of family they enjoyed for many years at the school was a result of the insularity of the community rather than an effort to establish collegial relationships. As the community and student population changed, the teachers began to lose the familiarity that once anchored them. No system was in place to support and sustain the teachers in times of change.

Overall, the staff's reception of these interviews was positive and inviting. Rather than being resistant to change, the teachers communicated that they were looking forward to new leadership and they were eager to learn and implement new ideas. Most had a sense that things were going on in other schools that were not happening at Coal Mountain. They had a real sense of pride in the school and felt a deep connection with the students and parents. The more time we spent with the teachers at Coal Mountain, the more optimistic we became about the potential of the school. We felt that the strengths of the staff far outweighed the weaknesses, and that with some direction and training, the teachers could lead an exemplary school.

A FRESH START WITH WHOLE-FACULTY STUDY GROUPS

During the spring of 2003, we attended an orientation about the Whole-Faculty Study Groups (WFSG) System (see Murphy & Lick, 2005) along with three teacher leaders from Coal Mountain. The more we learned about WFSGs, the more we realized the potential that the WFSG process had for the teachers at Coal Mountain. However, in order to effectively implement the WFSG process, we would have to build a foundation of trust with the faculty. We planned to be highly visible in the school, supportive of teacher efforts, and responsive to teacher concerns. We also wanted to have *fun!* Coal Mountain Elementary needed an infusion of joy and levity to regain the camaraderie teachers and staff had lost.

The school had a leadership team already in place made up of grade-level and departmental representatives. These teacher-leaders were enthusiastic about guiding the school in a new direction. We met with the leadership team over the summer of 2003 to create a plan to communicate the vision of a professional learning community. We planned to build on the strengths in the school—strong sense of community, stability, and knowledgeable and experienced teachers—to incorporate focused collaboration for the purpose of school improvement and increased student achievement.

Also that summer, we attended the WFSG Summer Institute in Augusta, Georgia, along with the three teachers who had accompanied us to the WFSG orientation in the spring. Our group was the first focus team for WFSGs at Coal Mountain. During our time together in Augusta, we developed a step-by-step plan for how we would work with the faculty to implement the WFSG process.

We began by introducing the concept of teacher collaboration in the context of WFSGs during our faculty meetings early in the year. We discussed WFSGs in more detail with the Leadership Team members, and used their feedback to calibrate our meetings with the faculty. Six weeks into the school year, we began the WFSG process by gathering the faculty for four consecutive weekly meetings. In the first meeting, the focus team taught the principles of WFSGs. In the second meeting, we examined student achievement data. In the third meeting, we determined areas of student need. In the fourth meeting, we formed groups and created agendas for the first four meetings of WFSGs.

As we went through the process, it became evident that these teachers had never been asked to analyze student data. They did not have experience with reading state and national testing reports; they were not aware of the achievement levels of the students; and they had never used data to determine areas of academic strengths and weaknesses. Sharing this information created a powerful connection: For the first time, the teachers were able to view their work from a whole-school perspective and relate their practices to the school improvement effort.

THE FIRST YEAR OF WFSGs

The teachers began meeting with their groups early in October. They were divided into twelve groups of three to five members. The groups were cross-sectional, made up of teachers from different areas: Classroom, guidance, special education, media, art, music, physical education, and student support. Each group met weekly after school for three out of four weeks in each month. We divided the twelve groups between us, both of us taking responsibility for overseeing six WFSGs.

Most of the groups struggled through the first several meetings. How do the media specialist, a kindergarten teacher, a speech teacher, and a third-grade teacher work together to improve student vocabulary? How can they monitor and measure student achievement so that they know the strategies they implemented are working? What should the action plan look like? Working together, we helped the groups by responding to their logs and by occasionally attending their meetings. Some groups went through several drafts of an action plan before they arrived at one that defined measurable goals and outlined specific strategies for meeting those goals.

At leadership team meetings, progress within the WFSGs was discussed, monitored, and even debated. We asked the teachers on the leadership team to share the progress of their groups and talk about the difficulties they were encountering. We discussed how they could help their groups negotiate through difficulties and how they could model a positive attitude when working with their groups. The information our leadership members shared was important, because it let us know where the teachers were frustrated and when they had hit a brick wall. We used the feedback from the leadership team to talk about WFSGs in faculty meetings, to provide encouragement to the teachers, and to recognize and celebrate their efforts even as they struggled.

About halfway into the year, the leadership team suggested that we bring all the WFSGs together to share what they were doing in their groups. Although we had had two Instructional Council meetings (consisting of the administrators along with one representative from each group), the teachers felt that everyone would benefit more from a "group share." We planned a faculty meeting in which we structured a "jigsaw" activity. In the activity, the teachers rotated three times among small groups to share what they were doing in their WFSGs. Everyone had the opportunity to hear from someone in each of the twelve WFSGs.

This activity gave the teachers a tremendous boost, because in discussing their work in WFSGs with other teachers, they came to realize that what they were doing *did* impact their students' learning. Many of the groups decided to share strategies and combine efforts. Looking back, this was the turning point for WFSGs at Coal Mountain. After sharing with each other, the teachers had a renewed sense of purpose and increased confidence in the process. It still was far from perfect, yet it seemed that the fog had lifted and we were able to see where we were headed.

We finished the year by asking each group to document descriptions of best practices that they implemented as a result of working in their WFSGs. These descriptions were compiled into a "Best Practices" book that was copied for each teacher in the school. Each WFSG also submitted the results of their action research and evidence of their accomplishment of student achievement goals. This brought closure to the process and allowed teachers to share their successes.

WHAT THE TEACHERS SAY ABOUT WFSGs

At the end of the year, we met with individual teachers to talk with them about their progress during the year and discuss their plans for continued professional growth. We asked teachers to complete a written reflection that included their thoughts on the following: their exhibition of leadership, their best use of resources and student achievement data, their design and implementation of quality work for students, and their success in differentiating instruction to meet all students' needs. The teachers were also asked to suggest how to continue to improve Coal Mountain.

The feedback we received from the teachers at the end of the 2003–2004 school year was overwhelmingly positive. The efforts to unite the faculty and keep the focus on *what students need us to do* had a tremendous impact on the school culture. We discovered through our discussions with the staff and our review of their written reflections that WFSGs played a vital role in the change at Coal Mountain Elementary. Documentation from the groups' action research projects revealed consistent student gains in the areas that were targeted by the WFSGs. Teachers observed that they had formed relationships with other staff members that enhanced their working and learning environment.

Following are specific comments about WFSGs that reflect the teachers' feelings about their personal and professional growth:

- Continue the great work with WFSGs
- I was able to be a leader in WFSGs
- Through WFSG I have initiated new writing ideas with my students, increasing their interest and achievement
- I adapted lessons based on discussions in WFSGs
- The feedback from my WFSGs in terms of professional student review and Looking at Student Work has greatly assisted me with fine-tuning previous lessons, leading to improvement of existing lessons
- Being a WFSG team member has helped me look introspectively at my own skills in lesson preparation, strategy development, and implementation. My ability to partner with WFSGs has been effective in increasing student achievement
- Collaboration is the key to improving the learning in our building
- In WFSGs, I share ideas with teachers in other grades and participate by assuming the leadership role every fourth week

- As a result of WFSGs, I have been documenting, comparing, and monitoring student growth on the CRT. Looking at student work has helped me reflect on my teaching strategies
- My idea for improving Coal Mountain is to build a positive, productive, and collaborative working relationship between grade-level colleagues and cross–grade-level colleagues
- Our WFSG has researched different rubrics to use to evaluate our students' developmental stages in writing and ideas for different writing techniques and prompts to encourage their writing. We have looked at each student's individual writing level and used different techniques to encourage improvement in their writing stages
- From the media specialist: Through my work in WFSGs I designed a vocabulary test with media terms and I work with students on analogies and "word of the week"
- Our school is on the right track for improving test scores, cohesiveness of the faculty, and a trust for each other. With WFSGs, we are looking at areas of weaknesses and conducting action research to improve student knowledge. My idea for improving Coal Mountain is to make sure the study groups continue to grow and change as the needs of the students do. The groups should continue to share with each other so that we can benefit from the research of others
- Looking at Student Work in my WFSG has helped me to reflect on my teaching of writing
- My idea for improving Coal Mountain is to continue to use WFSGs to improve instruction
- WFSGs have helped me incorporate new ideas and teaching strategies
- I feel that we have made great strides in unifying our staff and building morale. To improve we need to continue to celebrate success on a regular basis, developing a mindset of collaboration, communication, and sharing of resources
- As a result of our WFSG, I have focused particularly on reading comprehension and fluency and developing skills in that area. I have planned and reworked lessons due to findings in our research to make them more appropriate
- I work to improve student achievement through study, research, and discussion in WFSGs
- Some important information has been brought to my attention through WFSGs. We have used the data to try to target specific needs in the writing process
- From the speech pathologist: I have done more reading comprehension activities this year since it is the focus of my WFSG. Through these activities I believe I have learned more about my students' strengths and weaknesses than by just doing drill work in speech.

REFLECTION

How did WFSGs change the culture of Coal Mountain Elementary? By shifting the focus from what we do *to* students to what we do *for* students, we impacted all areas of learning in our school. Previously, the culture of Coal Mountain supported the things teachers could do *to* students: failing them, retaining them, sending them to the office and referring them for testing. The past system required teachers to respond reactively to student concerns.

With WFSGs, we now have a system whereby teachers are able to do things *for* students, such as improving instructional practice, differentiating instruction to meet the needs of all students, developing student achievement goals, monitoring and assessing student progress, and creating classroom environments that are conducive to learning and that minimize the potential for discipline problems. By implementing this one change, the power of the teachers has increased exponentially, and they are able to take proactive measures in anticipation of student concerns. Examining student work, talking with each other regarding best practices, and focusing on learning, not teaching, are now understood as the way we do business at our school.

LESSONS LEARNED

Coal Mountain Elementary School is in its second full year of WFSGs, and the change in the school culture is remarkable. Our inaugural year was full of changes, yet these changes energized the school. We had fun, we celebrated successes, and we were *present* for the teachers and for the students. Simply introducing a new "thing" such as WFSGs would have been ineffective if we had not laid the groundwork for empowering teachers by bringing them together to work toward a common goal. We created the conditions for teachers to recognize the value and power that their collaborative efforts had on our students' learning.

The change at Coal Mountain can be attributed to a variety of factors, and as leaders of the school, we reflected on events that led to the success of WFSGs at our school. Our reflections resulted in "lessons learned" for creating a school climate of mutual respect, student-focused decision making, and ongoing professional growth. Key components that contributed to the growth of the staff and led to the success of WFSGs included listening to the teachers and being considerate of their concerns, having fun, being visible and present, creating opportunities for teachers to share with each other, being available, and celebrating successes. Perhaps the most important lesson learned is that the success of WFSGs depends on the leadership of the school and the steps that school leaders take to create a culture that is conducive to meaningful teacher collaboration.

14

Using Data to Improve Student Achievement in Mathematics

Teri Roberts

O ne of the key areas in discussions of school improvement is the use of student data. As an integral part of these discussions, this chapter focuses on the important uses of student data, through the implementation of Whole-Faculty Study Groups, to improve student achievement in mathematics.

LINCS SCHOOLS

In Louisiana, schools can apply for a grant for school improvement through a state initiative called the Learning-Intensive Networking Communities for Success—LINCS. LINCS is a multidimensional professional development partnership in association with the Louisiana Department of Education (LDE), the Louisiana Systemic Initiatives Program (LaSIP), and the Southern Regional Education Board (SREB).

The LINCS process is a whole-school reform initiative that focuses on site-based professional development and requires and supports common study time for teachers. The LINCS process has the potential to establish professional learning communities in the schools to develop a culture of high expectations and to strengthen teaching and learning.

In this grant process, the major vehicle for local school improvement is provided through the implementation of the Whole-Faculty Study Group (WFSG) System (see Murphy & Lick, 2005). LINCS schools use the WFSG model's seven-step Decision-Making Cycle:

Step 1: Collect and Analyze Data

Step 2: State Student Needs

Step 3: Categorize and Prioritize Student Needs

Step 4: Organize Study Groups

Step 5: Develop Action Plans

Step 6: Implement Study Group Process

Step 7: Evaluate Impact of Study Groups on Student Learning

This chapter discusses how the LINCS process uses student data to improve student achievement in mathematics. In Step 1, the process begins with collecting the data. Louisiana currently administers criterion-referenced tests in Grades 4, 8, 10, and 11. Norm-referenced tests (NRTs) are given to students in Grades 3, 5, 6, 7, and 9. These tests have served as the basis for Louisiana's School and District Accountability System. Also, each school system can choose to give a norm-referenced test in kindergarten and first and second grades, but presently such scores are not included in the state's accountability system.

LINCS School Team

Each LINCS school has a school team trained in the WFSG process. WFSG professional development is provided by Regional LINCS Coordinators.

The school team consists of a minimum of four members: the principal and three teachers in areas of content focus, including one special education teacher.

Each school also has a LINCS Content Leader on the school team.

Subsequent discussions in this chapter will reflect the perspective of an actual LINCS school whose focus area was mathematics and whose student scores were at the lowest level.

DECISION-MAKING CYCLE

In August, there was a two-hour meeting scheduled for the whole faculty. The LINCS school team led the faculty through the first four steps of the seven-step Decision-Making Cycle (DMC). The school team planned this activity during the LINCS Professional Development held in July.

Step 1: Collecting and Analyzing the Data

The school team "collected the data" from standardized test results for each grade from the makeup of the school's configuration. All test results were copied and placed in folders for each faculty member. Recording charts were also placed in each folder for each grade. For example, in the first column of the third-grade chart, the skills tested were listed (e.g., number properties and operations, algebra, geometry, measurement and estimation). Faculty members worked together in groups (though not the same grade or discipline) and recorded the correct percentage for the school for each skill in one column, and in the next column provided the correct percentage for the nation.

The next action was to find the differences between the school and national scores for each skill. Where school scores were higher, they were reported as positive numbers, grade-level strengths, and where school scores were lower, negative numbers, grade-level weaknesses.

Step 2: State Student Needs (Schoolwide)

Using the analyzed data from Step 1 for the NRT results for each grade level, they identified and recorded the top five (positively marked) skills tests where the class percentage correct exceeded the national percentage correct. Also, they identified and recorded the lowest five (negatively marked) skills tests where the class percentage correct was less than the national percentage correct. For the criterion-referenced test (CRT) results for each grade level, they took each of the four subject areas and identified the two strengths, as well as the two weaknesses for each of the disciplines.

For the sample school, the top five weakest areas for grade levels 3 through 5 are provided in Table 14.1.

Starting with the lowest grade level at the school, they listed the five weaknesses as the first five schoolwide student needs. Then they went through the remaining grades and identified additional schoolwide student needs. They did not repeat a student need that had already been identified on the list but did put an asterisk beside any need for each grade level that was weak in that area (e.g., need area 1 below had three grades with this need as a weakness). Schoolwide, students must:

Table 14.1 The Five Weakest Areas in Grade Levels 3 Through 5

Third Grade	*Fourth Grade*	*Fifth Grade*
1. Vocabulary	Measurement	Problem solving
2. Estimation	Constructed response	Measurement
3. Reading comprehension	Vocabulary	Vocabulary
4. Measurement	Reading comprehension	Geometry
5. Data interpretation	Estimation	Reference materials

1. Improve and enlarge vocabulary***
2. Make reasonable estimations**
3. Have the ability to read and comprehend information/tasks**
4. Develop and practice measurement skills***
5. Interpret data*
6. Solve and respond in writing to constructed-response items*
7. Become better problem solvers*
8. Relate geometry to real-life items*
9. Use reference materials effectively*

During the remaining part of the two-hour whole-faculty meeting, the school team led the faculty through the WFSG Decision-Making Cycle Steps 3 (categorize and prioritize student needs) and 4 (organize study groups).

Step 3: Categorize and Prioritize Student Needs

For this step, they referred to the list developed in Step 2 of the DMC.

The needs list from Step 2 had only nine schoolwide student needs, even though there could have been as many as thirty or more student needs, according to the data. They were asked to take the nine schoolwide student needs and group them into categories of study; that is, needs could be studied under each particular category. (This is where regional coordinators or content leaders can usually provide assistance by giving an example, such as for the measurement category.) See Table 14.2 for the faculty's selection.

With only nine schoolwide student needs, three categories were sufficient to study the identified needs. There is no set number of categories that should be used; what is important is being certain that all schoolwide student needs are assigned to one or more categories of study, as is true in Table 14.2.

The second part of Step 3 is to prioritize the categories. This is when faculty members look at the number of student needs under each category. The Measurement and Geometry categories each had seven student needs, while Reading Comprehension had only four student needs.

A first pass at setting priorities might suggest that measurement and geometry were the school's top priorities because these categories have the most student needs. But when reading comprehension was discussed, it was felt that reading

Table 14.2   Student Needs Grouped as Categories of Study

Category	Needs to Be Studied
Measurement	1, 2, 4, 5, 6, 7, 9
Reading Comprehension	1, 3, 5, 9
Geometry	1, 2, 5, 6, 7, 8, 9

comprehension also was a priority since it was needed to improve both of the other areas. In addition, the group referred back to the asterisks noted in Step 2 and reaffirmed their conclusion that all three categories were important for school improvement and should be choices for study groups.

Step 4: Organize Study Groups

This step of the Decision-Making Cycle was the last procedure completed during the initial two-hour meeting in August with the entire school faculty. As the final item of business, the school team requested that all faculty members write their names on Post-it notes, think about what categories they might choose to study, make their individual choices of categories that they want to work under and learn more about, and then write their choices on their Post-it notes. During this last part of the process, it is wise to have each faculty member list first and second choices. Finally, chart paper was used for displaying the categories, and faculty members were asked to place their Post-it notes on the chart under their first category choice.

After the meeting was adjourned, the school team organized the study groups according to first choices, where practical, and second choices otherwise. Study groups were to consist of at least three but no more than six members. For instance, if seven faculty members chose the measurement category, they formed two WFSGs of three and four members, respectively. If a category had less than three faculty members, then those members were asked to move to their second-choice category. If a category did not make it, then the student needs for that category were addressed in one or more of the other categories, so that all student needs were covered.

Step 5: Develop Action Plans

In September, study groups met for one hour every two weeks. During the first two meetings, they developed their action plans. Action plans guide study groups through their course of study for the school year.

The action plans were divided into six sections to record information. The top section was for the category of student needs that the group was addressing, such as measurement. Each study group created an essential question for its category that was to help guide its work during the school year.

The top left-hand side of the action plan was for specific schoolwide student needs that were included in the study group's category from Step 3 above. For example, the measurement group had seven schoolwide student needs listed, including improve and enlarge vocabulary, make reasonable estimations, develop and practice measurement skills, interpret data, solve and respond in writing to constructed-response items, become better problem solvers, and use reference materials effectively (e.g., CRT reference card).

In the top right-hand portion, proposed teacher actions were listed based on what the group members would study when they met. Below, in another section, resources, both human and material, were listed. The final section of the action plan contained the documentation sources and evidence demonstrating that the study group work increased student learning.

Grades 3 through 5 of the demonstration school for this chapter utilized a variety of data and implemented the WFSG System to improve student achievement in mathematics. The work of the measurement study group was emphasized. Study group members used data to improve student achievement in mathematics by, for example:

- Keeping a journal
- Compiling a portfolio of measurement activities
- Making measurements, beginning with familiar objects and progressing to numerical understanding
- Understanding which measurement unit is appropriate for a particular situation
- Making reasonable estimations of measurements
- Converting units of measurement
- Knowing how to use measurement tools
- Developing measurement concepts, vocabulary, and processes
- Researching best practices
- Observing others teaching measurement lessons
- Reviewing state standards/benchmarks/grade-level expectations for the measurement strand
- Examining student work

Resources for teachers in the measurement WFSG included:

- State standards/benchmarks/grade-level expectations
- Measurement lessons on video
- Professional mathematics journals
- Mathematics content resource books
- State mathematics lesson plan database
- LINCS regional coordinators
- LINCS district content leaders
- Supervisors

Step 6: Implement the Study Group Action Plan

By October, each study group was working on implementing its action plan. Teachers charted in their action plan what they did to improve student achievement in mathematics. An implementation and meeting schedule for the year for the study groups was as indicated below:

- *August:* One two-hour meeting with the whole faculty for a LINCS and WFSG overview and to form study groups
- *September:* Two one-hour WFSG meetings per study group, and an Instructional Council (IC) meeting (see the discussion of IC below)
- *October:* Two one-hour WFSG meetings per group
- *November:* One one-hour WFSG meeting per group and an IC meeting
- *December:* One one-hour WFSG meeting per group
- *January:* Two one-hour WFSG meetings per group and an IC meeting

- *February:* Two one-hour WFSG meetings per group
- *March:* One one-hour WFSG meeting per group and an IC meeting
- *April:* Two one-hour WFSG meetings per group
- *May:* One two-hour evaluative summary meeting involving the whole faculty

With the above schedule, teachers participated in seventeen to twenty-one hours of job-embedded WFSG professional development.

The Instructional Council (IC) provided coordination and assistance to the school's study groups. A part of Step 6 included Instructional Council meetings, in which attendance was rotated among study group members and the agenda was tied to what the study groups were doing or needed at the time. LINCS School Teams planned and conducted Instructional Council meetings at least every four to six weeks.

These meetings, which also involved the principal, assisted study groups and their action plans and guaranteed that study logs were displayed.

Step 7: Evaluate the Impact of the Study-Group Work on Students

Study-group work was assessed from time to time throughout the school year by examining student work. In May, a second two-hour meeting involving the whole faculty was scheduled; the collective faculty began the year together and ended the year together. During this final meeting, each WFSG made a presentation of no more than thirty minutes. Presentations shared with others the impact that their study group's work had had on student achievement. These presentations were quite competitive among the school's study groups. Various presentation styles were used, including skits, PowerPoint presentations, songs, poems, dances, and lessons.

CONCLUSION

For the particular school studied in this chapter, the work that was done in its measurement study group used data to help the school improve student achievement in mathematics, which was one of the schoolwide student needs. Among key findings at the study school discussed in this chapter were:

- Student data must be kept in view all year
- The focus throughout the school year was always powered by the needs of the students
- Action plans were continuously an important part of the discussion
- Examination of student work was reflected in a journal from the measurement group
- Group members were able to chart the growth of students through an analysis of their work from the beginning to the end of the school year
- Test scores were analyzed at the end of the year to summarize the successes of the study group's work, according to the documentation sources contained in the group's action plan

In addition, two critical findings from both the focus school study and from other grant-recipient schools in the Learning-Intensive Networking Communities for Success (LINCS) program were the following:

1. The Whole-Faculty Study Group process leads to the empowerment of teachers, bringing about mathematics improvement according to student needs.

2. The effective use of student data to identify needs to improve student achievement has been the power behind school improvement efforts.

15

Making Data-Based Decisions for Student Success

Karl H. Clauset

Sherman H. Parker

Marcia R. Whitney

Teaching can be a lonely and isolated profession. Often the teacher is alone with the students and makes decisions on learning strategies with no collaboration with other adults. Using Whole-Faculty Study Groups (WFSGs) to analyze data and study student work allows teachers to cooperatively develop successful strategies for student learning and to create a more collaborative environment for effective learning.

This chapter describes how data about their students' learning is an essential resource for WFSGs and how such study groups continually make data-based decisions as they address student learning needs. Five types of data-based decisions that WFSGs make are discussed. The study-group process for making data-based decisions is highlighted with illustrations from a WFSG school.

TYPES OF DATA-BASED DECISIONS

As WFSGs begin to implement their action plans, they make five types of data-based decisions:

1. Analyze student needs to decide what to focus on.

2. Establish baseline performance and set targets.

3. Decide whether specific interventions work.

4. Monitor student progress and make mid-course corrections.

5. Assess end-of-the-year results and plan for next year.

The first four decisions are part of Step 6 in the WFSG Decision-Making Cycle the WFSGs engage in as they address the student learning needs they have selected (see Murphy & Lick, 2005, pp. 253–266, pp. 130–132). The first two decisions, which analyze needs and establish baseline performance and targets, usually occur at the beginning of a study group's work. The third and fourth decisions, determining whether interventions work and monitoring student progress, occur as study-group members try out interventions in their classrooms. The fifth decision is part of Step 7 in the WFSG Decision-Making Cycle and takes place at the end of the school year.

By data, we mean both qualitative and quantitative data about student learning. Quantitative data are numerical data on student performance on an assessment or performance task. Qualitative data are all the other information we collect about students' learning.

For example, in New York state, the English Language Arts (ELA) assessment for students at Grade 8 requires students to read passages, answer multiple-choice questions about the passages, and write short essays related to the passages. Quantitative data consist of each student's performance on the multiple-choice questions and essays, as well as demographic information about students to analyze subgroup performance.

Qualitative data include the actual student work, observations of students while they are working on the task, and notes they generate while reading the passage, answering questions, and planning the essay. These data might also include information gathered from students through interviews or class discussions about what they were thinking and feeling while working on the task.

For each type of decision, we will answer two key questions: (a) What questions do WFSGs ask, and (b) What do groups do to answer these questions? Each decision type will be illustrated with examples from a WFSG at the Cohoes Middle School in Cohoes, New York. Team 6 was a study group of teachers working with eighth-grade students; it included two special education teachers, and a science, social studies, mathematics, English, and technology teacher. The examples are in shaded text boxes.

Cohoes Middle School serves about 550 students in Grades 6 through 8 in a working-class community about ten miles north of Albany, New York. The school has 40% of its students on free lunch and an increasing ethnic and linguistic diversity. The 2003–2004 school year was the school's second year with WFSGs and ATLAS Communities. Most WFSGs were grade-level teams and included special education, art, music, and technology teachers. Study groups met weekly during common planning periods.

ANALYZING STUDENT NEEDS TO DECIDE WHAT TO FOCUS ON

WFSGs may choose to do this at the beginning of the year for all the student learning needs in their action plan, or start with the need they want to tackle first and return to this step later in the year for other needs. Most groups find it easier to start with one learning need.

What Questions Do WFSGs Ask?

- What are the key skills and concepts embedded within this need?
- What is our students' performance in the need we have identified?
- Which skills and concepts do they understand and how well?
- Which skills and concepts do they not understand and why?
- Are there different levels of understanding for different groups of students and why?

What Do WFSGs Do to Answer These Questions?

The WFSG must "unpack" the student learning need to determine precisely in which areas students' performance is strong or weak, and must agree on:

- The content skills and knowledge required to demonstrate proficiency for the need
- What students should be able to "do" with the skills and knowledge—the performance tasks that demonstrate understanding
- The level of quality that students should reach to demonstrate proficiency—the scoring rubrics for each performance task

The WFSG also should think about how these items vary by grade level (if they are working in a cross-grade WFSG) or by content area (if they are working in a cross-content WFSG). Since members often have different opinions about each of these areas, WFSG meetings are a forum for sharing perspectives and reaching consensus on how they will collectively define and use each area.

Depending on the need, teachers may not have the information they require to define each area and may have to search for or create materials, such as a performance task, scoring rubric, or grade-by-grade set of expectations. Study-group members also might search for or create materials between study-group meetings and bring the drafts to meetings for colleagues to review and "tune."

The choice of tool to use to collect data depends on what skill or need is being assessed and whether the group wants qualitative data, quantitative data, or both. Finally, the WFSG should decide when, how, and from whom they will collect data. One important decision WFSGs make is whether to collect data on all students in all their classes or only on representative samples of students.

We have found it helpful to collect initial baseline data on all students and to set targets based on all students. However, to make ongoing monitoring easier, we suggest that WFSGs track a representative sample of students throughout the year on a specific student learning need.

Cohoes Team 6 Analyzes Its Student Need

Team 6 focused during the 2003–2004 school year on seventy-one at-risk eighth-grade students—about half of the eighth-grade cohort. The students also participated in a voluntary, daily, before-school academic support program. These students—including students with disabilities and/or not proficient in English, and economically disadvantaged students—were at risk for not achieving proficiency on the state assessments in the eighth grade. Team 6 decided its primary student need was to improve reading comprehension skills for at-risk students.

In looking at samples of its students' work, Team 6 decided to focus within reading comprehension on students' being able to (1) identify the key words that were the subject and main ideas for each paragraph in reading passages in English Language Arts, mathematics, science, social studies, and technology; and (2) identify at least two supporting details in a paragraph.

ESTABLISHING BASELINE PERFORMANCE AND SETTING TARGETS

WFSG members collect baseline data on where their students are with regard to specific components of the student learning need they are addressing and repeat this process for each student need they address during the school year.

What Questions Do WFSGs Ask?

- How would we describe the performance of our students relative to this need right now?
- What improvements in student performance do we desire at year's end?

What Do WFSGs Do to Answer These Questions?

Determining baseline student performance and setting performance targets requires quantitative data based on scores obtained from having students complete one or more tasks related to the specific student learning need or from teachers' codifying their observations of students. Ideally, data should be linked to levels of proficiency and disaggregated for important student subgroups.

Cohoes Team 6 Collects Baseline Data

Team 6 collected baseline data on its students' reading comprehension by giving each student a pretest from the previous year's state ELA test and by asking students to read the passages, underline or highlight key words that were the subject and main ideas in each paragraph, highlight key words in the multiple-choice questions after each passage, and answer the twenty-five questions. The team calculated for each student the number of correct responses to the multiple-choice questions and examined each work sample to see whether students were able to correctly underline or highlight the subject, main ideas, and supporting details. The team decided that if students correctly answered eighteen out of twenty-five multiple-choice questions, they had a good chance of reaching proficiency on the state test.

Data can be summarized in tables or charts to show where students are in the baseline assessment. Baseline performance data can also be presented in graphical charts. If the baseline data are captured in an Excel spreadsheet, the information can easily be displayed in a variety of chart formats.

> ## Cohoes Team 6 Baseline Data Results
>
> On the pretest in September only 20% of the at-risk students were able to answer correctly eighteen or more multiple-choice questions, while 61% of the other eighth-grade students answered eighteen or more questions correctly. In examining student work, the team confirmed its hypotheses about the areas to focus on in reading comprehension. Teachers noticed that many students were not correctly identifying the key words in the passages and even when they did, they were not using the key words to correctly answer the multiple-choice questions. They also found that students did not understand what the questions were asking them to do with information from the reading passages.

Once WFSGs have collected data on students' baseline performance, they then set performance targets that they hope their students will achieve. Charts for performance targets should be in the same form as those for baseline data. As with baseline data, teachers create target charts for their own classes and then create a composite target chart for the study group.

Each WFSG should develop a chart for each skill or need it is addressing. In addition, the study group might disaggregate the data for important subgroups of students, based on such criteria as special needs, income, language proficiency, or ethnicity, to track each group's performance during the year. Performance targets should be challenging but attainable; targets should represent levels of performance that cannot be achieved simply by teachers' doing "business as usual."

Setting performance targets also involves analyzing the baseline data. If the data describe different levels of proficiency, then teachers might ask: "Are most of our students in Level 1 or Level 2? Do we need to move more students from Level 3 to Level 4?" Answers to these kinds of questions help the WFSG decide what its targets should be and on which students it should focus.

> ## Cohoes Team 6 Performance Targets
>
> Team 6 decided that its performance targets for 100% of its at-risk students would be: Each student will demonstrate an improvement of three points or more between both "September and November" and "November and January," as measured by the number of correct responses on the multiple-choice sections of the January state ELA test for eighth graders and practice tests given in class in September and November.

DECIDING WHETHER SPECIFIC INTERVENTIONS WORK

This set of decisions occurs in the midst of the action research cycle as WFSGs try out interventions in their classrooms to address the specific learning needs they have identified. "Intervention" here means a combination of teacher actions and student activities designed by the study group to target a specific learning difficulty that students are having. Each intervention has an expected outcome in terms of improved student performance and must include appropriate assessments to determine whether the outcome has been achieved. This set of data-based decisions is also related to the next set of decisions, monitoring student progress and making mid-course corrections, because as WFSGs check student learning to see if specific interventions are working, they should also be monitoring progress.

Typically, WFSGs try out several interventions during the school year and collect and analyze data on the effectiveness of each intervention. Study groups need to decide how to plan for such interventions. Some groups decide to focus on only one intervention at a time—trying out the intervention and assessing its effectiveness before moving on to another intervention. Other groups, like Team 6, decide to launch several interventions concurrently. Each WFSG needs to think about what is appropriate and manageable for its members. It is about working smarter—using data to improve instruction—not working harder.

Cohoes Team 6 on Interventions

Team 6 tried a number of interventions. One strategy was the voluntary, daily, before-school academic support program. Teachers provided an informal environment with individual and small-group help for students in writing, solving word problems, and completing homework assignments.

A second strategy was to encourage students to read more on their own. Students were asked to read from a book every night and write out connections they made to the nightly reading. These could be as short as three sentences. Students were expected to read thirty books of at least 150 pages during the year.

Team 6 implemented other strategies in all members' classrooms, regardless of content area:

- Underline key words in questions and in each paragraph of the reading passages
- Number paragraphs and write the main idea of each paragraph in the margin
- Underline supporting details in paragraphs
- Rewrite questions on quizzes in their own words
- Write paragraphs with main ideas and at least two supporting details
- Analyze responses to multiple-choice questions to eliminate wrong answers and distracters
- Use a common rubric in all subjects to assess writing samples

Team 6 also asked students to give feedback on what students felt they were learning and where they needed to improve.

What Questions Do WFSGs Ask?

- Are the interventions we are trying out in our classrooms helping students build and demonstrate understanding?
- Are the interventions interesting and engaging for students?
- Why do we think these interventions work for our students?
- What should we do to maintain the gains from the interventions we tried?
- How might we improve the interventions when we use them again?

What Do WFSGs Do to Answer These Questions?

Each of the questions requires different kinds of data.

- Are the interventions that we are trying out in our classrooms helping students build and demonstrate understanding?

To collect data about changes in student performance, WFSGs compare data on student performance from before and after the intervention; in research, this is called "pre-post" data. If the intervention is focused on only one specific skill or concept, then the performance tasks given to students before and after the intervention might be simpler than the tasks, or only one of the tasks, used for collecting baseline data.

The study group already has two types of "before" data: the quantitative baseline data for each of its students on the specific learning needs being addressed and qualitative data in the form of student work samples collected for scoring. The "after" qualitative and quantitative data come from similar assessment tasks given to students during or immediately after the intervention. The "after" quantitative data are collected and analyzed in the same way the baseline data were collected and analyzed. The "after" student work samples for a representative set of students is compared with work samples from the same students collected during the baseline assessment. It is important that the "before" and "after" tasks be the same types of assessment tasks. In the Cohoes Team 6 example, the "after" task was another version of the state's ELA assessment.

- Are the interventions interesting and engaging for students?

To collect data about students' interest and engagement in the intervention, teachers could observe or videotape students during the intervention and/or interview or survey them after the intervention. One strategy for observing students during an intervention is to invite other members of the WFSG to observe students while one member is teaching. Another source of data on the impact of specific interventions is the results of student self-evaluation, peer reviews, and reflective journals kept by students over time.

- Why do we think these interventions work for our students?

Data to answer this question might come from looking together at samples of student work and talking with students about the thinking they were doing as they participated in the intervention.

- What should we do to maintain the gains from the interventions we tried?

Data to answer this question come from what teachers learned from students about their interest and engagement in the intervention and from the understandings teachers develop about why the intervention worked.

- How might we improve the interventions when we use them again?

Data to answer this question come from what teachers learned about what parts of the intervention worked better than others and from students' observations and reflections on the intervention.

Cohoes Team 6 on Intervention Effectiveness

Team 6 used several strategies to determine whether interventions were working and to monitor changes in student performance. The teachers monitored students' homework and book reading daily during the before-school time. Since students were asked to identify key words and restate questions in their own words on weekly and biweekly quizzes in all subjects, these quizzes provided evidence of whether students were improving. Teachers also examined the students' responses to multiple-choice questions on content area tests to look for changes in test-taking skills. Writing samples were assessed using the common rubric, and students were given targeted instruction in areas of weakness. In addition, team members brought student work samples from a representative group of students to study-group meetings. They used a protocol to examine the work samples and discuss strategies for strengthening the work.

MONITORING STUDENT PROGRESS AND MAKING MID-COURSE CORRECTIONS

This set of decisions occurs near the end of an action research cycle as a WFSG determines whether student performance actually improved for the learning need being addressed. These decisions are also related to the previous set, deciding whether specific interventions work, because as teachers check student learning to see if specific interventions are working, they are also monitoring progress. The difference between these two sets is that the one about interventions focuses on whether specific interventions really work, while the one about monitoring progress focuses on whether student performance is improving.

What Questions Do WFSGs Ask?

- Is student performance improving in the area of need we have identified?
- Are all of our students progressing at the same rate?
- Why are some students progressing more slowly or more rapidly?
- What changes do we need to implement to help students who are lagging?

What Do WFSGs Do to Answer These Questions?

To collect data about changes in student performance, WFSGs compare data on student performance from the baseline assessment with data collected periodically throughout the year. These periodic assessments to monitor progress can either be scheduled at fixed intervals, such as monthly, or after specific interventions. The WFSG already has two types of baseline data, the quantitative baseline scores for each student on the specific learning needs being addressed and qualitative data in the form of student work samples collected for scoring.

The quantitative data on student progress should be collected and analyzed in the same way the baseline data was collected and analyzed. The qualitative data on student progress from student work samples, for a representative set of students, should be compared with work samples from the same students collected during the baseline assessment. It is important that the "baseline" and "progress" assessment tasks be the same type of task.

Another element of monitoring student progress is to monitor changes in student engagement and attitudes toward learning. We suggest that teachers observe students during interventions and interviews or discuss with them their reactions to the interventions. These qualitative data from different interventions provide another lens on student progress: Have attitudes and engagement improved over time, stayed the same, or declined?

These strategies for collecting and analyzing data to monitor student progress are similar to the strategies used to determine whether a specific intervention is working, because in both cases, teachers are looking for changes in student performance and attitudes.

Cohoes Team 6 on Monitoring Progress

In November, Team 6 gave students another practice ELA test; this showed that 41% of the at-risk students got eighteen or more out of twenty-five correct compared with 20% in September. After the November practice test, the team realized that some students were making more progress than others, and that the low performing students with disabilities required different supports than the other low performing at-risk students. The team divided students into groups of five to seven and provided small-group instruction during ELA classes. The special education teachers worked with the lowest performing group regardless of classification. The higher achieving students were given more practice with inference skills since they still struggled in this area.

ASSESSING END-OF-THE-YEAR RESULTS AND PLANNING FOR THE NEXT YEAR

This set of data-based decisions by WFSGs directly relates to Step 7 of the WFSG Decision-Making Cycle: The whole faculty evaluates the impact of study groups on student learning. Assessment and evaluation of study groups occurs at two levels, individual study-group and whole-faculty levels. In this chapter, we are focusing on assessment and evaluation of work by individual WFSGs.

Assessment and evaluation should occur throughout the year, but less intensively. WFSGs ought to take stock of their progress at least once or twice during the year, asking themselves the questions indicated below.

What Questions Do WFSGs Ask?
- Did we do what we said we would do in our action plan?
- What changes in what we teach and how we teach has each of our study-group members made as a result our work together as a WFSG?
- Did our WFSG work result in improved student performance in the learning needs we addressed?
- Did our study group follow the WFSG process guidelines and did we work together effectively?

What Do WFSGs Do to Answer These Questions?

- Did we do what we said we would do in our action plan?

The data for this question come from comparing different versions of the action plan with the work reported in the WFSG's logs. If the WFSG didn't do what it said in its action plan, then the group should identify gaps and discuss why the gaps occurred. Was the action plan overly ambitious? Did the action steps take longer than anticipated? Were appropriate resources available? Were WFSG meeting times cancelled?

- What changes in what we teach and how we teach have each of our WFSG members made as a result our work together as a study group?

Data to answer this question should be found in the study group's logs where members have described what changes in teaching they have made. WFSG members should be able to create a list of the changes they made in their classrooms. Evidence of the effectiveness of interventions should be seen in the WFSG logs for the meetings where interventions were analyzed and in the supporting documentation in the WFSG binders.

- Did our WFSG work result in improved student performance?

To answer this question, the WFSG gives students at the end of the year the same performance tasks they used in their baseline assessments for each learning need addressed. To determine whether the group achieved its performance targets, the group compares the end-of-the-year results on performance tasks with the targets set. To think about why performance improved or didn't improve, the group reflects on how the instructional decisions they made influenced student learning and understanding. Data to answer this question come from the study group's discussions about the effectiveness of specific interventions and their examination of student work samples. This reflection and analysis of student work samples also leads the group to identify the skills and concepts students still do not understand well.

- Did our study group follow the WFSG process guidelines and did we work together effectively?

WFSG members review their study-group logs for evidence of process guidelines and group effectiveness/synergy. Then they can rate the group on each guideline and their level of synergy individually first and then share and reach consensus on each indicator.

An end-of-the-year assessment and evaluation by WFSGs that addresses these questions may require more than one meeting. The process should begin with a planning meeting to decide what questions to address, who will collect what data, and when and how discussions of the data will be conducted.

Groups usually devote one or two meetings to examining their impact on teaching and learning, assessing the group's effectiveness and use of the process guidelines, and looking ahead to next year. Some of the data collection can be done between meetings. Murphy and Lick (2005, pp. 225ff) provides examples of assessment forms WFSGs can use to assess their work.

Cohoes Team 6 Results and Reflections

Team 6 used data from state assessments in ELA (in January) to determine whether it had achieved its performance targets. The teachers found that between September and January: 34% of the at-risk students reached the Team 6 performance target and demonstrated an improvement of six correct questions or more; 37% had gains of three to five correct questions; 11% had gains of one or two correct questions; 10% had no gain in the number correct; and 8% had a decrease. The scores for the at-risk students improved more from September to January than did the scores for other students.

The ELA teacher on Team 6 assessed students' progress in independent reading and making connections, and found that 89% of the students read the equivalent of thirty 50-page books during the school year, and 100% of the students were able to write about connections for their reading.

In analyzing the data, the team felt that the interventions shown in Table 15.1 had the most impact on improving performance.

Table 15.1   Team 6: Successful Interventions

Intervention	Reason for Success
Individual conferences about their writing	The students got very specific feedback
Rewriting questions	It was a great way to check for understanding
Highlighting the key words in questions and in the passages	This helped the students read for information as well as eliminate wrong choices

The team plans to use these same interventions next year with the new cohort of at-risk eighth graders. It also plans to identify and work with a new at-risk group in September, continue the before-school program, and continue the independent reading of thirty books and of writing about connections. The team realized that there were some skills and concepts that students still did not understand well. These were inference skills and understanding poetry.

In reflecting on its work this year, the team realized that collecting, analyzing, and using data to shape instruction helped keep the focus of its work on what the students required rather than being "curriculum-driven" work. Team 6 also decided that next year it wants to stay together as a study group to work on similar student learning needs.

CONCLUSION

This chapter has described and illustrated five types of data-based decisions that WFSGs make as they work during the school year to address student learning needs. The five types of data-based decisions are:

1. Analyze student needs to decide what to focus on.

2. Establish baseline performance and set targets.

3. Decide whether specific interventions work.

4. Monitor student progress and make mid-course corrections.

5. Assess end-of-the-year results and plan for next year.

For each of these decisions, we described the questions WFSGs ask and what study groups do to answer these questions.

There are several key points to remember as WFSGs use data:

• Data are both quantitative and qualitative. WFSGs use quantitative, numerical data to help identify where the learning problems are and qualitative data such as student work samples, observations, student self-reflections, and interviews to reveal strengths and weaknesses in students' thinking and understanding and their levels of interest and engagement.

• WFSGs use data to improve learning, not to blame, believing that all students can achieve standards of proficiency and that every teacher can improve instruction.

• The most useful data for WFSGs to use to identify specific student learning needs are disaggregated data that pinpoint which students are experiencing learning problems with which type of performance tasks and for which standard and associated skills and concepts.

• Charts and tables that group students by subgroup, performance level, and skill help WFSGs monitor progress and spot successes and challenges.

• WFSGs use the same performance task to monitor student progress throughout the school year. Content for the task can vary.

• WFSGs look at student work together, using protocols to identify what skills students should learn, reveal students' thinking and level of understanding, and assess the effectiveness of instructional strategies and assessment tasks.

• WFSGs assess the effectiveness of each intervention used with students to decide whether the strategy was successful and how it might be improved when they use it again.

• Less is more. We strongly recommend that WFSGs focus on one specific student learning need and a few interventions as they start to use data to improve learning.

• Document your work. WFSGs document their work in these five data-based decisions through the WFSG action plan, meeting logs, and the binders each member maintains. Keep samples of student work during the year and record key decision points as the group plans, acts, and reflects.

• Schools that are successful in making data-based decisions foster a climate of respect and collegiality among students, parents, teachers, support staff, and administrators.

With these key points in mind, every WFSG can successfully use data to make good decisions, improve practice, and increase student learning.

PART V

Instructional Strategies

Current expectations for our schools are that they should raise student achievement in every subject and at every level. What is easy to state is often difficult to accomplish. This is the situation with these expectations. Raising student achievement will be a major challenge in all subjects and at all grade levels. What will be required will be serious commitment and deliberate action for this goal, across the board in schools and their support base, including policies, procedures, and strategies. At a minimum, school personnel (teachers, staff, and administrators) and district-level leaders must accept responsibility for this goal, commit themselves to its accomplishment, and collaboratively work together to make increased student achievement a reality.

This section of the Fieldbook, *Instructional Strategies*, contains six chapters devoted to illustrating the successful application of *instructional strategies* in the WFSG process for improving student achievement in the classroom. An overview and sense of flow for part of the "implementation of instructional strategies," described by one author, was:

> As implementation continued and teachers gained control over the initial strategies and levels of use increased, new strategies and techniques were introduced. These strategies were introduced, modeled in their classrooms, and practiced within their small groups before they actually tried them in the classroom; this allowed the teachers an initial level of comfort with the strategies.

The six chapters in this section: (a) cover primary, elementary, middle, and high schools; (b) focus on such things as: strategies and activities, application of ideas in "real-life," first-hand case studies, implementation of the WFSG System, action plans, rubric development, gap closing, data-based decision making, creation of quality teaching, lesson development, instructional troubleshooting, examination of student work, peer observation and mentoring, effective and ineffective lesson sharing, current literature, and action research; (c) contain several content areas, including reading, mathematics, English Arts, and languages; and (d) have among their success factors: a consistent and supportive administrative team, strong instructional leadership from within, a belief that study groups work, a decision to bring in "expert voices" for the writing instruction and meaningful practices, use of data to drive instructional decisions, a commitment on the part of all faculty members to make a difference in the life of a child, a study group intent on content "that matters," and an instructional focus.

The *bottom line* is: *When we enhance our teachers' performances relative to instructional strategies, we will increase our students' achievements.*

16

Improving the Quality of Student Performance

Steve Keyes

I believe that in these times of super accountability, every school everywhere is looking for ways to increase student achievement. This chapter describes how the faculty at Destrehan High School has done just that. By highlighting some of the difficulties encountered during the process of learning how to enhance the quality of student performance at Destrehan, others may benefit by not having to go through the same growing pains.

The chapter discusses successes with the Whole-Faculty Study Group System (see Murphy & Lick, 2005), Destrehan's journey to developing effective study groups, and how these groups have helped improve student performance. Keep in mind that one of the beauties of the Whole-Faculty Study Group System is that it is a process that can be molded to fit the exact needs of your students and faculty.

WHAT IS REQUIRED

For decades, the idea has been lurking around that improving instruction will somehow improve student performance. Education has gone through many years of frustrating teachers by giving them "new ways" to teach. Of course, each new way was, surely, the silver bullet that would alleviate all their teaching woes. Oftentimes these methods were delivered by highly paid, inspired, and inspiring presenters who truly believed that they were doing a great service by imparting the information. The sad truth is that most of this did little to change instruction and even less to improve student achievement.

In this time of high-stakes testing and accountability, this method is just not acceptable (actually, it never was). I am not insinuating that we do not need to offer new ideas to teachers in order to impact their instruction. What I am stating "loudly and clearly" is that what we have done in the past is simply not enough. Not only do teachers require new ideas, they must also have meaningful, paid time to have professional dialogue about what they are doing and the results they are experiencing. This chapter describes why one of the best ways to ensure this type of effective professional development is to make the move to adopt and implement the Whole-Faculty Study Group System.

SUCCESS WITH WHOLE-FACULTY STUDY GROUPS

Since we have implemented the Whole-Faculty Study Group (WFSG) System at Destrehan High School (DHS), we have seen a pattern of continuous growth in every assessment area. Every score on every high-stakes test is higher than it has ever been. One example is that since 1999, our ACT scores have risen from 19.8 to 20.4. They have consistently risen 0.1 each year. Our ITED scores have also been constantly rising. In just the past year, our composite score went from fifty-seven to fifty-nine. This has been the pattern for several years. Our scores on each subtest also increased this past year. I could spend ten pages giving data and charts to substantiate these findings, but rather than waste that much paper, I simply am going to give you the facts and let you know that I am still at Destrehan, as the Staff Development Coordinator, and that you can contact me for specific data at skeyes@stcharles .k12.la.us. The passing rate of students in class is also higher and improving as we continue down this road. These are wonderful results for which I applaud our faculty.

Another great benefit of the WFSG System is what it does for teachers when they get to choose what they learn.

Cherie Hebert, an English teacher at DHS, puts it this way:

> Having the chance to select my own study group topic and the members of my study group has empowered me to grow as an educator based on my own needs. This has made study groups much more powerful and authentic. Also, this has allowed me to choose a topic which directly impacts my students' learning every day!

When I state that WFSGs have revolutionized many facets of Destrehan, I am not exaggerating. Such strides are not made overnight, however, and I must not fail to mention that the way we develop and perform in study groups has evolved over the seven years that they have been the centerpiece of professional learning at our school.

DEVELOPING EFFECTIVE STUDY GROUPS

Developing effective study groups is an ongoing, arduous task, but the rewards are immeasurable. As with any other high school, our faculty changes each year when some of our teachers leave and new ones arrive. Therefore, each new school year marks the first time some teachers experience study groups. After reflecting on the effectiveness of our groups following each school year, we have often chosen to tweak our plan in order to increase the impact that the groups have on student achievement. Therefore, the way we carry out study groups has been fluid. That is not to say that we do not adhere to the basic tenets of WFSGs. I am stating, rather, that we have grown, and study groups have evolved in order to more effectively meet the needs of our students and faculty.

The first year we implemented WFSGs (1998–1999), we spent most of the time just learning the process. In that first year, we had groups that met before school or after school. This was done because we did not request a schedule change from the district that would make our schedule different from any other school in the district. Do I need to describe the confusion caused by having some groups meeting at 6 A.M. and others meeting at 5:00 P.M.? Some were meeting on Monday while others chose Tuesday, Wednesday, or Thursday. Imagine trying to motivate a group who had to be at school for a study group at 6:00 A.M. on Monday because of other afterschool responsibilities, such as coaching. Now imagine attempting to get a group that could only meet at 5:00 P.M. on Thursday afternoon to discuss what they could do to improve their instruction. Do you know people who are at their best that late in the day after having taught for six hours? Although our study groups that year spawned positive classroom changes and increased student achievement, it became clear that the structure had to be changed.

After that first year, the faculty was so pleased with our results that we did ask the district for permission to rearrange our school calendar so we could have almost two and a half hours every other week for our groups to meet. We would have loved to have had one and a half hours each week, but as in many districts, buses were a problem. Therefore, we settled for two and a half hours every other week. We still follow that schedule today. On study-group days, teachers begin school at 7:10 A.M., as usual, but the students do not arrive until 9:30. This is the plan that we developed to create time, but there are many other ways to make time for WFSGs.

The time issue is one of the biggest obstacles to implementation. Schools all over the nation have found creative ways to provide the time. If I may, I would make one suggestion here. Those who are contemplating implementing WFSGs should think through the time issue carefully and come up with several viable proposals before bringing the idea to a faculty. This could keep your ideas from getting bogged down because of that one issue and make them much more palatable to the teachers. Keep in mind that some teachers are going to want to know, "what's in it for me?" So please learn from our mistakes and think the whole process through carefully before proceeding.

Not only has the time factor evolved, but other aspects of our groups have changed also. One year, our school governance board decided that study-group membership should come from within our smaller learning community groups rather than the whole faculty. That did not result in the improvements that were anticipated, and many faculty members resented the change, so we changed that back after only one year.

Another thing that has evolved over time is the number of members of the groups. We have also learned that, for our faculty, groups of five or six are too large. We have found that, for our school, smaller groups of two or three work better. Again, our school governance board has recommended this change. They wanted this because they felt that a member could become a wallflower more easily in the larger groups. They have also asked that I meet with a member of each group after each study-group meeting so that I know exactly what the groups are doing. This creates a situation where everyone gets to discuss, with me, the work of her or his study group, and the expected impact that such work should have on student achievement. Thus, smaller groups have proven more desirable to all concerned. We have, however, found that some teachers still want and need to meet in larger groups. Our solution is to say that two groups may meet together, but they must keep separate logs and a member of each group must meet with me after each group session. This still allows me to have personal contact with at least one third of the faculty after each study group day.

IMPROVING STUDENT PERFORMANCE

I truly believe that in any school building anywhere, there is enough knowledge among the faculty to seriously and immediately improve the performance of students. But how in the world does that knowledge get disseminated in the average school? It doesn't. What we have learned at Destrehan High School is that as we allow teachers time to share their wealth of knowledge and create research-based activities, instruction does, in fact, improve, and students do perform at higher levels.

As mentioned, the model of WFSGs that our school has adopted allows teachers to choose their topics as well as the members of the faculty with whom they meet. One drawback to this is that teachers sometimes do not make wise choices about how to spend their time. Our experience has taught us that to ensure optimal efficiency at our school, we often have to encourage teachers to choose groups that do not necessarily include their best friends. So we ask teachers to meet in groups of two or three. If two groups want to meet together, that is fine. They are also encouraged to choose topics that are directly related to their students' areas of need rather than random, general topics. We facilitate this by conducting a needs assessment survey at the end of each year. Furthermore, teachers are offered opportunities to attend mini-sessions on research-based strategies that they feel they should strengthen in order to better meet the specific needs of their students.

Let's see what some Destrehan teachers have to say about the choice of study group topics and group members, as well as the impact of such choices on the achieved results. First, Chuck Hughes, a speech teacher, says that:

> I am constantly telling the students in my Speech I classes that they must be interested in and like the topics they choose for their speeches. I tell them if they are not happy with their topics, they will put off the preparation of the assignments. I find that in Whole-Faculty Study Groups, this is also true. Sometimes, in the past, I have not always been happy with areas of study

I have chosen and the groups with whom I have met. Hence, I have been slow to implement new ideas in my classroom. This year is much different. I have chosen to study reading strategies in a public speaking class. I have two English teachers in my study group who can relate to my situation. By working together, presenting new reading and vocabulary strategies to each other, and examining student work, I am able to bring a new dimension to my classroom. My students are reading more and are therefore gaining new experiences of which to speak.

I must add this little sidebar. Chuck Hughes has not always been as positive about professional learning. A few years ago, he was one of the teachers who strongly resisted staff development. He has dramatically changed his thinking about the benefits of good staff development.

The implementation of WFSGs has impacted the lessons planned and taught by Shannon Diodene, a science teacher at DHS. It has also helped provide well-planned and challenging instruction for her students, as she indicates below:

> One of my main goals in my classroom is to increase the use of higher order thinking on assessment and activities so that my students may achieve at optimum levels. Through Whole-Faculty Study Groups, I have been given the opportunity to analyze student work with a team of my peers. This has allowed me to make modifications and improvements on assessments and activities as well as gain ideas from my colleagues. As a result, higher order thinking skills have become integrated into my daily lessons.

You will note that in each teacher's remarks, examination of student work is at least alluded to. This is such an essential element of the process. It must happen early and often in order for the groups to succeed. It is too late to make changes in instruction if we wait until the end of the year for the results of standardized tests. Our faculty has learned the importance of using students' work as a guide to direct change in their instruction; much of this is due to the implementation of WFSGs.

CONCLUSION

In the preceding pages, I have attempted to describe our journey at DHS with WFSGs by mentioning some of our obstacles and successes, which have been many. Although we have adhered to the basic tenets of the Whole-Faculty Study Group System, our study groups have evolved from fledgling, often poorly focused groups, to groups that are on a mission to improve student performance. As indicated in the facts previously stated, we have been able to positively impact the quality of instruction at DHS. As with anyone else in education, we realize that we have not arrived, but have certainly taken some positive steps toward providing every student the opportunity to receive excellent instruction.

If you or anyone you know is considering implementing WFSGs, I have only two words for you: "Get started." If we sit around and try to work out all the details before getting started, nothing will ever happen. After instructing a faculty in the process, we still must seek those who will lead the faculty in implementing the process. When this is done with some forethought, the probability of success will surely increase. Once the groups are working efficiently and the purpose is well understood, teachers will instruct better and students will achieve at higher levels. This is a fact.

Since I am not a believer in the "silver bullet" theory, I am not suggesting that simply having some semblance of WFSGs implemented in your school will make all your problems disappear. But if a school's faculty will use the WFSG System for groups of teachers to address weaknesses indicated by data, there is enough knowledge among the faculty to meet any challenge. I have been fortunate enough to work with other schools that have implemented WFSGs and have seen results similar to ours. I have seen improvements in schools from every group: elementary, middle, and high; rural, suburban, and urban; and large and small schools. So, please be aware that this system can enhance instruction at your school and make a major impact on your students' performances.

17

Implementing Instructional Strategies

Terri L. Jenkins

Lynn K. Baber

As practitioners involved in the work of Whole-Faculty Study Groups, the greatest rewards are (a) the knowledge that study groups are self-perpetuating and ongoing, (b) the outcome that services and support provided will impact the lives of children for years to come, and (c) the realization that this structure will forever change the way teachers work. The following chapter chronicles the journey of one Georgia middle school and elaborates just one of its many successes.

CONTEXT FOR STRATEGY DEVELOPMENT

In 1992, the Washington County Schools, under the leadership of Grace Davis, contacted Carlene Murphy in order to begin training in what was then called "Models of Teaching" (and that later evolved into the Whole-Faculty Study Group System). For one week during the summer, two entire faculties were initially trained in three instructional strategies based on the work of Bruce Joyce and colleagues (Joyce & Weil, 1986; Joyce, Weil, & Showers, 1992). In order to ensure implementation of these strategies, each of the faculties was given parallel training in the formation and essence of Whole-Faculty Study Groups (see Murphy & Lick, 2005).

It was in the fall of 1992 that the "real" work began. As the study groups began the school year, consultants provided consistent follow-up and support to best ensure the integrity of the models as well as schoolwide success. This unwavering support continued throughout the 1992–1993 school year.

Six years later, in the spring of 1998, we were again contacted by Washington County. This time, Lisa Franklin, Assistant Principal of the Thomas Jefferson Elder Middle School (usually called simply Elder or TJ Elder), sought professional development for her staff. Upon receiving less-than-satisfactory results on the statewide writing test, a determination had been made that all study groups would focus on the teaching of writing and the improvement of writing skills in a struggling student population. This deficiency in writing had existed throughout the history of the school and had shown little or no improvement over time. In fact, the school had never once met the state standard in the area of writing.

When the authors first talked to Lisa regarding her needs, it was evident that the study-group structure was still in place and still operational. In fact, Principal Bern Anderson stated, "It [study groups] has become just the way we do things at Elder Middle." Though the task at hand was considerable since scores in written communication had never met standards, as consultants and instructional support personnel, we knew that our battle would be much more easily fought and won. A number of factors were working in our favor, including the following:

- The faculty at Elder Middle School was now accustomed to "whole school" staff development; it was "the norm"
- The study group structure remained intact and would facilitate the continued study and implementation of writing techniques and strategies we would introduce in the summer
- During our follow-up visits to the school, the study-group structure provided the perfect organization for the dissemination of added strategies throughout the year
- The administration was aware of the need for consistent gentle pressure, with the necessary support, to fully execute a change in instructional delivery methods and had already demonstrated its willingness and ability to provide this type of pressure and support

Using the data provided by the state, as well as a needs-assessment plan completed by individual members of each study group, together with administrators, we developed a yearlong, multidimensional plan designed to:

- Increase the number of opportunities students were provided for writing
- Enlarge each teacher's repertoire of writing strategies
- Enhance the faculty's understanding of the writing process
- Develop awareness, in both students and teachers, of the scoring and structure of the state writing test

Summer Staff Development

The first step of the plan began with the summer staff development session that we provided. For this training, we purposely chose two strategies easily incorporated into any content that were nonthreatening in nature. During this three-day session, attended by all faculty members, the new strategies for teaching writing were introduced to the teachers and administrators. To ensure implementation across the curriculum, demonstrations of each strategy were provided in several content areas and at all grade levels. Teachers were also given the opportunity to practice the strategies through peer teaching, first with lessons we provided and later with lessons they had developed together.

Before our summer session ended, with the support of administrators and discussions with teachers, clear expectations were established in regard to the implementation of these strategies for the fall. All teachers were expected to utilize these strategies a minimum of twice weekly, and lesson plans were to reflect their use. In addition, study-group logs were to indicate a continual study of these strategies as well as others in order to improve each teacher's capacity to teach writing. It was understood that administrators would check both lesson plans and logs for indications that these expectations were met. In addition, administrators were committed to the following: (a) frequent observations when plans indicated these strategies were used and (b) initiation of recurrent conversations with faculty regarding the teaching of writing. It was also established that we would visit the school monthly in the capacity of consultants to further ensure successful implementation of the writing strategies.

Fall Strategy Implementation

Actively monitored by school administrator Lisa Franklin, implementation began in earnest in the fall. Teachers were expected to employ writing strategies in classrooms across the curriculum, incorporating these into lesson planning. To ensure consistency throughout implementation, lesson plans were checked specifically to note the inclusion of such. In addition, administrators actively reserved time for classroom observations that ensured implementation.

Administrators also provided articles containing current research in the field that could be read and discussed by the study groups. Teachers continued to meet in their study groups weekly. Initially, a teacher survey indicated that early meetings were productive and regularly included the following:

- Lesson development (joint work)
- Instructional "troubleshooting"
- Sharing of both effective and ineffective lessons, accompanied by discussions of why the lessons were effective or ineffective
- Reading of current research in the field

Implementation Follow-Up

Because we worked in tandem, our monthly follow-up visits accomplished two purposes. One consultant met with every study group over the course of the day. During these meetings with study groups, the consultant addressed problems, issues, and concerns regarding the Teaching of Writing and any "snags" during the implementation of the initial strategies utilized. Strategies were also revisited and reinforced, and additional demonstrations were provided when needed.

The other consultant spent a full day modeling one or more of the strategies in various classrooms, with the teacher acting as observer. Building administrators were active in determining the classrooms in which demonstrations might have the greatest impact. They considered a number of factors when making these decisions, including:

- Voice and influence of the teacher
- Maturity of the teacher's instructional knowledge
- Areas of greatest need (both teacher and student)
- "Show me" attitudes

Once it had been determined which classrooms were to be utilized on a given monthly visit, lessons that modeled the strategies we were asking the teachers to use were developed on the appropriate grade level and measures were taken to ensure that the content of the lessons would flow smoothly with the current instruction being provided in those particular classes. Administrators again were instrumental in not only selecting demonstration classrooms, but also aiding in the process of securing information regarding the "level" of the students to be taught as well as the current concept being covered. Often one of those same lessons would be demonstrated in the study group and discussion would ensue. Commentary and insight from classroom teachers who had actually seen students actively engaged in that particular lesson were invaluable. In some instances, work resulting from the lessons was provided by the study group for examination by other teachers.

As implementation continued and teachers gained control over the initial strategies and levels of use increased, new strategies and techniques were introduced. These strategies were introduced, modeled in their classrooms, and practiced within their small groups before teachers actually tried them in their classrooms; this allowed the teachers an initial level of comfort with the strategies. In addition, over the course of the year, techniques designed to enhance particular skills in writing, such as slotting and slanting, were taught and demonstrated by the consultants. In January, a new Editing Checklist (Jenkins & Baber, 1998) was introduced and explored, and both teachers and students began to engage more actively in the editing process. This list was not designed to emphasize traditional proofreading elements of writing, but editing elements to improve style and technique.

In the absence of consultants, ensuing study-group meetings focused on lesson development utilizing the strategies and their implementation for the following days. Each study group and its members concentrated on writing within their content. Together they practiced the strategies, developed lessons, and "reported back" on the resulting lessons. Teachers discussed successes, student reactions, resultant student work, and the less-than-successful lessons.

After discussions of why lessons did not produce expected behaviors, teachers participated in peer observations to coach and mentor each other. These experiences were discussed with the consultants during each visit. Lessons were pulled apart and rebuilt so that each lesson acted not only as a teaching tool for the student, but a learning tool for the teachers.

RESULTS OF THE INSTRUCTIONAL STRATEGIES

Finally, upon the publishing of the state test scores in May, the results were evident. A schoolwide increase from the preceding year's score of 198 to 216 placed them well above the state average for the first time in the school's history. The state average at that time was only 208. Only 4% of the student population scored in the at-risk category, and most of these students received special education services. Sixty-three percent of the student body scored beyond the adequate range as Good or Very Good overall. For the entire school, the following results were recorded:

- 81% scored good or very good in content/organization, up from 67%
- 60% scored good or very good in style, up from 36%
- 67% scored good or very good in sentence formation, up from 54%
- 63% scored good or very good in usage, up from 47%
- 55% scored good or very good in mechanics, up from 50%

A subsequent note from administrator Lisa Franklin reflects the school's and the faculty's feelings of success. "Needless to say, we are over the moon. Thanks for everything you did to make this possible. These results exceeded all my expectations!!"

CONCLUSION

As consultants we recognize that the phenomenal success at the Elder Middle School is the result of many factors—the first being the sound use of study groups as a structure to provide teachers the opportunity to practice and hone their skills as educators. In addition, we believe that the following greatly increased their chance of success:

- A consistent and supportive administrative team
- Strong instructional leadership from within
- A belief that study groups work
- A decision to bring in "expert voices" for the writing instruction and sound practices
- Use of data to drive instructional decisions
- A commitment on the part of all faculty members to make a difference in the life of a child
- A study group focus on content "that matters" and an instructional focus

The ultimate success at Elder Middle School is neither that of those at the school nor the consultants, but belongs to the true beneficiaries of the work, the students of the Elder Middle School.

Purposefully and planfully attacking instructional needs, study groups at TJ Elder persist today. While presenting during the 2003 National WFSG Conference, Principal Bern Anderson answered a question often asked: "Why has this process worked so well for so long? His response was:

- Study groups have become a part of the school's culture.
- Study groups are just "the way we do things at Elder."
- We are committed to professional development for all members of the staff.

18

Implementing Reading and Mathematics Programs

Julie J. Nall

have to share with you that I am a very good teacher and love working with students of all ages. The reason I am sharing this fact with you is that I almost quit teaching after my first year. I was saved by the grace and guidance of many talented colleagues. I began my teaching career at one of Baton Rouge, Louisiana's, largest inner-city elementary schools. Our students were poor and had little adult support at home. I went home crying every day because I felt inadequate as a teacher and had no one to turn to for help.

The only reason I am still in education today is that I was lucky enough to be rescued by the Exxon Elementary Mathematics Specialist Program. The program provided time for collaboration and opportunities to participate in quality professional development. I observed my peers, and they observed me. We developed lessons together, had expert voices attend our meetings, and attended conferences. We studied together and learned good instructional strategies proven to be effective with low-performing students. The collaboration not only saved my teaching career, but the next year I was chosen mathematics teacher of the year at my school. I later became a mathematics specialist and taught mathematics to all the students in Grades PreK–6.

I was one of the lucky few in my district. Several years ago in my job as districtwide mathematics/technology specialist, I worked with teachers every day who felt as I had in my first year. They had no opportunities to network with other teachers, and, subsequently, we lost quite a few talented young professionals. I was becoming depressed because I could not save them. My good fortune returned when I became a LINCS (Learning-Intensive Networking Communities for Success) Regional Coordinator and learned about Whole-Faculty Study Groups (see Murphy & Lick, 2005). I now see teachers consistently being supported and mentored in all thirty-three schools that we serve in our region and in the 170 schools involved in the LINCS program across the state.

This chapter will attempt to describe the passion and commitment of the teachers I work with in Louisiana's Region II school districts, and the multiplying effects of the collaborative efforts of the LINCS partnership that consists of the Louisiana Department of Education (LDE), Louisiana Systemic Initiatives Program (LaSIP), local districts, local schools, universities, and the Southern Region Education Board. The heart of the LINCS process is the Whole-Faculty Study Group (WFSG) System that enables us to successfully implement more effective reading and mathematics programs in our schools.

THE SETTING

My experience with schoolwide reform began five years ago when I was recruited as part of an innovative pilot project that evolved into Louisiana's present-day LINCS program. It was overwhelming at first as we had to try to find ways to help schools understand that the best staff development is job embedded and must address specific student, teacher, parent, and community needs. The LINCS program is a support program that has incorporated the best practices as outlined by the National Staff Development Council, and, of course, one of the strongest links in LINCS is that 100% of our schools are firmly committed to developing professional learning communities using the Whole-Faculty Study Group System.

Table 18.1 shows the correlations between the LINCS process and the National Staff Development Council standards.

I am now a firm believer in the Whole-Faculty Study Group (WFSG) System, and my vision of the future of our public education system is becoming brighter. Properly implemented, the WFSG process empowers teachers and administrators to make instructional decisions based on the needs of their students as indicated by student achievement data. When teachers become leaders and are involved in instructional decision making at their school, they rise to the challenge and grow professionally at a very rapid pace.

Louisiana is sectioned into eight educational regions. As a Region II LINCS regional coordinator, I work with thirty-three schools located in five districts. LINCS schools modify their instructional focus based on the specific needs of the students. Successful schools consistently analyze student achievement data to use as they write school improvement and WFSG action plans. One of my low-performing middle schools recorded increased mathematics scores for three consecutive years and

Table 18.1 Correlation of Learning-Intensive Networking Communities for Success (LINCS) and the National Staff Development Council (NSDC) Standards for Staff Development

NSDC Standards for Staff Development	LINCS Process Components (LINCS is a multidimensional, whole-school, professional development process for school improvement)
Learning Communities	WFSGs give LINCS Schools the structure and time to establish professional learning communities whose goals are aligned with those of the school and district. LINCS study groups (WFSGs) work during the school day (or after school) at least twice each month for a minimum of one hour per session. Instructional councils and evaluative summary sessions allow the entire faculty to network.
Leadership	Principals must be willing to faithfully implement the LINCS process: serve on the LINCS school team, attend PD, ensure time for WFSGs, approve SG action plans, review/comment on SG logs, and partner with LINCS/LaSIP university professional development projects. LINCS regional coordinators, district contact persons, school content leaders, LINCS school teams, and university project site coordinators guide the continuous improvement.
Resources	The Louisiana Department of Education (LDOE) awards funds to the LINCS schools to pay for substitute teachers, stipends, in-state travel, and materials in order for schools to provide time and resources for study groups and other LINCS professional development. LINCS regional coordinators are also provided by the LDOE to work daily in school classrooms, with study groups, content leaders, and university staff to ensure the full implementation of the LINCS professional development/school improvement process. LaSIP funds the university PD Projects for two or three teachers from every LINCS School. District contact persons assist LINCS schools secure resources that must be committed by the school district to participate in LINCS.
Data-Driven	WFSGs require all on the school faculty to analyze student data to organize study groups of 3-6 teachers, develop/implement SG action plans, plan classroom instruction, monitor progress, and sustain improvement. LaSIP university PD projects use the student need summaries to inform their instruction.
Evaluation	LINCS has a comprehensive evaluation process that uses multiple sources of information (including teacher content knowledge assessment, classroom observations, and student test data) to guide improvement and demonstrate its impact on student achievement.
Research-Based	The LINCS process components were selected by combining research-proven PD strategies that are high quality, sustained, intensive, and classroom-focused to improve teaching and learning. The LINCS process is aligned to the NSDC Standards for PD and NCLB requirements.

Design	The design of the LINCS process uses learning strategies appropriate to the intended goal to establish professional learning
NSDC Standards for Staff Development	*LINCS Process Components (LINCS is a multidimensional, whole-school, professional development process for school improvement)* communities where classroom teachers build content knowledge and strengthen their ability to design and implement standards-based, technology-enhanced lessons into their daily instruction in order to improve student achievement.
Learning	LINCS School Teams assist school leadership to guide each school's focus on issues that are current and relevant to classroom practice and based on student needs. LINCS regional coordinators, LINCS content leaders, and LaSIP university staff model lessons in teachers' classrooms, assist study groups with ongoing learning, and assist faculties to apply knowledge about human learning and the change process.
Collaboration	LINCS regional coordinators provide school faculties with the knowledge and skills to implement the collaborative WFSG process during the school day for teachers to deepen content knowledge, plan instruction and assessment, and analyze student work to improve student achievement. University PD projects also encourage and support collaboration.
Equity	LINCS regional coordinators and LINCS/LaSIP university PD project staff prepare school faculties to understand and appreciate all students, create safe/orderly/supportive learning environments, and hold high expectations for their academic achievement.
Quality Teaching	Regional coordinators work daily in school classrooms to model lessons, coach teachers, assist WFSGs, and provide professional growth experiences for Content Leaders. University content PD provides content-focused PD and follow-up support for teachers. LINCS expands the supply of high quality teachers by providing structure for teachers to become highly qualified.
Family Involvement	LINCS regional coordinators provide educators with knowledge and skills to involve families in family mathematics, family literacy, and family science nights.

decided that English/language arts (ELA) should be this year's schoolwide focus. My responsibilities as a LINCS regional coordinator include:

1. Assist the LINCS School Teams with establishing and facilitating Whole-Faculty Study Groups (WFSGs) in each LINCS School.

2. Work alongside teachers in the classroom modeling and observing lessons and providing the necessary follow-up and one-on-one coaching.

3. Plan and present professional development for LINCS schools during the summer and school year.

4. Plan and conduct monthly LINCS Content Leader professional learning meetings and facilitate state Department of Education-sponsored Compressed Video Conferences.

5. Schedule collaborative office time once a week to attend Regional Education Service Center (RESC) staff meetings, plan professional development and model lessons, participate in online discussions via blackboard sites, research best practices, and handle routine itineraries, e-mails, and paperwork.

6. Attend LINCS Regional Coordinator professional learning meetings and other professional growth opportunities as requested.

7. Assist schools and universities with the development of content-focused professional development projects.

8. Attend state conferences to deepen content knowledge in the content area(s) of the assigned LINCS schools.

THE "WOW" EXPERIENCE

In the first year, the eight schools that I supported all found that their students were weak in the areas of problem solving and completing constructed-response tasks in which students have to explain their work using pictures, words, charts, and graphs as is required by our statewide high-stakes assessment at Grades 4, 8, and 10. Schools formed WFSGs around the areas of weakness. The first year, I was invited to attend a WFSG meeting of all fifth-grade teachers at South Boulevard Elementary School. They wanted me to help them plan lessons to address student weaknesses in problem solving. I was not excited about offering advice on this topic since the problem-solving process I had used seemed to be ineffective. I pulled every resource I could find and looked at strategies on the Internet, and showed up for the meeting. Many of the resources I found showed teaching problem solving one strategy at a time; for example, this week we'll be learning to work backwards. I didn't think this was the best approach, since the problems on state-level tests don't identify problems by strategy. We discussed this in our WFSGs and decided that we should present the problem, let students solve it any way they wanted, and, as the "working backwards" strategy occurred, we'd let the students name it and display the problem and the strategy in the classroom. It would then belong to the students. We all felt encouraged that collaborating together was helping. Quite by accident, while working on a complicated problem, I asked one of the teachers to explain the problem in her own words. She quickly got the problem and *really* started reading the problem for understanding. We all looked up at the same time and our eyes met. We experienced a huge "WOW!" moment. The teachers began to discuss our realization: "Think about the behaviors we observe when our students are trying to solve complex word problems. They rush through reading the problem, paying very little attention to the words; pick out numbers, and then randomly select an operation to use."

Figure 18.1 Math Gumbo and R.I.C.E.

Math Gumbo and R.I.C.E.

Restate
Illustrate
Compute
Explain

Julie Nall Region II Lincs Coordinator

We concluded that, "If we could teach our students to first explain the problem in their own words before attempting to solve it, they would have to read for understanding. They would have to process the information orally, explain it in writing, and, consequently, have a much higher chance for success." It was decided that each teacher would try this process with her students in the next two weeks and bring a collection of student work to the next WFSG session so the group could discuss and refine instructional strategies. We left the meeting excited and hopeful!

MATH GUMBO AND R.I.C.E.

The following week, I shared this "wow" moment with members from a WFSG from another school who were also studying problem-solving strategies. They were planning lessons and were asking their students to illustrate the problem, make necessary computations, and then explain their thinking. During the meeting, I shared the "wow" moment experienced at South Boulevard Elementary. They felt a similar reaction and wanted to add the power of restating the problem to their schoolwide problem-solving plan. The faculty decided that "Restate, Illustrate, Compute, and Explain" was the perfect acronym for Louisiana problem solving because it would bring in our Louisiana culture and make it fun for the students. This was the birth of "Math Gumbo and R.I.C.E." The teachers found clip art on the Internet and made the R.I.C.E. poster shown in Figure 18.1.

WFSGs provided the system for teachers to become empowered instructional leaders at their schools. I am convinced that when teachers get together and collaborate concerning improving education, miracles happen. I have seen it over and over.

R.I.C.E. FOR KINDERGARTENERS

I began sharing the R.I.C.E. story with other WFSG groups at the schools I serve. The process was conceived for third- to fifth-grade students. While sharing how collaboration helped teachers address a specific student need, a kindergarten teacher spoke up saying,

> Wait a minute, this is not only for upper grade students; let me explain how I could use "R.I.C.E" with my kindergarten children. I will seat them on the carpet in front of me and orally present a problem such as: Two students were building with blocks. Three students joined them. How many students were building with blocks? The students will then act out the problem and I will have them retell what happened orally. After retelling, I will ask them to return to their table and draw a picture of the problem. To finish the process, the children will explain their drawing to a friend. This is how R.I.C.E will begin in Pre–K and kindergarten.

ACADEMIC GUMBO AND R.I.C.E. ACROSS THE REGION

The networking among schools in my region rapidly began to blossom. Teachers across content areas got involved. Science, social studies, and English/language arts teachers began to share how this process could help their students learn to explain their ideas on open-ended assessment tasks. I began to see revised R.I.C.E. posters for "Reading, Social Studies, and Science Gumbo and R.I.C.E." The teachers in Region II in Louisiana discovered a way to improve learning for all students at all grade levels in all content areas at no extra expense and with no additional work. Quite an accomplishment for their first year! The accomplishment was made possible by teachers being provided time for job-embedded staff development as defined by the WFSG system. The R.I.C.E. problem-solving procedure evolved from natural discussions among teachers all focusing on the common problem of how to improve their students' ability to solve complex problems and explain their strategies. It is a perfect example of how teachers can work together to address specific student weaknesses. The R.I.C.E. problem-solving method is now used in schools throughout the entire state of Louisiana.

RECOMMENDATIONS

If I am asked to make one key recommendation based on what I have learned during the past five years helping schools effectively implement the WFSG System, I always share how the LINCS/WFSG process makes it possible for schoolwide improvement efforts to succeed. Principals and district-level administrators must provide time and support for teachers to:

- Study their school improvement plans (SIP)
- Develop a punch list of goals that can be addressed during job-embedded WFSGs (see Figure 18.2 for an example punch list from one of my elementary schools)

Figure 18.2   The 2004–2005 School Improvement Plan: Strategic Action List

---

Goal 1: Improve student mathematical skills schoolwide

- Focus on number sense, developing a deep understanding of concepts by first using concrete materials
- Create a learning atmosphere open to student solution methods and student interaction in a variety of groupings
- Encourage student use of calculators
- Implement ten-minute math strategies that spiral concept practice all year
- Implement problem-solving strategies; R.I.C.E. problem solving
- Integrate technology into math instruction

Goal 2: Implement activity-based math instruction, "Investigations in Number Data and Space," an exemplary elementary mathematics curriculum developed by universities, and TERC with funds from a National Science foundation Grant.

- Teachers will meet in WFSGs every other week for one and a half hours to:
  1. Analyze student work and create lessons based on the group's action plan and students' greatest needs in the area of math
  2. Review student work and tests to monitor the impact of teaching strategies discussed in WFSGs on student learning
  3. Discuss effective classroom procedures
  4. Create teacher-made tests, performance checklists, and rubrics
  5. Find ways to communicate effectively with parents about new math curriculum

- In order to support the WFSG process:
  1. The principal will review WFSG action plans and logs and conduct classroom observations to evaluate the implementation of Math Investigations and the use of calculators
  2. The LINCS coordinator will provide demonstration lessons
  3. The Content leader will model lessons and facilitate WFSG

- Write group action plans that will directly impact the objectives described in the SIP

To summarize, I found that this system of ongoing support and the gift of time for collaboration provides the structure for faculty members to work in WFSGs to accomplish several tasks simultaneously.

1. Teachers will have no misunderstandings as to the tasks to be addressed during WFSGs because they were part of the process of designing the tasks around specific student needs.

2. Principals will have excellent documentation that all of the faculty have read and faculty will understand the school improvement plan (SIP) goals and objectives.

3. Principals can easily stay informed about the progress each study group is making by reading and responding to WFSG logs.

4. A system of accountability occurs naturally as groups get frequent feedback on their efforts to implement schoolwide reform.

5. The whole faculty can see how all of the staff development is aligned with student needs and designed to effectively improve student learning.

CONCLUSION

As I reflect on my five-and-a-half years as a LINCS regional coordinator, I realize how fortunate I am to be involved in education. This is an exciting time to be an educator in Louisiana. We have made incredible progress in our goal to improve learning for all children. We have moved from consistently being at the top of every negative educational list and the bottom of most positive ones to being national leaders in many measures of academic growth. It is quite a relief to now be reading headlines like the ones listed below:

> BATON ROUGE, LA—Louisiana ranks 12th in the number of teachers receiving National Board Certification this year, outdistancing 38 other states.

> BATON ROUGE, LA—Louisiana's 4th- and 8th-grade students improved at a faster rate than students across the nation in Reading on the National Assessment of Educational Progress (NAEP), according to results released today by the U.S. Department of Education. "These scores show that Louisiana continues its trend of steady educational improvement and that is quite encouraging," State Superintendent of Education Cecil J. Picard said. "Our 8th graders ranked 4th, and our 4th graders ranked 11th in the amount of improvement—and that's outstanding."

> BATON ROUGE, LA.—Louisiana's testing program ranks 6th—up from 7th last year—when compared to the 50 states and the District of Columbia, according to a report issued today by *The Princeton Review*.

> BATON ROUGE, LA—Louisiana ranks among the top states in the country for its efforts to improve school and student performance, according to a new report from the nation's foremost K–12 education publication. *Education Week's* Quality Counts 2003 ranks Louisiana 5th among the 50 states for its accountability and standards efforts and 12th for its efforts to improve teacher quality. Louisiana's grade of A– in Standards and Accountability trails only four states.

I know that our LINCS school improvement process, which is centered on improving student achievement by increasing teacher content knowledge and incorporating best instructional strategies, has helped Louisiana in this positive growth. Our LINCS process is working because we are implementing the WFSG System of creating learning communities as the structure for job-embedded staff development. Teachers, administrators, parents, community members, and, of course, students of Louisiana salute the efforts that allowed us to learn about the WFSG System and to become national leaders during this historic time for education. Louisiana educators no longer hang their heads, but stand up tall, proud to be Louisiana professionals leading the charge for improving education for all students.

19

Enhancing Performance in the English Language Arts

Charlotte Ann Buisson

Teaching has always been my passion. When asked to explain "how" to enhance student performance in the English Language Arts, I felt excited to know I would be able to share my passion. Enhancing students' performance depends on being an effective reader. I believe this is the basis for *all success* in school. My mission is to share a passion for reading, writing, discovery, inquiry, and the pure joy of learning. This chapter will guide you on my path of joy.

The key areas of focus will be: strategies and activities, application of ideas in "real life," first-hand case studies, application of the Whole-Faculty Study Group (WFSG; see Murphy & Lick, 2005) System, closing gaps, data-based decision making, creating quality teaching, examining student work, and action research.

GENERAL FOCUS

Strategies and Activities

As a teacher, I continuously seek new strategies and activities that might assist me in my efforts to enhance my students' performance in every subject I teach. In this chapter, I share some strategies that proved to enhance *my students'* performance, attitudes toward reading and writing, and a marked improvement in their social skills.

Application of Ideas in "Real Life"

Students often ask, "When are we ever going to use this? Why do I have to learn this?" Students pay attention to those who hold celebrity status and have amassed great wealth and fame. As a result of these questions, I chose to deliver a famous TV personality's implementation of a reading strategy. This chapter explains my version of Oprah's Book Club (Literature Circles).

First-Hand Case Studies

Nothing speaks more loudly to me than testimonials by students. By listening to students, educators can learn what students need, and by listening to each other within Whole-Faculty Study Groups, we can learn how to address those needs. Read first-hand accounts by my former students to learn how I responded.

Lessons, Strategies, and Tips

Lessons, strategies, and tips are what teachers seek in an effort to enhance their curriculum. I do not believe in *adding* anything to a teacher's already overwhelming workload. I do believe in working smarter by addressing standards, benchmarks, and state mandates through students' writings and student-selected reading material. This chapter addresses "working smarter."

THE WFSG SYSTEM APPLIED TO SCHOOL IMPROVEMENT

Within Whole-Faculty Study Groups, I work with educators reviewing students' strengths and weaknesses, addressing action plans, researching, and implementing strategies directly affecting students' learning. This collaboration benefits all. Each time I visit a school, teachers pick my brain in an effort to discover the strategies in this chapter.

Gaps, Data-Based Decisions, Teachers, Student Work, and Action Research

In an effort to close achievement gaps among students, I share strategies that are applicable for all ability and grade levels in English Language Arts. With data-based decision making, teachers focus on the needs of their students by examining student work. This leads to action research. This chapter reveals the results of my personal research: "Can students' attitudes toward reading and writing be altered through student choices?" Join me as I share my reflections on teaching and learning experiences.

STUDENTS DESIRE TO BE SUCCESSFUL

In the beginning are the words . . . "Mommy, I'm going to learn to read and write!" The goal of most kindergarteners is to learn to read and write, and they fully expect to return home from the first day of school, reading and writing. When I taught fourth through eighth graders, I utilized the Readers' Workshop and Writers' Workshop methods introduced by Nancie Atwell (1998) in her book *In the Middle*. My students completed a Reading Survey and a Writing Survey during the first days in the workshop. My prediction was affirmed; students *do want to be successful* and from their early years have a desire to be proficient readers and writers. So, what happens along the way that interferes with many students' success? What roadblocks and obstacles arise? I have my own thoughts on this subject, but I have chosen to share reflections of my former students.

Case Studies

"When I was little, my mom read to me all the time. As soon as I learned how to read, she made me read to her. I missed my mom reading to me." This explanation from a seventh-grade boy led me to realize that as a teacher of English Language Arts, it was vital that I read to my students daily. The subject of the reading was not nearly as important as the fact that I continued to model what successful readers do—they read, voraciously, continuously, and they read a variety of genres, making reading a lifelong habit.

Another young man observed that I had looked around the room cautiously and then attempted to hide a novel beneath my grade book. At the end of class, the grade book was in its place, but my new copy of *The Chocolate War* by Robert Cormier was missing. I did not mention the book, and then on Friday, three grinning, acned faces returned my book to me.

"Sorry," one boy said sheepishly, "but we thought you didn't want us to read your book, and so we figured it MUST be good."

"Well, what's the verdict?" I responded curiously.

"It was great! All three of us read it this week!" They had passed on their guilt and their joy of reading with bursts of laughter and grins.

"Is anyone interested in reading the sequel?" I grinned, holding up three copies of *Beyond the Chocolate Wars*.

The novels were snatched from my hands; now they knew their teacher was a seventh grader trapped in an adult's body. I knew middle school students had a difficult time demonstrating self-discipline if they were told they could not do something. From that day forward, those three boys were the best advertisement I could have had for promoting young adult literature. They read everything I brought to class and then began bringing in their own selections after visiting bookstores with their very surprised moms.

The voracious readers became excellent writers—no surprise! After reading a wide variety of genres, they drew upon the styles and vocabularies of their favorite authors, emulating styles and developing their own. This correlation has been affirmed every year I have taught. Students *do want* to be excellent readers and writers, but they require motivation and modeling in order to develop desire.

Regardless of what we teach, we must teach with passion. As a teacher of English Language Arts, I modeled a love of reading, a satisfaction with writing, and an ability to communicate effectively in order to teach those skills to my students.

After becoming a writing consultant through the National Writing Project, I realized how futile it was to try to separate reading from writing and that it was even more futile to *not expect teachers* to read and write. Now, as a LINCS (Learning-Intensive Networking Communities for Success) Coordinator, I have the responsibility to work with administrators and faculties in schools in five different school districts. My position is directly under the Louisiana State Department of Education's Office of Quality Educators. Within my region, I am one of the coordinators working with School Improvement initiatives. Each of my schools was awarded a state grant that provides it with my services and money for professional development, substitute teacher stipends (for job-embedded staff development or for teachers attending conferences), teacher stipends, and materials for professional development. I use my experience and expertise as a National Writing Project Consultant to enhance my mentoring of teachers in English Language Arts. Each school I serve has one or two content leaders. These positions are held by highly effective teachers who redeliver to their faculty members the strategies, research, and content that I provide at monthly meetings. During each month, I visit the schools and provide a wide variety of services to them, including: facilitating WFSGs, teaching model lessons, planning professional development based on the schools' needs, and providing professional development as requested by the school. Each visit is guided by the needs of the students within that particular school. I spend 80% of my time *in my schools*, facilitating, presenting, and teaching model lessons.

Every teacher understands that the highest performing students on standardized tests are those who are competent readers *and* possess a desire to *demonstrate* their knowledge. Now, as I share my experiences with teachers in WFSGs, they acknowledge their own observations of the competent readers who are successful students. We agree that the self-motivated students who have maintained their passion for reading have become excellent writers. We also agree upon the challenge to motivate the struggling reader and the student who claims, "I don't care." Within WFSGs, teachers research various strategies for motivating their students, assisting them with weaknesses in reading, and analyzing the students' work in order to discover how to proceed in raising their achievement levels. The most powerful sharing that I have observed has been when a teacher brings students' work to a WFSG for analysis. Within a set protocol, colleagues provide the critical analysis in a risk-free environment that encourages all to grow: teachers and students. In addition, teachers observe peers who provide high quality instruction to students creating those projects and then follow up with discussions of the strategies and techniques observed. I have often heard teachers muse, "It worked so well in first and second period, but then it bombed in third period. Why?" Through analysis with colleagues, we can find the answers to the questions we pose while driving home or gulping coffee in the lounge.

Content Leaders are selected by their district or administrator based upon their ability to mentor teachers and provide professional development for faculties. At the present time, these teachers serve as a school's Title 1 Coordinators, Curriculum Facilitators, and/or Master Teachers. When schools join the LINCS program, district superintendents assign content leaders their responsibilities. Our hope is that in the future, content leaders' salaries will come totally from the grant, but for now, the individual districts cover their salaries.

In the schools I serve, content leaders attend monthly meetings in which teaching and learning strategies are modeled and analyzed. Upon returning to their schools, content leaders: (a) meet with teachers in WFSGs and share the strategies; (b) teach model lessons in classrooms used as "goldfish bowls" for other educators; and (c) provide mentoring to those teachers willing to try the strategies in their own class, with their own students, and with guidance from a successful teacher. Some of the lessons provided by content leaders are: "Writing to a Prompt," "Reading and Responding to Literature," "Poetry for All," "Responding to Constructed Response Questions," and "Literature Circles." Through sustained job-embedded WFSGs, teachers learn about instructional teaching strategies; discuss the strengths and weaknesses of a strategy; agree to try the strategy in their own classes; arrange a model lesson or observation of the lesson; and then, finally, return to the WFSG where student work is analyzed in order to assess the strategy.

English Language Arts teachers have moved far beyond the red pen strokes identifying misspelled words, incorrect grammar, and overused commas. We must look at the students' content to determine the level of comprehension of concepts, the ability to describe or explain, and the ability to persuade a specified audience with opinions and facts. Oral communication became written communication in order to share ideas with members of an audience who read. For everything there is a season, and the season for effective communication through speaking, reading, and writing is at the forefront of standardized testing.

Once I was asked why I thought students did not do well on standardized tests. I responded as many seventh graders did at that time: "Why should they? There is neither consequence nor reward for the results. No one gives you feedback, and no one cares how you do." This statement is no longer true. With *high-stakes testing* gaining more significance with policy makers and accountability demanding more of both students and teachers, educators do care. WFSGs analyze student work to determine: *what* strategies worked, *how* they worked, *why* they worked for some and not others, *what* we can do *differently* so that *all* will be successful and those who were successful gain even more.

Strategies and Activities

Examples of strategies that worked for me include the following:

- Silent sustained reading at the beginning of every class
- Silent sustained writing at the beginning of every class
- Shared excerpts from readings and writings

- Mini-lessons to address common needs of students (e.g., comma usage, quotations, premature closure, and overuse of pronouns)
- Writing as a process continued from the previous day (students work at their own pace on a genre assigned by the teacher), with the teacher becoming the facilitator and monitor

Self-discipline and self-motivation were required of everyone. Modeling preceded all work, cooperative learning was taught, steps in the process were taught, structure for assignments was taught, and as the teacher, I provided organization of materials and assignments in a very structured way that could be easily explained by any one of the students if a new student joined us or a visitor asked.

Reading was purposeful for some assignments and for pleasure in others. I assigned the genre, and students selected the book and author. This structure gave students voice and choice—desired by students. Writing was purposeful for all assignments, constructed response items on tests and for pleasure (e.g., personal journals).

Assessments contained three major parts:

1. Items specifically for editing (e.g., mini-lessons)

2. Constructed responses (e.g., specific to topic discussed from novel)

3. A final draft of a writing with all parts of the process attached

Rubric, final draft, rough draft with revisions, editing, brainstorming, and prompt were all attached in order. Each part received a specific number of points for completion of tasks for formative grades, and the final draft received a summative grade.

These grades were weighted: 60% formative and 40% summative. The emphasis was on the *process*, and students' summative grades improved vastly as their *effort in the process improved.*

Students maintained records of the books they read and the writings they completed. In addition, my students wrote friendly letters to their classmates and me in response to the books they read. Publication was always important to us; bulletin boards, anthologies, contests, and oral sharing in "The Authors' Chair" were among our favorites.

As an avid reader, I have always enjoyed sharing books with friends and coworkers. When I heard Harvey Daniels present Literature Circles at the International Reading Conference, I knew I had discovered a way to mesh my passion for reading with my students' need to read and share. After showing Harvey's video, I asked my students if they would be interested in participating in this process. The students responded overwhelmingly, "Yes!" They were hooked. Sixth graders love to move and talk. With this process, students move from whole-group discussions to small groups for Literature Circles. I provided a modified set of task sheets (using Harvey Daniels's model), and demonstrated how to select the tasks and then rotate the tasks within their cooperative groups. I planned a specific time during each class for the circles. The circles averaged fifteen minutes per class and included the opportunity for the following tasks to be shared: Discussion Director, Passage Master, Connector, and Illustrator.

Since first using these strategies, I have shared Literature Circles with teachers and students in Grades 4 through 12 with equal interest and success. As with all effective strategies, the success comes from a deep understanding of the process, organization of materials, enthusiastic explanations, and modeling of expectations. These items are time-consuming up front, but pay off tenfold in the long run.

I strongly advise teachers interested in implementing Literature Circles to begin by setting high expectations for social conduct and to stay with the process even when students resist it. Literature Circles require intensive work from the students, and they may be unaccustomed to the level of involvement you require of them. In addition, your level of organization and enthusiasm will be contagious. (For additional information on Literature Circles, see *Literature Circles: Voice and Choice in Book Clubs & Reading Groups;* Daniels, 2001.)

Assessment

Students learn in advance the criteria and standards for their final products through a Writing Checklist. This checklist is written in "Kid Friendly" terms for clear understanding of assessment. Writing is assessed using a checklist that is completed for self-assessment *prior to* my assessment. Following my assessment, I meet with students to review the results and collaboratively list personal strengths and weaknesses followed by setting goals for improvement in future writings. These one-on-one conferences are time-consuming but highly valued by students. Each student expects this personal attention and respects others while waiting for his or her special time with the teacher. Monitoring must be continuous throughout the writing process.

While waiting, students continue to refine writing pieces in progress and to read for pleasure, to continue work on a long-term project, or to seek peers for revisions or editing. No student can ever truthfully say, "I don't have anything to do" or "I don't know what to do." By following the advice of Harry Wong (1998), structures and routines are in place. Students are familiar with their role as a self-initiator of learning. They "ask three before they ask me" what they can do if they are unsure.

A classroom where students are self-motivated, self-disciplined, and self-initiators does not happen by accident. Every structure, role, responsibility, and process is taught explicitly and implicitly. No easy task for a teacher, yet vital for students to achieve their potential for success.

Carl Nagin (2003), in his book *Because Writing Matters,* cites Strickland and colleagues:

> State curriculum documents and assessments are carrying a new message: writing should no longer be "the silent R" of learning, or the poor cousin of reading. The standards movement has helped to focus attention on writing in all disciplines and to push for consistency within standards, assessments, and rubrics. (footnote, p. 71)

I agree completely, and know for a fact that my students' writings demonstrate their mastery of all standards in English Language Arts.

CONCLUSION

My passion continues as I motivate teachers and students, modeling my love of reading, writing, and learning. Enthusiasm is obvious to students, and a teacher who is observed reading and writing, shares excerpts from books, refers students to young adult literature with genuine knowledge of the content, and shares personal writings is like a "fisherman with the ultimate bait." Baiting students with success and then hooking them with great literature leads them to become the writers they are meant to be. Successful writers are readers, and effective readers write with ease. You cannot separate one from the other. *The goal: a literate America. The cost: highly effective teachers who teach their "passion with passion." The result: priceless.*

I genuinely believe that we must nurture our teachers through highly engaging and job-embedded staff development, and then continue to support them through collegial networking and modeling. Whole-Faculty Study Groups provide the vehicle for school improvement by developing our teachers, the heart of education. Literate students are the heart of America. *When we enhance our teachers' performance, we will enhance our students' performance in English Language Arts and across the curriculum.*

20

Raising Student Achievement in Reading and Mathematics

Lisa S. Smith

Raising student achievement in any subject, particularly reading and mathematics, is possible, probable, and even expected in America's schools today. Unfortunately, there is no "magic bullet" for educators to use to achieve this. Yet there are, indeed, strategies, policies, and procedures that can be implemented to make a difference with students and schools, to ultimately raise student learning levels and test scores. A cooperative effort, though, is required to actually make it happen. Cooperation between home and school must be noted, because it has been proven to have an effect on student achievement, but the cooperation I am emphasizing is that within the hierarchy of the education community. Teachers, school support personnel, school administrators, and district-level administrators must cooperatively accept responsibility and work together to make increased student achievement a reality.

Developing Common Attitudes

Having been appointed as principal in one of Georgia's lowest performing schools the fall of 1999, the first thing I noticed was that all of the teachers and staff had to be on the same page as to their beliefs of what children *can* do. Teachers, teacher assistants, administrators, secretaries, custodians, cafeteria personnel, and bus drivers, virtually everybody who comes into contact with students at school, must sincerely believe that the students CAN be successful, and then provide them the opportunities and tools to prove it. I personally believe that children are "pleasers" by nature; that children want to please the adults whom they love and respect, and those whom they believe *sincerely* love and respect them—those who encourage them, believe in them, and set high, yet reasonable, expectations for them. *Adult attitudes toward students, school, and student successes at school are the most crucial underlying factors in improving student achievement.* Adult attitudes largely determine student attitudes, and student attitudes largely determine their successes.

School Setting and Achievements

In a school where more than 80% of its students were served free or reduced-priced lunches, more than 60% were of minority races, and more than 40% of those minorities were Hispanics whose families spoke little or no English at home, we had plenty of excuses for being "low performing." Yet, after three years, with a terrific staff that I would assemble again if attempting the task anywhere in the nation, our school was removed from the three "low-performing schools" lists that haunted us daily. The school motto became: "Where diversity is an opportunity, not an obstacle." Monthly student attendance percentages reached as high as 97%, PTA attendance increased 133%, and community volunteers increased 200%. Student achievement in fourth- and sixth-grade reading, language arts, and mathematics, on the Georgia Criterion Referenced Tests, increased as shown in Tables 20.1 and 20.2.

Table 20.1 Percentage of Students Meeting or Exceeding Standards: Fourth Grade

Fourth Grade	1999–2000	2000–2001	2001–2002
Reading	40	48	82
Language Arts	57	51	65
Mathematics	20	37	71

Table 20.2 Percentage of Students Meeting or Exceeding Standards: Sixth Grade

Sixth Grade	1999–2000	2000–2001	2001–2002
Reading	63	69	84
Language Arts	19	48	60
Mathematics	38	42	72

Our Commitment

As we moved through the three years, we accepted the painful truth that our test scores were the lowest in our school district and among the lowest in the state. We talked about this reality and pored over school, grade, and student data, and then determined plans of action to address specific weaknesses. We realized, acknowledged, and attacked head-on the probability that we could not go from our current scores to the 80th or 90th percentile in just one or two years. We did, however, believe that we could make steady steps upward and eventually have our students above state averages in reading and mathematics. We made a commitment to identify our specific problem areas, attack our weaknesses with a vengeance, and celebrate our successes, regardless of how small.

Research shows that the most important single influence in student achievement is the teacher. The key for school and student success lies within the classroom walls: *teachers whose attitudes and sincere beliefs are that students can and will learn, and who are passionate and energetic in the cause of educating each individual child.* In Jim Collinss (2001) research for his book *Good to Great,* he found that "good-to-great leaders first got the right people on the bus, the wrong people off the bus, and the right people in the right seats—and then they figured out where to drive it." His analogy is more than applicable in a school working to raise student achievement. In order for a school to move forward and to make changes to increase student performance, the commitment for improvement must be embraced by every member of the school staff. "Every child can learn" cannot simply be a cliché, but must be the *sincere* core of educational beliefs for each school employee.

Administrators attempting to lead a school reform effort must "load the bus" with knowledgeable, dedicated teachers who help create a vision for success and are willing to make it happen. It *can happen* if the right people are on the bus *and* in the right seats. Then, these "right" people must be given the tools, support, and authority they need in order to make it happen.

How We Raised Reading Scores

Our first reality check confirmed that students who couldn't read showed little success in their other subject areas. Success in science and social studies, and even mathematics word problems, was virtually impossible if students could not read. So, reading became our first priority.

Required Change. Our focus on reading required a change in practically every aspect of school operations. Changes in curriculum, instruction, scheduling, personnel, professional development, budgeting, and even discipline were all vital components of our new focus. In the spring of 1999, before I became principal, district-level administrators and the teachers adopted a new reading series to be implemented the following fall. A *direct instruction program,* with initial focus on phonemic awareness and phonics, was adopted for only one school in the district, ours. Professional development and training were provided for teachers and paraprofessionals, and monthly coaching was scheduled to support and promote success in the program. These costly decisions were made to *meet the needs* of the students at our school. We were fortunate to have had a knowledgeable and visionary superintendent and a board of education whose philosophy was "to provide unequal resources to meet unequal needs." This profound philosophical change had an effect on several areas in our school that made a difference for our students. *If superintendents and boards of education are serious about removing schools from "needs improvement," then they must assume some of the responsibility and adopt a similar philosophy.*

Listening to Experts. Adopting the new reading program was a wonderful beginning. Providing training and monthly "coaching" support for our teachers were other vital initial steps. We realized, however, that in order for a new program to be successful, we had to pinpoint every opportunity to make it so. We consulted with program directors and followed their advice for implementation. *Whenever beginning a new program, listening to the experts and specifically following their program design will more likely ensure its success.*

Scheduling. We began program implementation by creating a schedule to make the most effective use of our reading time. Each day, all of our K–2 students were taught reading during our first reading block, and our third- to sixth-grade students were taught reading when the first block had finished. Each student received two fifty-minute, back-to-back, uninterrupted reading periods. Thus, each homeroom teacher would teach two back-to-back reading groups or levels. Our physical education, art, media, and music teachers did not teach reading, but maintained a regular schedule with students not scheduled for reading during each block.

Direct instruction is exactly what the title implies; the teacher would spend fifty minutes with her first group, following the scripted lesson, with pacing determined by the program, while her other group worked independently on supplemental materials and lessons created for the program. After fifty minutes, the groups rotated. The independent work time was a challenge at first, particularly with the younger students, but they *can* be taught how to work independently. If you think they can, they will. If you think they can't, they won't. So, we expected it, showed them how, gave them opportunities to practice, and then required it! Kindergarten classes, which had paraprofessional assistance, had three rotating groups: a teacher-led group, an independent group, and a language group led by the paraprofessional. The language component was part of our curriculum adoption to strengthen language skills for language-deficient students. For those kindergarten students who entered school with a language-rich background, the teacher provided a different, content- and skill-appropriate activity center.

Placement and Pacing. Scheduling students based on the program-designed initial placement assessment became another challenge. Placement was so specific that it not only prescribed the child's level, but also the specific lesson within each level. Teachers would request or be assigned to teach levels that included most students in their grade levels. However, within a few months (and even more frequently after we had implemented the program for more than a year), the student groups would change. Students were allowed to move "up" to the next level or future lessons of the same level if they were showing exemplary mastery and passed a program-generated assessment. Likewise, students could be moved "back" a level or a group of lessons within a level if they were struggling and not showing mastery. Thus, our more fluent readers were never held back while waiting for others in the group to master a skill or lesson. Through this multiage grouping and frequent monitoring and assessment, students were allowed to move forward or backward, changing groups and progressing at an independent pace based on individual performance.

Staffing and Coordination. The challenge of this process, other than with scheduling, was staffing. At one time, we had 57 reading and language groups for our 301 students. *Pause now and do the math!* That's right; it's an average of 5.3 students per group and is another HUGE contributing factor to raising our reading scores. Small groups, more individual attention, and the teacher's direct, focused instruction for fifty minutes every day made a difference. Some of our third- through sixth-grade reading groups who were on or above grade level, had more than the average of 5.3 students. Many of them had between seven and fourteen students. But still, isn't that considered a *small* reading group?

On our staff, we had two teachers per grade level. With our schoolwide Title I status, we were able to hire two additional teachers. One of those served as our Direct Instruction (DI) coordinator who tested children as they moved between reading levels, maintained the inventory of reading materials, tested new students for program placement, and taught up to six reading classes (two in each of our reading blocks and often one or two additional classes for our non-English-speaking children for whom we "created" reading classes when they enrolled). She also trained with our reading coaches and became an onsite coach for our teachers.

An alternate plan, if we had required additional reading teachers, was to hire two teachers who wanted to work only part-time (new moms or retired teachers are a perfect fit). I planned to have both of them work during our two reading blocks, teaching two groups during each block. This would have provided teachers for an additional eight reading groups.

Language Classes

A final strategy we implemented, using our new reading program, was to provide the kindergarten-designed language program for our new, non-English-speaking children, regardless of their ages. We frequently had students enroll in our school who spoke no English, so we created *additional language classes,* adapted the kindergarten language program, and had a paraprofessional work with these students. In addition to their regular reading class with our DI coach as their teacher, they received this language class, as well as their English as a second language (ESL) class, taught by dynamic, highly qualified, ESL-endorsed, certified teachers. This scheduling challenge provided these students with three daily doses of reading/language arts, and since more than 40% of our student population qualified for our ESL program, this was considered another HUGE contributing factor to our improved reading scores.

Daily Practice Exercises

Even though the direct instruction approach to teaching reading was undoubtedly a major contributing factor in increasing our student achievement in reading, there were other strategies that were implemented to aid in the process. We began a routine of *daily practice exercises* in grammar, analogies, and vocabulary

(Grades 1–6) each morning as the students arrived. Having this written on the board before teachers left each afternoon was an administrative expectation, so that regardless of how hectic the morning was for the teacher, students would enter the classroom each day with assignments already posted. After completion, an oral review of the activities was conducted in each class. This took no longer than ten to fifteen minutes per day, yet contributed to student success in recognizing and correcting grammatical errors, thinking through analogies, and learning new vocabulary.

Media Program

We believe that creating a focus and emphasis on our school *media program* also had an impact on our students' reading improvement. Media specialists should be among the strongest and most important teachers in your building. Our media specialist created an inviting atmosphere where children felt welcomed, and managed a creative program that instilled in our students a love of reading. By offering an open schedule for student and teacher use, and by utilizing various competitive contests in conjunction with a well-known reading software program, we saw media center usage and circulation statistics greatly increase.

Being a former media specialist, I knew the administrator's attitude toward and support of the media program could contribute to the success or failure of its implementation. Support included providing financial resources and identifying community organizations to make contributions to our media center. A percentage of our Title I budget was earmarked to provide a current and wide variety of reading materials for students on all ability and interest levels. English/Spanish books were also purchased and heavily circulated within the ESL population. These students frequently shared that their parents were also enjoying learning to read English through our English/Spanish collection.

To ensure reading success, an active, well-supported school media program needs to be at the center of your school reform efforts. You may be surprised by how much better children read when they read often. "Practice makes perfect" is certainly applicable to reading and will contribute to increased student achievement across the content areas.

Language Development and Experiential Opportunities

Language development and experiential opportunities outside the school were encouraged for our students. Many children enter our schools without an array of experiences outside the home or neighborhood, and much of what they should see and experience cannot be provided within the walls of the school. We looked for occasions to provide schoolwide opportunities and encouraged teachers to explore avenues for learning experiences in outside settings. Teachers connected the experiences with state standards, and then we worked together to find the resources to make it happen. We were most fortunate to have created a "sister school relationship" with a more affluent school in our district and would frequently be invited to participate in their special Cultural Arts, Career, and Georgia Day activities. They even provided bus transportation for our students to travel between the two schools. Now, that's a relationship!

HOW WE RAISED MATHEMATICS SCORES

Mathematics was identified as our second most critical area of weakness and recognized as the second indicator for our school performance status.

Additional Time and Pretests

As in reading, we had to make adjustments in the way we approached most areas of school operations. We began by scheduling *additional time* so that no mathematics class received less than sixty minutes of uninterrupted, instructional time. Grade levels and teachers divided their classes into groups of students based on student performance. Effective use of *pretests* for each introduced skill determined group placement for each child; thus, groups varied depending on the skills being taught.

Special Practices

We added a *problem of the day* to our daily morning practice exercises where, through teacher-led, oral, step-by-step procedures, students were able to discover multiple ways to think through problems and then solve them. We also provided teacher training to implement a *daily, fifteen-minute program* that reinforced a blanket covering of mathematics skills including tallying, place value, patterns, grouping, graphing, time, and money for all K–6 homerooms. This incredible program provided consistent, instructional, and entertaining support for the mathematics skills required by the state and National Council for Teachers of Mathematics (NCTM) standards.

Research-Based Computer Program

With district financial and technology support, we implemented a *research-based computer program* to increase fluency in basic mathematics skills. This individualized program also provided interactive practice in both computation and application strands of mathematics. Again, seeking advice for success from program specialists, we required seventy minutes per week for all students in Grades 3 to 6. Our K–2 students also *consistently* used the program, but were not required to adhere to the minimum seventy minutes.

Mathematics Study Group

For an additional focus on increasing student mathematics scores, our *mathematics Whole-Faculty Study Group* worked to address specific content weaknesses of our students. Through research, observations in other schools, and careful analysis of student and program strengths and weaknesses, the group led us through major changes that improved opportunities for our students. Students identified as "struggling," those who were not showing measures of success in mathematics, were offered alternate textbook options. Again, district support allowed us to *meet our students' needs* by excluding these students from the system textbook adoption. I believe this is crucial, since a textbook should be only one of the references used for teaching. *In order to meet student needs, we must not allow textbook publishers to determine what and how we teach, confining ourselves to either running out of chapters or months of the school year as the basis for our curriculum.* If we follow state and NCTM standards, textbooks alone cannot provide what students need!

COOPERATIVE LEARNING AND MANIPULATIVES

Cooperative learning activities, increased *use of mathematics manipulatives,* and even playing cafeteria background music of *multiplication songs* made a difference for our students. We believed that some made more of an impact than others, but the combination probably created the greatest contribution. Regardless, administrative support was necessary for any of these to be effective. Cooperative learning requires movement and discussion in the classroom. Administrators cannot expect this to be effective if the anticipation is that student desks must be in rows and students must be quiet in order to learn. I once had a teacher tell me that her former principal had come to her mathematics class to conduct her formal, required evaluation. When he saw students talking and working in groups, he said he'd come back when she was "teaching"!

Engaging students in meaningful, hands-on activities is how they learn and retain information. We must encourage what I refer to as "organized chaos" and quit viewing manipulatives (even blocks and colored candy pieces) as toys. When used instructionally, manipulatives can assist students in *learning the process* of mathematics and help them to begin to understand the basic concepts of geometry and probability, even in kindergarten. Administrators must also support mathematics teachers (science, social studies, and other disciplines, as well) by providing funds necessary to *equip classrooms for hands-on instruction.* Ask teachers what they need in order to provide their students with better opportunities for success, and then make sure they get it.

Financial resources may hinder the school improvement process unless the administration is willing to find the additional resources that are needed. District support (remember, "Unequal resources for unequal needs"), community support, and numerous grant opportunities are available to schools if administrators are willing to take the time to pursue them. Don't be fooled; this is time-consuming, exhausting, and oftentimes frustrating, but necessary and worth the effort when it pays off! *Having resources to provide what teachers REQUIRE is absolutely crucial and may take time to amass.* When resources are provided, administrators should follow up by visiting classrooms frequently to see them in use.

Teachers Bring Coherence to Multiple Initiatives

With all the curricular and instructional initiatives, a schoolwide system should (a) provide the opportunity for teachers to collaborate, (b) share what is and is not working, (c) bring coherence to multiple initiatives, (d) support the implementation of new materials and strategies, and (e) monitor the effects of the materials and strategies on students. To accomplish these purposes, beginning in January 2001 all certificated personnel in our school became members of Whole-Faculty Study Groups. The groups provided teachers of varying grade levels, attitudes, understandings, knowledge, and skills with the opportunity to collaborate and support each other in their efforts to improve student achievement. We found that it is not enough just to have study groups; it is what teachers do when the groups meet that makes the time and energy that go into "group work" pay dividends for students. *It is the responsibility of the principal to know what the study groups are doing and to provide whatever resources, support, and feedback that the groups require.*

ADMINISTRATIVE RESPONSIBILITIES

Teachers are the most crucial factor in student achievement, but administrators have huge responsibilities to support and provide teachers with optimal opportunities to do their jobs. Administrators, both school and district level, must assume some of the responsibility to make it all happen.

Protect Instructional Time

Perhaps the most important contribution a school principal can make to student success is to seriously protect the instructional time for teachers by eliminating classroom disruptions. Principals should make this a top priority and prohibit anyone—secretaries, counselors, parents, and even administrators—from making intercom calls schoolwide or to classrooms during instructional times except in emergencies. There are workable plans, regardless of the school schedule, that can be created to eliminate interrupting instruction. It may take an administrator, secretary, or counselor longer to walk to find a student, but this one person's time is much less than the time it takes a teacher to refocus an entire class of students after an interruption is made. Consistent support of this policy reinforces an *administrator's commitment to students and teachers that teaching and learning are the most important things the school is doing.*

An additional way to protect instructional time is to minimize the number of days out of the same class period for pictures, assemblies, and other activities. Alternating schedules for these is time-consuming for the administrator, but will continue to emphasize the importance of instructional time. Since this chapter focuses on increasing student achievement in reading and mathematics, then I suggest specifically working around such classes for these inevitable interruptions. It isn't always possible, but every attempt should be made to protect these instructional times.

Provide Collaboration Time

Another administrative responsibility must be to set aside time for teacher collaboration within the school. Grade-level meetings are crucial for teacher planning and collaboration: An effective piece of the student improvement puzzle is missing when teachers do not have the opportunity to unify a focus on specific areas of the curriculum. Whole-Faculty Study Groups are an effective means for accomplishing this.

Based on school data and trends, Whole-Faculty Study Groups provide an avenue for teachers to focus on specific areas of need, provide time to study the research, engage in meaningful discussion and decision making concerning alternative strategies, plan lessons and activities, and then evaluate actual student work to determine the impact on student learning. They are an opportunity for teachers, concentrating on specific areas of the curriculum, to try new, perhaps unconventional, strategies in an attempt to improve student learning. They provide and encourage collaborative risk-taking opportunities that must be supported by the administration in order to have a possible positive impact on student achievement.

Create the Right Atmosphere

It is imperative for administrators to create an atmosphere where the hallways are quiet and students respect the schoolwide learning environment. Administrators should make conscious and frequent efforts to talk about the learning environment with the students, consistently emphasizing a "we're here to learn" mindset. Having a clear understanding of acceptable behaviors and consequences for each classroom, grade level, and schoolwide area is the first step. But, unless these are compatible—so students won't ever be confused as to what is appropriate and acceptable—with consequences that are firm, fair, and consistent, they will be useless. The staff should come to an agreement and then be willing to enforce the decisions. *Strong administrative support will determine the success of all discipline efforts.*

Provide for Awareness of Data

Administrators should lead the effort to create an awareness of the importance and implications of test scores. In our school, we believed that students should be made aware of the importance of the tests, so we created an effective way to involve them in understanding the purpose and benefits of testing. Through individual conferences, we disseminated testing information to students and conveyed strengths and areas needing improvement to the individuals. Students were told, before testing, that they would have an opportunity to see their results and learn about their own strengths and weaknesses as soon as scores were available at the school.

Promoting the idea that individual results would be discussed with them before the year ended encouraged additional effort from our students. Furthermore, conducting individual student conferences provided students with the opportunity to see, understand, and appreciate the time they spent testing. Spending three to five minutes with each student, explaining the test domains and reviewing individual strengths and weaknesses, gave students the feedback they required to set personal goals for the next school year. We kept these documented goals, along with yearly test scores, in individual Academic Improvement Plan (AIP) folders and moved them from grade to grade, using them each fall for an additional AIP conference. The fall conference would serve to remind students of the goals they set, and also as an accountability measure knowing that someone actually reviewed the goals that were set at the end of the previous year. These conferences also provided important insight for current teachers.

Administrative scheduling for individual AIP conferences requires priority in setting aside a schoolwide block of time (e.g., extending the homeroom period for a few days). Regardless of when the conferences are set, their definite need and benefits exist. Given the opportunity to discuss the results, students will more likely become cognizant of their personal accountability.

Determining how to use test scores to improve instruction begins with evaluating school, grade, classroom, and individual-student results to determine strengths and weaknesses in the curriculum, focus, instruction, and learning. Rerostering data, creating lists of students who were weak in each domain, and examining weaknesses reflected in longitudinal studies are crucial for pinpointing specific areas to address when determining how to improve instruction, student achievement, and test scores.

Schedule Test Practice Time

Another important way an administrator can contribute to increased student achievement is to include, in the weekly schedule, a period for "test practice" time. *If a schoolwide testing environment is created for thirty to forty minutes every week, where all students are in the classrooms working on test-taking skills, they will learn to be comfortable with the testing environment, procedures, and successful test-taking practices.* Practice in timed activities, such as reading questions looking for key terms, learning various testing vocabulary, and eliminating wrong answers, can make a difference on actual testing days.

There are a variety of test practice materials available on the market, and Georgia even provides Web-based test practice activities for teacher and student use. In addition to scheduled practice activities, teachers should be encouraged throughout the school year to create some of their assessments in the format of standardized tests, using a variety of styles, "bubbling answers," and vocabulary to prepare students for state assessments. Sometimes students do not understand the direction "add numbers" when they are asked to "find the sum." Then again, some students can add $5 + 5 = $ _____, but cannot complete the problem when written as:

$$\begin{array}{r} 5 \\ + 5 \\ \hline \end{array}$$

Students require exposure and practice in these test-taking competencies.

Fostering Flexibility and Confidence

Flexibility and confidence in the school administration and staff to make decisions at the school level based on needs determined at the school is a district-level responsibility that can definitely make a difference in the success of the school. Allowing professionals who work "in the trenches" to make research-based, professional decisions concerning budgets, curriculum, staffing, scheduling, and general school operations creates a climate that encourages identifying needs, seeking solutions to problems, and acquiring resources necessary to address specific issues, thus creating a climate conducive to student success. Schools, like students and teachers, have different personalities, needs, strengths, and weaknesses. *If, indeed, no child is to be left behind, then districts must encourage schools to "think outside the box" and support flexibility within the district, based on individual school and student needs.*

CONCLUSION

There is no magic bullet for raising student achievement, but a conglomerate of strategies, policies, and procedures made it happen for us. Are these the best or the only answers? Probably not, but these are what worked at our school. *Once we decided what needed to be done, we made a commitment to do it. Programs were implemented by everyone, every day.* Teachers did not haphazardly implement pieces of the programs; they all made a commitment to seriously and correctly implement them together.

Our reading and mathematics grouping of students, even in our fourth- through sixth-grade departmentalized schedule, was always determined by performance. There is always a lot of controversy over grouping, but we believed that performance grouping for these subjects was important for our success. When specific skills, strengths, and weaknesses of *individual students* were identified, instruction in those areas was more specific. *Teachers "raised the bar" as far as expectations from students, but they began instruction at the students' level of understanding.* All classes, other than reading and mathematics, were heterogeneously grouped.

Bell-to-bell instruction in a school working toward academic excellence must be the norm, not a novelty. Instructional time must be taken seriously, management issues handled expediently, and the "main thing"—teaching and learning—must always be the main thing in the classrooms. These were expected procedures to which we adhered consistently. Seldom, if ever, did I hear our teachers say they "didn't have enough time" to teach.

Raising student achievement in reading and mathematics is not an easy task. Schools do not want the label "needs improvement," but most important, they do want their students to learn and be successful. Educators lack access to a magic bullet to achieve this. *Yet, with the right people in the right places in the school and a collaborative, identified direction and concentrated efforts from school-district personnel, school administrators, teachers, and staff, success can happen.* Make up your mind, prepare your school, roll up your sleeves, and get busy.

You Can Make It Happen—It Can Be Done!

21

Improving Reading in Primary Grades

Angela S. Dillon

All children will read at grade level by the end of third grade. This was the goal that our school system set when it rolled out the new Monroe County Balanced Literacy Initiative in the fall of 2002. It was a major initiative meant to support the school system in meeting the requirements of the No Child Left Behind (NCLB) Act. NCLB forced school systems to take a good, hard look at the way they ensure student success. Excuses were no longer accepted, if NCLB and students were to succeed. "How do we reach this lofty goal?" asked Hubbard Primary School teachers four years ago when it was presented at a faculty meeting. The teachers knew that they would be primarily responsible for ensuring the success of meeting this goal. As instructional leader, I knew that this question must be answered with strategies that would bring success, and these are discussed in the balance of this chapter.

HUBBARD PRIMARY SCHOOL BACKGROUND

Hubbard Primary School opened in January of 1995, with approximately 850 students in kindergarten and first and second grades. The poverty level has always been fairly high, with a 50% free and reduced lunch rate. Minority groups make up 35% of the student population. Monroe County is a rural community, with many parents working at the local fast food restaurants, grocery stores, or traveling out of town to find work. Parents support the school, but are often unable to support their children academically. When looking at the test data from 1995 to the present, it became obvious that to increase student success, it would not be enough just to continue to work hard. Fortunately, I was invited to attend an overview of the Whole-Faculty Study Group System of professional development, which led us to study the school's test data in search of patterns that would point us to specific areas in which we should focus our instruction.

IMPLEMENTATION OF WHOLE-FACULTY STUDY GROUPS

The teaching of reading is a complex, ongoing endeavor that involves myriad strategies. The task is daunting if attempted alone. Whole-Faculty Study Groups (WFSGs; see Murphy & Lick, 2005) enabled teachers at Hubbard Primary School to work together to focus on critical strategies that helped to effectively address how students learn to read.

Teachers work hard to help all children become successful. Although all teachers want to achieve a high level of success with their students, the constraints of time and daily demands often prevent this from happening. When WFSGs were introduced to Hubbard Primary, they were seen by the administration as a method of lending strong support through the best practice of local staff development. In addition, WFSGs supported efforts to work together across grade levels and across the curriculum to look at data to determine students' needs. Our school system developed a framework for literacy a year earlier that aligned improvement efforts, making them integrated and results oriented. WFSGs assisted us in sustaining this framework and maintaining a focus on student achievement.

Initial WFSG Meeting

The initial WFSG meeting was used for the faculty to look at the previous year's test results. Ten of the twelve groups focused on various reading skills, which included phonics, comprehension, writing, vocabulary, research, and critical thinking. The previous year's efforts to improve reading included the newly developed framework, and also provided explicit instruction in phonics. Teachers were interested in continuing to develop their skills in order to reach the school system's three-year goal: *that every student would be able to read at grade level by the end of the third grade.*

ACTION PLANS

Action plans were developed, and essential questions to be considered were included: How do we effectively teach students to apply phonemic skills? What specific skills can we teach students so they will comprehend what they read? And, what skills must students master to be able to read for meaning? These questions represented a strong focus, yet the action steps required more student involvement and better assessment. Although our initial action steps were relatively weak, they developed during the year. As teachers became more familiar with how to (a) use student data, (b) develop rubrics, (c) look at student work, and (d) develop formative tests for each specific skill, their ability to write action steps improved.

USING STUDENT DATA

Initially, a test that was given in the fall and the spring of the year was identified as providing the data teachers would use to improve teaching strategies. They quickly discovered that looking at student data would have to occur much more often if the results they anticipated were to become a reality.

DEVELOPING RUBRICS

Rubrics were developed by the teachers to identify specific benchmarks that students must meet to become proficient in certain skills. Soon, students began developing their own rubrics, providing the teacher with distinctive insight into the knowledge base each child had acquired. Classrooms began using graphs to show overall growth in learning letters, sounds, and sight words. Many individual student graphs were used when it became evident that graphing helped students set goals and improve motivation to learn. Kindergarten teachers decided to do away with the "letter of the week" because they found that students were learning at a much faster rate than they had expected. The decision to teach consonant and vowel sounds earlier in the year was a direct result of student success with graphing. Kindergarten and first and second grades improved sight word recognition, as well, by observing the results of each grade level and finding that there was little consistency in the words that were taught each grading period.

Graphic organizers became more evident in the classroom as a result of research in the area of comprehension. These would then be copied and placed in a folder on the network for easy access. Students learned to develop their own graphic organizers as they began to improve in comprehension and, ultimately, in test taking.

LOOKING AT STUDENT WORK

"Looking at student work" is one of the most important forces driving the work of a study group. It is also difficult to do it effectively. A paradigm shift has been taking place at our school, from the "evaluation of teaching" to the "evaluation of learning." The success of WFSGs depends largely on how well we succeed in shifting our focus from the teacher (i.e., from teaching) to the student (i.e., to learning) so that the "looking at student work" component will be most effective. If not done properly, teachers may feel threatened by the remarks that are made or the questions asked by others. Each study group had at least one member with training in the use of "looking at student work" protocols. This provided some support, yet required much practice to become effective. Further professional learning is planned for teachers in the future to hone this skill.

MODELING INSTRUCTIONAL STRATEGIES

"Teachers modeling instructional strategies for other teachers" is another skill that requires both trust and confidence. An expert sees the distinctions in teaching that a novice often misses. Therefore, it is important that study-group members take time to observe each other and share important strategies that work with their students. A five-minute walk-through, with a five-minute debriefing of effective instructional strategies, is becoming the norm for our school. Small groups of teachers and an administrator take time to walk through five classrooms, observing for five minutes, then following up with five minutes of questions and comments for each visit. This has provided our teachers with a valuable resource to gain knowledge and share effective practices. Also, Guided Reading and Writers' Workshops are two components of the locally developed framework for literacy. By observing effective strategies used by teachers who have experience in these areas, a much faster and more effective implementation for other teachers is taking place. WFSGs are able to identify teachers with special instructional-strategies knowledge and use them as resource people to make other teachers more effective.

CONCLUDING EXERCISE

As a final exercise for the year, each WFSG is asked to develop new action steps for the school's Continuous Improvement Plan, based on what the members found to be effective action steps in their study group. This provided a schoolwide sharing of actions that supported student success. The school's targeted goals are more likely to be met with such recommendations from the WFSGs in place.

LESSONS LEARNED

As we completed our second year with WFSGs, it became evident that the administration must participate strongly in order to support successful group work. WFSGs want and require immediate feedback on their meeting logs. Care must be taken to identify groups that are not functioning at an effective level. Dialogue must take place in a nonthreatening way with the group members to determine specific needs that will make them successful. Each year, at least one group had to be reorganized by moving members to successful groups. Although this increased the other groups' sizes, reorganized group members gained significantly in the work they were able to accomplish. It has been important to our school staff to continue staff development to increase the knowledge of the various components of WFSGs.

Another important aspect of successful WFSGs is the membership of each group. Speech teachers were of tremendous support for groups working to develop phonics skills. Vertical teams resulted in excellent discussions and planning to improve students' writing skills. Groups working on improving reading comprehension should include teachers who are successful at teaching this skill, as well as teachers who may require much support.

CONCLUSION

Teachers are not able to achieve the goals of NCLB by working in seclusion each day, nor should they be expected to. They must be provided with an organized method of developing collegiality so that the focus of students' needs can be determined, studied, and researched. Teachers must be provided with time to observe each other, learn from each other, and work together to achieve the skills necessary to ensure student success. Just as no student wants to fail, neither does the teacher. Success for all students is possible within the time frame given us by the federal government. Our school has seen evidence of the possibilities within the past three years. The state test scores for our third-grade students in reading have risen from 88% of the students meeting or exceeding the state standards in 2002 to 97% in 2004. The gap between minority and white students has decreased to only 2% in reading, and 93% of our students with disabilities met or exceeded the state standards in third-grade reading.

We continue to work to increase our success in mathematics and writing, however. WFSGs help to keep us focused on our areas that require improvement. Teachers have become more adept at using available resources, such as special education and speech teachers, the instructional coach, professional books, and Web sites. Professional books, such as *Guiding Readers and Writers* by Irene Fountas and Gay Su Pinnell (2001); *Writing Essentials: Raising Expectations and Results While Simplifying Teaching* by Regie Routman (2004); *Bringing Words to Life* by Isabel Beck, Margaret McKeown, and Linda Kucan (2002); and *Learning Focused Schools* by Max Thompson and Julia Thomason (http://www.learningconcepts.org), are excellent resources as well. These have brought us success with our students, and success is a strong motivator and energizer for both students and staff!

PART VI

Perspectives for Teachers and Teaching

I n terms of student achievement and student success in school, teachers are the most critical element. Teachers' preparation and professional development, their mindsets, the environment they function in, their motivation, and how they teach, are evaluated and hold themselves accountable all have a major influence on their overall effectiveness and their students' achievement.

This section of the Fieldbook, *Perspectives for Teachers and Teaching*, provides five chapters that offer perceptive stories relating to the above factors and their consequences. In particular, these five chapters: (a) tell how meaningful professional learning for teachers is required for effective student learning; (b) explain how changing teachers' beliefs on students and learning can positively impact student learning; (c) recount a teacher's first-hand point of view of the transition and journey toward achieving school success; (d) describe the team efforts of a Principal and Instructional Specialist in planning and implementing school improvement that led to true collaboration, different learning styles, opposing viewpoints, and clashing personalities, all uniting together at one school for the purpose of improving teaching and learning and student achievement; and (e) introduce teacher evaluation into a model of sustained teacher collaboration that integrates the expectations for self-directed professional growth and the elements of shared instructional leadership, empowering both processes and providing a consistent and cohesive focus for increasing student achievement.

22

Increasing Teacher Learning to Improve Student Learning

Beverly S. Strickland

A guiding principle of the Whole-Faculty Study Group (WFSG; see Murphy & Lick, 2005) student-based, professional-development philosophy is, "Students are first." The maxim that to be able to take care of others, one must take care of one's self holds true in education. The most significant way to affect student learning and increase student achievement is to affect those who facilitate learning, *the teachers*. When teacher learning becomes a priority, student achievement increases. When teachers learn, students learn.

As society changes, the needs of our students also change. Teachers must identify and implement research-based practices that address the needs of today's students. Professional learning is required to meet these needs. However, finding time to read professional literature and conduct research to increase professional learning calls for a scarce resource—time. Teachers find it difficult to continue professional learning outside of the workday. Their daily lives are filled with the activities of family life, hobbies, and interests. The WFSG model is an excellent vehicle to provide the professional learning designed to meet the specific needs of teachers because it can be scheduled at the convenience of teachers.

In her study of the use of best practices in teaching reading, Aspinwall (2003) found that teachers' "professional learning activities" were more important in determining the use of best practices than their level of education or years of experience:

> Yet, when the occurrence of staff development classes or workshops in reading was compared with teachers who utilized best practices with those teachers who did not report a high percentage of use of best practices, an important difference was noted. Ninety-three percent of the teachers who reported a high percentage of use of best practices also reported taking a staff development class or workshop in reading within the last six months compared with only 63% of the teachers who did not report a high incident of use of best practices. (p. 39)

Although these findings are specifically related to reading instruction, they have implications for the use of best practices and staff development in all subjects. Meaningful professional learning is vital to improving teacher skills. Murphy and Lick's WFSG System is a new way of implementing staff development for the purpose of increasing teacher learning and practice and increasing student learning.

WFSGs are effective for professional learning because they focus on students' needs and can transform schools into professional learning communities. This chapter outlines the steps to effectively implementing the WFSG process and describes additional benefits of this process. Finally, a description is included of how St. Marys Elementary School prioritized teacher learning by becoming a collaborative, results-oriented school rich in professional learning communities.

ROLE OF THE PRINCIPAL

The role of the principal is continually changing. In the past, the role of the principal was that of school manager. Today, that role has evolved and broadened into the roles of *instructional leader* and *transformational leader*. The principal has become the *lead learner* and the *leader of change* in the school. When the principal serves as the lead learner of study groups, professional communities become "learning communities," and a transition unfolds as the school culture becomes more of a *culture of learning*.

When highly committed professionals are led by highly committed leaders who place student learning as a priority, changes in the learning culture take place. Principals have a responsibility to shift the focus from teaching to learning. Students are first when teachers are first, and teachers are first when their leader shifts the focus from teaching to learning that involves the entire school. "Only principals who are equipped to handle a complex, rapidly changing environment can implement the reforms that lead to sustained improvement in student achievement" (Fullan, 2002).

CHANGE AND THE CULTURE OF LEARNING

Sustainable reform in the learning culture of schools can be created when the lead learner acknowledges the need for change, becomes willing to initiate change, understands resistance to change, and develops relationships that will endure the change. An astute leader will recognize that the key to improving academic achievement lies not in the demographic makeup of the student body but within the professional practices of the school community's teachers and leaders. Students are first when teacher-leaders recognize the need for cultural change. Schools often become stagnant, and student performance stabilizes or even decreases when there is a lack of quality professional development and follow-up. Adults in school communities must grow and develop to meet the changing needs of students. Teachers' needs for growth are met through relationship building and the provision of quality professional learning. WFSGs offer an effective strategy to build collaboration, cooperation, and community, where members of the faculty become leaders in the process, new relationships are formed, and the culture of learning changes.

Resistance to change is always a part of implementing new ideas. There will be resisters to change because change brings discomfort, uncertainty, and doubt. Leaders must plan strategies to convince doubters and resisters to accept the change. Zmuda, Kuklis, and Kline (2004) suggest that the change must be explained to the staff, opportunities must be given for role playing and practice, and feedback must be supplied by a knowledgeable and nonjudgmental coach. Time must also be provided for discussing the change, brainstorming desirable modifications, and revising the use of new approaches.

THE LEARNING CULTURE AND WHOLE-FACULTY STUDY GROUPS

The professional community in the school must adopt and support the unique style of professional learning seen in WFSGs. When teachers understand that assessment data can be used to identify strengths and weaknesses of the instructional program and develop professional learning that meets students' needs, they understand the importance of data analysis. As learners study longitudinal and demographic data, they learn that there are common threads of achievement throughout the data. They find common areas for instructional improvement. Once these areas are identified, WFSGs allow teachers to plan learning for themselves. Performance strengths and weaknesses are made evident, and when the entire faculty chooses areas of study pertinent to their needs, teachers share learning. Effectiveness and shared leadership combine to create a participative culture in which professional learning can begin. Teachers realize that their effectiveness can be improved through their own action research.

The learning culture is changed when professional educators realize that personal-professional development is required to enhance student achievement. The learning culture becomes a "me" culture in the sense that teachers see the need to improve their instructional practices and strategies. Adult learners develop a collaborative culture through participation in WFSGs. Barth (2002) discusses school culture and its importance for reforming and improving schools:

> A school's culture is a complex pattern of norms, attitudes, beliefs, behaviors, values, ceremonies, traditions, and myths that are deeply ingrained in the very core of the organization. Many school cultures are indifferent to reform. And all school cultures are incredibly resistant to change, which makes school improvement—from within or from without—usually futile. Unless teachers and administrators act to change the culture of a school, all innovations, high standards, and high-stakes tests will have to fit in and around existing elements of the culture. (p. 7)

Learners First

WFSGs are designed to provide personal professional development. The old saying, "A chain is only as strong as its weakest link," can be applied to classroom teachers. When teachers gain and apply new knowledge about best practices in instruction, students benefit because needs for personal development are identified by teachers. WFSGs differ from most professional development programs. A deeper commitment is established when teachers choose their own area of interest or personal need; they are more committed to the process. New professional relationships are developed when teachers come together to study a common, identified need. WFSGs bring teachers together who may not have developed an academic relationship otherwise. For example, a physical education teacher, a technology teacher, and classroom teachers come together to form a study group. The pre-kindergarten teacher, the speech-language pathologist, the counselor, and the media specialist meet to study listening strategies. Special education teachers meet with fifth- and first-grade teachers. Study group combinations are flexible and do not restrict themselves to the grade-level groupings that are often used for staff development.

PROFESSIONAL COMMUNITIES AS LEARNING COMMUNITIES

WFSGs lay the foundation for a change in the role of the teacher as the professional community becomes a learning community. When teachers become more active and focused learners, they experience a shift in attitudes and reflect on their responsibility and impact on student learning. Teachers see the need to gain the knowledge and skills necessary to ensure that students' needs come first. Teachers realize that they must continue to be willing learners who seek to apply new knowledge and skills to their instruction. As these deliverers and facilitators of knowledge begin to understand change and the need to update themselves on the latest, most effective teaching strategies, the culture of the learning organization transforms. Teachers join the principal as leaders of the transformational effort. The guiding question of WFSGs is answered when groups of learners continually ponder: *What are students learning and achieving as a result of what teachers are learning and doing in study groups?*

Learning Needs

The learning culture grows as study groups are formed from professional learning needs that are identified by teachers. Once an analysis of the data is completed and specific areas of improvement are identified, study groups are formed, not by grade level or subject area, but by the needs of the students and faculty. Study groups consist of teachers who may be grade levels apart, who teach various subjects, or professionals who specialize in specific areas. An example is the physical education teacher who seeks strategies to incorporate general vocabulary instruction into the physical education curriculum.

Action Plans and Logs

The study groups disaggregate the data and inquire: *Are there trends over time? How do our students compare with those of other local schools, our state, and the nation? What are the implications for our work with students?* Answers to these questions drive the action-research plans that are a part of the WFSGs. Teachers learn that it is their work with students that is being assessed. Teachers, therefore, must use the results of research and data analysis to improve their work.

Three concepts are key to action plans and logs in WFSGs: The lead learner, the principal, will *expect* action research from others. He or she will *inspect* action logs written by the adult learners and then respond with *respect* to the goals and relationships that are being built. Lead learners challenge others to set SMART goals and objectives (Danielson, 2002). "Good objectives translate broad, long-term goals into prescriptions for action. In addition to being short term, they are specific, measurable, attainable, relevant and time-bound—in other words, S.M.A.R.T.," states Danielson. In *Results: The Key to Continuous School Improvement*, Mike Schmoker (1996) states that "clear, measurable goals are the center to the mystery of a school's success, mediocrity, or failure." This approach works well because teachers have real data from their own classrooms to reflect their efforts. Action logs are complete with SMART goals, mini-assessments, and timelines. These measure progress and provide accountability for teaching and learning. The logs become the WFSG lesson plan and are one of the communication devices between the school leader and study groups. The logs are submitted to the principal after each study-group meeting. Principals respond to the work written in the logs by making recommendations and providing support for the groups' needs.

Research and Practice

The WFSG process is cyclic. Teachers plan, teachers practice, teachers assess, and finally, teachers plan again. Research guides the goals of the action plan. Research from books, articles, expert voices, the Internet, and other sources provides information about best practices on the topic studied in the action plans. Emphasis is placed on research, practice, and assessment for one reason: *placing student learning first*.

Teacher Collaboration

One of the most beneficial aspects of the WFSG process is the collaboration that develops between and among teachers. When a study group, composed of a kindergarten teacher, a fourth-grade teacher, a special education teacher, and a music teacher, forms to study listening skills, a variety of experiences and attributes are brought to the table. The group develops synergy as members research and share professional thoughts and opinions. Murphy and Lick (2005) state,

> In a truly synergistic group, people energize and inspire each other and the diversity of ideas and openness to them provide the basis of new creative ideas and approaches. The synergistic process is an extremely powerful approach for increasing the effectiveness, productivity, and quality of the work of study group teams.

Study-Group Time

The issue of time for professional learning is always important. Adult learners need time that is protected and dedicated to improving student learning. When principals of schools preserve a specific day and time for the purpose of professional learning, teachers and others see the value placed upon professional learning and academic achievement. Protected time enables teachers to meet regularly and allows a specific purpose to guide their meetings. Time is spent researching and planning for instructional improvement in areas that teachers have chosen. Teachers and administrators must think outside of the box to create time for WFSGs. Some schools replace faculty meetings with time that is designated for WFSGs. One key to success is to protect a specific day and time for study groups to do serious, highly personalized, school-changing work.

Celebrating Success

Celebration is a significant piece of the WFSG process. It is important to plan time to recognize the work of the learning communities. Schools choose to celebrate in a variety of ways. Groups share their successes by giving personal testimonies of their own growth and that of their students. Celebrating success in a variety of ways breeds success and an even deeper commitment to the process.

THE ST. MARYS ELEMENTARY SCHOOL STORY

In the spring of 2003, teachers at St. Marys Elementary School, a small school located on the coastal southeast corner of Georgia, heard an overview of the WFSG process. Administrators chose to initiate the process after realizing that benefits were limited from the current expensive, off-campus professional learning in which most teachers participated. Teachers readily agreed to embark on this new type of professional learning.

A focus group consisting of the principal, assistant principal, instructional lead teacher, a second-grade teacher, and the teacher of the gifted and talented students attended the initial WFSG training in the summer of 2003. When school opened in the fall of 2003, the process began with an orientation of the essentials of WFSGs. Meeting norms were created regarding the expectations of the groups and the administration. The cooperative, professional group of teachers had one request of the administration: refreshments at each meeting! A commitment to a protected day and time devoted to professional development and the promise of refreshments at the end of a long day of teaching was appropriately agreed upon. Thus the work began.

Beginning With the End in Mind

What does "begin with the end in mind" actually mean? In education, the end is increased student achievement. The critical question is where to begin on the journey to increased student achievement. The St. Marys Elementary School faculty found that the WFSG process provides a road map for a journey of professional learning, which is characterized by professional communities focused on the specific needs of both the teachers and the students.

Taking a Look at the Evidence

School personnel began the WFSG process by examining student work. Assessment data from a variety of sources—nationally normed tests, state tests, locally developed tests, and student products—were compiled for the purpose of analysis. All certificated personnel at St. Marys Elementary School examined Stanford-Nine results, the Georgia Criterion-Referenced Test results, and benchmark data, as well as writing assessment and other significant data. The time spent examining the results of recent and longitudinal data provided a clear picture of how well students at St. Marys Elementary School were achieving. This process, which provided an accurate picture of learning, was an invaluable piece of the work. Teachers actually delved into the data to determine strengths and weaknesses for themselves. A collection of longitudinal data is vivid evidence of the strength of the programs, practices, anomalies, and trends in student achievement. When schools recognize a specific area of need, an examination of the curricular and instructional practices occurs.

When explicit areas of need from the data were determined, work began to create a plan of action. Using achievement data, St. Marys Elementary teachers created a list of areas in need of improvement. Teachers then continued the process by grouping similar needs into categories. The comprehensive needs inventory yielded eleven areas in need of improvement. Faculty members were asked to identify an area in which they felt a need to know more. Teachers and other certified personnel were able to choose a focus area based on *their* needs and interests. This allowed each learning community member to design her or his personal professional development. Individual action plans, derived from the instructional needs of teachers, were combined to create group action plans when the groups formed.

The formation of study groups is an integral step in the WFSG process. At St. Marys Elementary School, groups were formed to meet the needs identified by teachers. Groups that were larger than five were split into two groups. Most of the eleven St. Marys Elementary School (SMES) groups averaged three or four members.

Figure 22.1

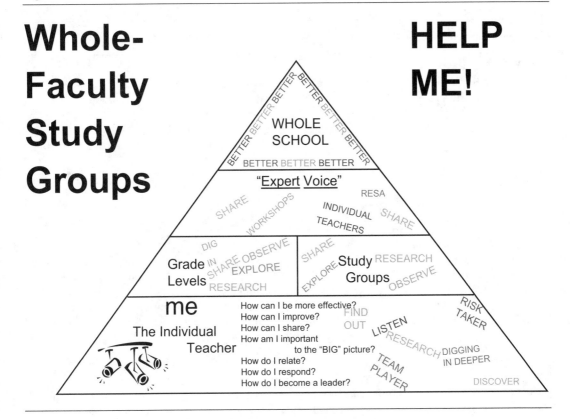

Although the faculty received an overview and orientation regarding the WFSG process, questions remained regarding the purpose and roles each member would play. Figure 22.1 is a visual created to demonstrate that the WFSG process is about highly personal professional development.

The information on the poster in Figure 22.1 was presented and seemed to be a turning point for the faculty. Teachers began researching via the Internet, books, and articles. SMES personnel were diligent in using their "expert voices." For example, teachers who were knowledgeable or talented in a specific skill shared information on successful strategies and practices regarding the work. One group's expert voice shared graphing software that was used by students in the gifted and talented classroom. Soon afterwards, students in first-grade classrooms were using the software. Students and teachers were excited about the learning. Evidence of student work generated as a result of WFSGs began appearing throughout the school.

Our work continued throughout the year. Action logs were completed after each meeting. The logs were filled with notes and responses from the principal on the implementation and success of new strategies and practices. Of particular interest was the research regarding listening skills on which one group focused. Teachers used methods gained from the research on listening to enhance their instruction by engaging the students through specific "whole body" listening strategies. These teachers reported positive results from the innovative approach.

The most exciting and exhilarating professional learning community meetings were the final two meetings of the year. Although group members shared regularly

Table 22.1   Whole-Faculty Study Groups' Assessment of Their WFSG Work

BEFORE the study group began its work:	*AT THE END of the study group's work:*
Group 1 • We rarely used center-focused teaching. • We did not use research to plan effectively.	• We regularly use center-focused teaching where children are intrinsically motivated to complete self-selected projects. • We use research to reflect best practices in teaching.
Group 2 • I rarely used available software.	• I always use The Graph Club! The students love it.
Group 3 • We used manipulatives primarily in math. • We rarely used research to improve our teaching practices.	• As a result of our collaboration, we have made a more concerted effort to use new strategies. • We are more cognizant of the importance of utilizing explicit research to improve our teaching strategies, specifically in developing higher-order thinking.
Group 4 • I didn't make a special effort to focus on rereading and setting a purpose for reading. • Students read AR books occasionally and many did not test on them. • I did not look as closely at benchmark scores and grouping.	• I am very aware of the need to let students read or listen to stories many times and to set a purpose for reading. • Most students read one or more AR books and score 80%–100% on tests. After reading short stories, students share answers to questions and listening seemed to improve. • I have grouped students according to weaknesses on the test.
Group 5 • Although we are not having the children write any more or less, we have shared different writing techniques and tried them with our classes.	• Power Writing • Hamburger Method • www.creativewriting.com
Group 6 • We never used direct listening activities. • We used technology during centers only. • We did not address vocabulary in depth.	• We use direct listening activities. • Frequently, we use technology for centers, word processing, and research. • We use weekly vocabulary activities.
Group 7 • We had no knowledge of the Web sites, software available or need to increase listening skills, vocabulary, and higher-order thinking skills (HOTS).	• We used less group work before—more group work now for higher-order thinking skills (HOTS). • Enthusiasm is up with cooperative groups. We see improved attitudes toward math.

	• We use Web sites to increase HOTS. • We use software to improve listening skills.
Group 8 • We did not use research materials to plan. • We did not always provide examples of higher-order thinking skills in lessons.	• Research articles from various literature sources to implement various problem solving strategies. The focus was promoting higher-order thinking skills from students in science and math. After modeling different problem-solving strategies, we observed and stressed the importance of using of various strategies to enable the students to reach an answer. • We searched and implemented more strategies that entailed illustration, writing, and/or manipulatives.
Group 9 • We were not regularly using the Internet as a resource for science/math activity ideas/ whole group and individual instruction. • Kindergarten was not completely aware of certain science/math skills that would be assessed in first grade. • Children were not given enough hands-on application of skills. • Kindergarten and first grade were not given time to share ideas and brainstorm together. • Our proven ideas were not always validated.	• We were exposed to and were using many more resources including internet resources. These resources and brainstorming allowed more enjoyable activities. • Weak areas that showed up in first-grade benchmarks were shared with kindergarten. • More time is spent to allow students to apply skills. • We enjoyed our sharing time and a bridge was built. • We validated what we knew worked.
Group 10 • We did not know about "Whole Body Listening."	• I always review "Whole Body Listening" components before beginning a lesson.
Group 11 • The majority of teaching was whole group. • The majority of computer instruction was in centers and not assessed.	• There is a substantial increase in small-group instruction. • A majority of computer instruction is remediation and direct instruction involving more logical/reasoning type of games correlating to concepts being taught and assessed. • The effectiveness of this teaching technique has been critiqued through student input with teacher-made rubrics on researched sites.

among themselves and within their grade levels, it was the formal redelivery that brought the SMES faculty to a high level of professionalism. Groups presented their study topics, their research activities, and their results to the remainder of the faculty during two meetings. Group members showcased their work with pride and enthusiasm. Requests for more information from the groups presenting made these meetings beneficial. The atmosphere of the presentation room was more like a college classroom than a professional development room. Teachers discussed their work and shared their success stories. Participation in the WFSG process proved to be one of the most beneficial forms of professional learning ever attempted by the faculty of St. Marys Elementary School. When teachers were provided time to grow and develop their skills, student achievement increased. Responses to a simple survey, shown above, reflect some of the growth that occurred during this process of personal-professional development.

St. Marys Elementary School's faculty continues the WFSG process with a commitment to provide the best possible instruction for student learning.

ADDITIONAL BENEFITS OF WFSGs

Table 22.1 provided a brief assessment of the professional learning community work. Comments indicate that time provided for professional learning set the stage for increased student achievement. Additional benefits were seen in the form of increased collegiality, communication, and collaboration. The benefits that resulted from the whole-faculty process would never have been gained in the traditional staff development model. The professionalism and collegiality exhibited by the teachers reached a new, higher level. St. Marys Elementary teachers were extremely professional prior to the WFSG undertaking; however, the collegial nature of the process opened new avenues for academic relationships and professional learning.

Improved communication at the St. Marys Elementary School was a significant result of the process. Teachers from different grade levels and subject areas came together to address common needs. These professionals built collegial relationships through communication and collaboration. As principal, I also had the opportunity to witness growth and respond to the needs of my faculty. Written and verbal communication throughout the year allowed the faculty to express concerns, excitement, and results of learning.

Collaboration was key to the success of WFSGs. Protected time allowed the learners to pursue research and sharing that brought about instructional change and improved student achievement. A culture of respect was built through the collaborative process, based on the value and dignity of each individual's contribution to the learning community.

CONCLUSION

I would encourage all schools to embark upon the WFSG journey. This initiative makes the most of professional learning in a manner unlike any the faculty of

Table 22.2 Whole-Faculty Study Group Results

Objective	Baseline*	Target	Results	Met Goal
Text factors	2nd gr. BM1 = 37%	+10%	95% Mastery	Yes
Comprehension	2nd gr. BM1 = 63%	+10%	70% Mastery	Yes
Extra Info	1st gr. BM1 = 24%	+5%	61% Mastery	Yes
Listening Action/reasoning/ sequencing	1st gr. BM1 = 61%	+5%	73% Mastery	Yes
Text factors	2nd gr. BM1 = 15%	+50%	62% Mastery	Yes
Employs problem-solving strategies	2nd gr. BM1 = 5%	+50%	14% Mastery	Yes
Thinking skills	1st gr. BM1 = 5%	+3%	58% Mastery	Yes
Spelling	3rd gr. BM1 = 0%	+3%	74% Mastery	Yes
Thinking skills	3rd gr. BM1 = 17%	+3%	73% Mastery	Yes
Listening	GKAP = N/A	+80%	94% Mastery	Yes
Higher-order thinking skills	GKAP = N/A	+80%	100% Mastery	Yes
Fragments	5th gr. BM1 = 58%	+5%	87% Mastery	Yes
Redundancy	5th gr. BM1 = 53%	+5%	89% Mastery	Yes
Run-ons	5th gr. BM1 = 31%	+10%	38% Mastery	Yes
Fragments	4th gr. BM1 = 43%	+10%	74% Mastery	Yes
Run-on sentences	4th gr. BM1 = 32%	+10%	74% Mastery	Yes
Run-on sentences	3rd gr. BM1 = 32%	+10%	67% Mastery	Yes

* BM1 means Benchmark 1.

St. Marys Elementary School had ever encountered. The results proved that the process was a beneficial endeavor.

Schools that are considering Whole-Faculty Study Groups should ask, "What are students doing as a result of what teachers are teaching?" If the answer is, "We don't know," then this will be a useful model. There will always be a place for traditional staff development courses, but Whole-Faculty Study Groups make changes within the classroom that are brought about by the people who affect the instructional process most directly, *the teachers.* When we place students first by placing teachers' instructional needs first, the returns on our investment will be evident. Table 22.2 documents the growth of students at St. Marys Elementary School.

23

Changing Teachers' Beliefs About Students and Learning

Danette R. Smith

In the play *Pygmalion* by George Bernard Shaw, a professor—Henry Higgins—insists that he can take a common girl who sells flowers in the streets of London, Eliza Doolittle, and train her to act and behave like a duchess. One of the most important and insightful lines in the play is a comment made by Eliza to the professor's friend, Pickering: "The difference between a lady and a flower girl is not how she behaves, but how she is treated . . . I know I can be a lady to you because you always treat me as a lady."

The play mentioned above is a commonly cited example of the Pygmalion effect or self-fulfilling prophesy that is essential to the success of students. Consciously or not, we exhibit thousands of clues about our expectations of others in ways that are often subtle, but usually picked up on by those around us. These clues can be as simple as tilting our head, raising our eyebrow, or flaring our nostrils and are the physical manifestation of our deep-seated beliefs that result in either a positive or negative effect on student performance.

This chapter describes the beliefs of a group of teachers participating in a study group relative to the achievement of transient students and the way in which their study group was effective in changing the beliefs that could have negatively impacted these students' achievement. The chapter includes related information from the literature, a description of both the study-group activities that were effective and those that were not effective in facilitating a change in the teachers' beliefs, and teacher comments that provide evidence of the change.

AN INITIAL EXPERIENCE

As a research project for a graduate program, I elected to initiate and observe a study group in which three fourth-grade teachers participated. My original intent was to investigate how the learning community developed among the teachers and the changes that occurred in the teachers' practices while participating in the group. While I did record my observations about the learning community and changes in practice, perhaps one of the most interesting observations was the difference in teachers' beliefs after reviewing data presented in print format (e.g., a journal article) about a school similar to theirs and their reaction to data presented from their own classrooms in a graphic format (e.g., a bar graph). Since my observations were part of a research project, I was able to capture comments made by participants during reflective interviews that revealed the teachers' "change in beliefs" relative to transient students. This change-in-beliefs discovery caused me to turn to the literature for related information.

BELIEFS AND A STUDY GROUP'S EXPERIENCE

Several authors (Ball & Cohen, 1999; Darling-Hammond & McLaughlin, 1995; Lieberman, 1995) suggest that if schools are to improve, teachers must have opportunities to challenge their conventional assumptions and beliefs surrounding teaching and learning, and to learn more about the students they teach. In addition, these educators suggest that this must be accomplished within a culture of collaborative inquiry such as study groups. Teachers engaged in such groups make their otherwise implicit assumptions and beliefs explicit as they reflect upon and discuss their individual teaching experiences (Kruse, 2001). This was certainly true in the study group I observed.

Prior to the inception of the group, the local newspaper printed an article emphasizing the high rate of transience in this particular school, stating that the transient students were low achievers and were likely to diminish achievement test scores in the school. As a result of the newspaper article, the teachers participating in the group, Emma Jones, Mitch Matthews, and Gail Williams (pseudonyms rather than their actual names) decided they wanted to study transient students and find more effective ways to meet their educational needs.

The teachers began by reviewing an article summary pertaining to standardized test scores titled "Turning Standardized Test Scores Into a Tool for Improving Teaching and Learning: An Assessment-Based Approach" (Chen, Salahuddin, & Wagner, 2000). The publication explained that research indicates it is not always the transient student with the lowest achievement-test scores, albeit that is a common assumption. Participating teachers had indicated opposing opinions, which were evident in comments made during the study group.

Emma's response to the article was, "First of all, I'm not big on research because anyone can say what they want. Someone else could have gone into the school and done the same thing and made it look bad for the transient students." Regarding his own students, Mitch offered, "When I get these kids, they are nowhere near where we are in our academic studies, and that's across the board." Regardless of the data presented in the article reviewed during the study group, which supported the achievement of transient students as being similar to the achievement of other students, the teachers did not accept this information as a foregone conclusion.

My role in the group was as participant-observer. I was curious about the scores of their students and how scores of the students who had arrived at the school as transient students during the school year differed from the students who had been enrolled in the school since the first day of the school year. I compiled reading and mathematics score data for each of the teachers' classrooms and fashioned a bar graph comparing the scores of the transient students in their classrooms to those of their other students. During the next study-group meeting the graphs were presented to the teachers in a matter-of-fact way with no comments made by myself. I simply suggested that they might be interested in looking at the data for transient and nontransient students in their classrooms.

The participants took a moment to look at the graphs, but made no comment about the obvious inaccuracy of their assumptions. Gail said, "You need to work here and do this stuff for us." Emma asked some general questions about testing, and Mitch suggested that it was really useful to have the data presented in a bar graph because he could readily see which students required remediation in which areas. Although none of the participants commented about the fallacy of their assumptions during the study group, when asked to reflect about their study-group experience, it was evident that the graph had impacted their beliefs about transient students. Emma indicated that she had previously used transiency as an excuse, but now believed she could not do so. Mitch explained that he had experienced "inward" changes. Gail concurred with Emma's statement about the use of transiency as an excuse, and provided further insight into the impact of her study-group experience. The comments of each participant are reviewed in the sections that follow.

CHANGES IN EMMA'S BELIEFS

When reviewing the journal article, Emma stated her belief that research data were not interpreted accurately, and therefore, they were not always valid. She made no connection between the students from the school presented in the article and her own students. At the conclusion of the school year, however, Emma was asked to share what had been the most valuable aspect of the study-group experience. She explained,

> Well, I really liked the transient thing that you did, the chart that you did.
> You know, you kinda have to see it more on paper. I think we knew it was all

the students [who were low achieving], but sometimes I think we use the transients as an excuse. Not an excuse, but it just adds on to the stress, and so we're thinking it was all these new students, but by the graph and the chart that you showed, it helps to see more that just, in general, it may be overall students, not just the transient students.

During a conversation between members of the study group, Emma confirmed her newly espoused belief.

Personally, with the transient issue that you were talking about, I've always thought that was an excuse too, and even at any school. "Well, we didn't do well because he's transient," or "I didn't do well because I'm transient," but when you showed us the data, actually broke it down and stuff, well, this is the difference. Well, there really isn't one, so in a way, transient really isn't an excuse because the other kids that we have are scoring the same [as those] who aren't transient. So what you did by actually showing it and [us] looking at it all compiled together did make a difference in how [pause] I can't say that's an excuse anymore. I can't say that. I've always wanted to say that, but now I feel like, after that, I really shouldn't say that anymore.

CHANGES IN MITCH'S BELIEFS

When initially discussing the purpose of the group—to study the issue of transiency and determine ways to more effectively meet students' academic needs—Mitch indicated that transient students were "nowhere near" his other students' level of academic performance. During the study group meeting in which the graph of student scores was presented, Mitch indicated that the graph was helpful because it revealed those students in need of remediation. During a group interview, Mitch talked about the changes he experienced as a result of participating in the group. He commented,

[I don't know] how much I changed outwardly, but inwardly, just looking at some of the stuff that we've done and some of the data that you presented for us, I got a better feel for the child, more so than just changing anything out. I mean, I know that they are going to try this and try that when, in the past, that did not even come across my mind. It [was] like, well, hey, I assigned it; you're supposed to have it—simple as that. And I kinda loosened up just a little bit.

Later in the interview, Mitch commented about the effect that reviewing the data and reading other articles describing the nature of the transient student had on his classroom practices. He said,

It affected me to the point where I have to take a second look at how I was doing things and kinda get another feel for what this child may be enduring or may be going through. Not to say that he or she can get away with anything, but it gave me another peek in at some of the things that I might need to do to help facilitate that child.

And indeed, he did make some changes in his classroom expectations that became evident during observations. During one observation Mitch distributed a homework handout to his students who were to cut out slips from the handout and glue them together on one edge to form a booklet. One student asked if he could take scissors home. Mitch responded by suggesting the students use their mother's scissors. The student commented that his mother did not have scissors at home. Mitch's reply was simply, "Sure she does." Another student asked if he could take one of Mitch's glue sticks home. Mitch commented that this was not necessary because a glue stick had already been provided to every student in a supply pack distributed to each by the school. Interestingly, this was the same day the study group read articles related to the home environment of transient students that had stimulated a response from Mitch indicating his appreciation and understanding of their circumstances.

While there was not an immediate change in Mitch's classroom behavior, later, when preparing for the science fair, Mitch explained that he asked his students to bring in fruits and vegetables for the science fair project; however, he also expressed his realization now that some students are just not able to bring such requested items to school. Mitch changed by altering assignments and tasks required at home to accommodate the needs of his students. Over the period of six weeks between the first observation and the second observation, the study group reviewed student data from the participants' classrooms and were involved in discussion about the obstacles transient students face. During this time, he changed his espoused theory of understanding the difficulties of the transient student into a theory in use as indicated by his change in classroom expectations.

CHANGES IN GAIL'S BELIEFS

During the initial group's discussion about transient students, Gail acknowledged her apparent understanding of these students' circumstances. She spoke of their moving from apartment to apartment to take advantage of special offers provided by landlords, such as "the first two months free." She also spoke of those students who lived in hotels or in shelters and moved from place to place each night. One would assume from these statements that she made accommodations for these students—and in some ways she probably did. After discussing the transient students, reviewing classroom data, reading articles about the nature of the transient student, and listening to group discussion, she commented in her interview:

> I think I just have realized that I have a lot more admiration for the people that I work with because we've been talking about things that we don't normally get a chance to talk about; and I realize that they're doing things in their classes I wasn't even aware they were doing, and it gives you some kind of an idea that some of these things you would like to try also; and I'm just very impressed with the kind of caring way that they have of dealing with their students. I knew that they were caring, of course, but talking about some of the things we've talked about makes me realize even more so.

When asked if any of the discussions in the study group had caused her to consider changes she might make to her own classroom practices, she responded,

> Yes, I think that, talking in the study groups, I realize that I don't know the children's families as well as I would like to know them, and I've made a real effort this time with parent conferences coming up. I've made a real effort to get parents over here. I've made phone calls and actually got people to come, and I was very pleased with the results that I got by doing this. One set [of parents]—well, they're not really parents, they're grandparents—came to a conference yesterday and they left at the same time I did; basically, at the end of the day, and I just assumed that they had come over in their family car, but when I left, I realized that they were walking down Aviation [Road] toward the loop [a main highway], and they must have had to take [public transportation] to get here, and that really impressed me that they made that big of an effort to get here, and they were one of the ones that I thought were not going to come, and I had called her and especially made an effort.

Gail shared with me that she had sixteen out of twenty families come for conferences and she had never had that many, but she had never made phone calls to encourage them to come to the school, either. As a result of participating in the group, she now acted on her espoused understandings of her students and made an additional effort to encourage their participation in their children's education.

REFLECTIONS

Sullivan and Glanz (2000) distinguish between espoused theories and theories in use, indicating that those theories or beliefs that teachers express are not always the ones that guide their actions; their espoused theories or beliefs are different from their actions. During this project, I learned two important factors to consider when implementing study groups: (a) a picture is really worth a thousand words, and (b) the discussion that takes place during a study group is vital to the process of changing teachers' beliefs and practices. The participants in the study group had to visibly see the performance of their transient students compared to their other students to dispel the belief that transient students achieve less that non-transient students. They also required time to listen to their colleagues and reflect on the groups' conversations in order to alter patterns of observable behavior. It is not so important to guide, direct, or control the conversation, but it is important to provide teachers an opportunity to explicitly express their concerns, their convictions, and their practices. In doing so, they are continuously evaluating and altering their beliefs and continuously improving practice.

24

Creating School Successes

A Teacher's Point of View

Beverly A. Gross

The *Mission Statement* for the Crooked River Elementary School is:

> The School will implement a quality, standards-based educational program that provides challenging learning experiences for students to succeed in a highly technological, information-based global society.

The Crooked River Elementary School realized that this statement was the impetus that guided the "achievement fire" of our school and its successes. As a part of this transition, this chapter, through the eyes of a teacher, will unfold a first-hand perspective of this journey, including the Whole-Faculty Study Group processes, personnel involvements, ups and downs, and exciting successes.

THE SETTING

Crooked River Elementary School is located in Southeast Georgia. The school name is derived from the Crooked River State Park, located three miles north of the school. Our school has forty-five certified staff and approximately 500 students.

It is through the dedication of the Crooked River Elementary School (CRES) faculty that this "fire of mission" has been maintained for success. Whole-Faculty Study Groups (WFSGs; see Murphy & Lick, 2005) were just one of many success stories that the CRES can offer to others. Dr. Shelia Sapp, principal, created a vision for the CRES after attending a WFSG workshop given by the WFSG System creator, Carlene Murphy. Dr. Sapp's vision led the CRES to the successful completion of its first year of implementation of the WFSG System. Without the principal's vision, the CRES would have continued on a narrow path without having the opportunity to grow and create new paths. Though the CRES has been successful, the successes did not come without difficulties or setbacks. It was through these difficulties and setbacks that the CRES clarified and moved forward with its vision—student achievement—and found impressive successes.

THE INITIAL WFSG PROCESS

When the CRES decided to implement WFSGs, it was the dedication of our coordinating group—the focus team—that helped the process appear smooth and consistent. Even during times of distress, the focus team maintained high expectations and guided the CRES faculty to a high level of achievement. After several effective meetings, the focus team decided it would be best to introduce the program during preplanning for the 2003–2004 school year. The principal developed a PowerPoint slide show that focused on key details of WFSGs. As a focus team, we delivered her slide show to the CRES faculty, hoping each member would be just as excited about it as the focus team. After the votes relative to adopting the WFSG System were tallied, the focus team discovered that the CRES faculty was not only in favor of it, but excited about implementing WFSGs.

Over the next few weeks, the CRES faculty completed the Decision-Making Cycle. The process included (a) examining school data (i.e., norm-referenced, benchmark, and criterion-referenced data), (b) determining student needs, (c) categorizing and prioritizing student needs, and (d) organizing groups based on the academic needs of the CRES. It was through the Decision-Making Cycle that the faculty realized there were *true* academic needs at CRES and that every faculty member had an opportunity to have an impact on these needs.

Setbacks

Once the focus team formed WFSGs, we felt we were off and running and had high hopes for success in the near future, only to find that we weren't running yet; we were simply at a crawl. The CRES discovered very quickly that an action plan can be a difficult task to implement. The majority of our WFSGs were struggling with this. The CRES faculty members were creating great action plans, but the school needs were too broad. After a couple of months, confusion and frustration had set in among the faculty, and members were wondering how effective their efforts would be if they couldn't narrow school needs down to a "specific" academic need. So, the principal contacted Carlene Murphy and asked for her input on the situation. With Murphy's assistance, the principal was able to create an effective plan to curb the distractions that had set in among the faculty. Murphy reviewed all of the new action plans and gave study groups a new sense of hope by guiding them through a period of revisions in which she offered ideas and suggestions to each group. Over the next few months, the WFSGs got back on track. From January until May, the WFSGs were very effective in meeting the needs of CRES students and implemented some wonderful solutions that positively affected the academic needs of each student.

It is through these efforts that one group, Mathematics, created a PowerPoint slide show that flashed mathematics facts on the computer screen. The PowerPoint slides were saved to the CRES network, which gave all teachers access to the materials for use in their own classrooms. Another group, Language, developed a K–5 editing/proofreading chart. Each member collaborated on what symbols were age-appropriate for K–5 students; the number of editing/proofreading marks was increased as the student advanced by grade. For example, kindergarten students would be responsible for one editing/proofreading mark (capitalization) and first grade students would be responsible for three editing/proofreading marks (capitalization, period, and question mark). One teacher offered the following comment about these efforts:

> I felt that the WFSG meetings really helped our students in editing/proofreading. We each created posters for our rooms of the symbols used in editing/proofreading. Students had a copy of these in their writing folders as well, to refer to during creative writing or journal times. I thought assigning different grade levels certain symbols to work on for that school year helped the students also. By doing this, all grades were able to participate and the symbols were age appropriate.
>
> —Virginia Wagner, Fifth Grade

In addition to editing and proofreading, the Language Group also created a scope and sequence for Language Arts (Grades 1–5). The Language Group reviewed Georgia's Quality Core Curriculum (QCC) and realized that many Language Arts skills overlapped from grade to grade. Using this information, each grade level decided which Language skills needed to be mastered and reviewed before students advanced to the next grade. Through this process, the Language Group coordinated two teams: K–2 and 3–5. Each team created a scope and sequence for the first semester of the 2004–2005 school year by examining and organizing the current Language Arts Series. Each scope and sequence didn't necessarily progress from one chapter to another, but from one skill to another. It was important that each skill was taught to mastery. Through this process, the Language Group members realized the importance of teamwork and confirmed that their actions were meeting the needs of each student at CRES.

One teacher offered the following comment:

> I was involved with the Language WFSG group. This group developed a scope and sequence for the language program Grades 1–5. The students will

benefit from a cohesive plan of mastery from grade to grade. Teachers are much more aware of concepts that simply need to be reviewed and those that need instruction. This allows a much better use of time during the academic day.

—Mrs. Cynthia Nelms, Fifth Grade

The Time Factor

One usually faces a time challenge, as did CRES. The focus team was trying to create an innovative use of time, but was limited by district requirements. The focus team elected to hold WFSG meetings on the first and third Tuesday of each month from 3:00 p.m. to 4:00 p.m. The one-hour time frame exceeded the normal-day hours. The principal wrote a proposal to the district office asking for permission to obtain "Professional Development Hours" for an extra hour per day. After a quick review, the district office approved the principal's proposal and agreed to give each staff member the opportunity to earn one Staff Development Unit for participating in WFSGs. With support from the district office and the focus team, the faculty rose to the challenge and was once again successful.

SUCCESS WITH PROTOCOLS

Though the CRES faculty encountered some setbacks, each setback eventually led to a great success. An important success due to the WFSG process was a program that focused on "looking at student work." This additional tool was developed and delivered to study groups, hoping that they would use the given protocol to look at samples of student work. This tool was developed after some focus team members attended a WFSG conference in February of 2004. At this conference, the members were introduced to a specific protocol (Tuning Protocol; developed by Joseph McDonald and Davis Allen) that guided individual groups in looking at student work. With this information, the focus team gathered a group of teachers and videotaped teachers reviewing a student work sample. This sample was edited and distributed to each WFSG. A member of the focus team visited each group and watched and discussed the video with them, providing groups an opportunity to discuss the protocol and how effective its use might be for each group. The video was also shared at the district level, giving other WFSG schools an opportunity to review and discuss the possibility of using it with their own faculty. During this time, the CRES faculty was able to use the process shown in the video to look at student work effectively. We found this opportunity to be successful because of the protocol. Many teachers expressed their need for the protocol because it helped keep them focused on student work. It was through this process that teachers became more focused on the true needs of their students.

A Success From Successes

Another success story developed from an activity in March of 2004 that focused on each WFSG's current successes. The focus team decided to create an activity that would include the whole faculty. It involved using the "WFSG Process, Content, and

Context Rubric" (see Chapter 10 in this volume). This was another idea that was adapted from the WFSG conference in February of 2004. The focus team worked together to create an eleven- by fourteen-inch poster that included each WFSG section (process, content, and context) of the rubric. The CRES faculty was invited to a celebration meeting; the members were given stickers and asked to place their stickers on a "chart of progress" where they thought their group currently resided. The rubric activity was done independently and anonymously. Because the activity was done independently and anonymously, it gave each faculty member an opportunity to respond truthfully and not feel pressured by other group members. Through a reflection process, the CRES faculty members realized how much progress each group had made since the beginning of the year. With this information in hand, the CRES faculty celebrated their progress with ice cream sundaes. The focus team later discussed this activity and realized that it would be important to implement it twice a year, once at mid-year and again at the end of the year. It is through these activities that WFSG successes are reinforced.

Other Successes

The Crooked River Elementary School strives to meet the needs of each individual student. Another success story was the collaboration among the faculty. In a normal school setting, teachers collaborate with their team, which is typically on their own grade level. It is not very often that a teacher gets to collaborate with other grade levels. When our principal, Dr. Sapp, organized our groups, she decided it would be beneficial to have teachers from across all grade levels in each group. Our Language group consisted of six individuals; one each from kindergarten through the fifth grade. This group discovered how beneficial it was to have a teacher from every grade level. When this group met and discussed what "student needs were going to be met" through their action plan, it was clear that each grade level was covered and discussed. It was through this collaboration that the group was able to create the editing/proofreading charts for each grade level. Our principal, Dr. Sapp, expressed her feelings about teacher collaboration:

> I feel the WFSG process is an excellent avenue to promote collegial collaboration and dialogue. I see teachers at our school sharing more ideas and strategies among different grade levels. Part of becoming a real learning community is learning and growing together as a school while focusing on students' needs.

Henry Ford once said, "Coming together is a beginning; staying together is a process; working together is success." This quote sums up what Whole-Faculty Study Groups are all about. The CRES's primary goal is student achievement, and when our school comes together and works through a process, we ultimately SUCCEED.

CONCLUSION

With new curricula being imposed upon us, teachers, administration, and parents must work together to meet the needs of their students. Whole-Faculty Study

Groups are the *answer*. This program is organized and user friendly. With a dedicated administration and faculty, a school will see many successes. As you read this chapter, you may have realized that it is the process that is critical to the success of any new program. When the going got tough, our administration and faculty worked harder because failing wasn't an option. It was through the setbacks of the action plans and time that our WFSGs became stronger. Our faculty came together in a time of need and continued to focus on student achievement. It was through our successes that the CRES realized what all of our hard work was moving us toward: *student achievement*. It is my recommendation that each school strive to meet the needs of each student, and, through Whole-Faculty Study Groups, any school can meet that ultimate goal.

The flavor of the Whole-Faculty Study Group process "in action" is nicely summarized in another teacher's comments:

I think the WFSG process of identifying students' needs schoolwide and focusing on these needs has been very beneficial to our students. Teachers are collaborating to address these needs not only in the current grade levels they teach but in others as well. This "linking" has given me the opportunity to address areas of learning differently in order to meet the needs of my students now and to prepare them for future learning. I enjoy researching new teaching methods and sharing ideas with my colleagues. I have high hopes for the upcoming year.

—Debbie Bailey, First Grade

25

Planning and Implementing Strategies for School Improvement

Emily Weiskopf

When teachers learn to facilitate faculty dialogue, they become better at facilitating classroom dialogue; when they listen well to colleagues, they pay the same degree of attention to their students; when they reflect aloud with colleagues, they enable students to reflect aloud; and when they expect to discover evidence to inform their own thinking, they begin to expect students to do the same on the path to problem solving and understanding.

—Linda Lambert (2003, p. 21)

I t is with this thought by Linda Lambert that I begin to tell about the school improvement journey of two leaders and a group of dedicated educators that continues today. As of yet, it can not be determined whether it is the leaders, the educators, or the students who have learned more or been changed the most by the extraordinary transformation that has taken place at this small Midwestern elementary school.

Don't let the positive tone deceive you; what began as a true mountain hike is still a strenuous uphill climb. Yet, there are no quitters in this story. Okay, maybe a few of us took several water breaks, but, even today, the learning and the reflection on the learning continues. What is presented here is true collaboration: different learning styles, opposing viewpoints, and clashing personalities all uniting together at one school for the purpose of improving the work of teaching and learning.

THE SCHOOL AND OUR UNDERLYING ASSUMPTIONS

The Springfield Public School System is made up of several small neighborhood elementary schools that are in essence homogenously grouped by income level. These elementary schools feed into larger, more heterogeneous, secondary schools. Ed V. Williams Elementary School is one of these neighborhood schools serving the north side of Springfield, Missouri. The school has a free/reduced lunch rate of 79% and a mobility rate closely mirroring this percentage. The school serves approximately 300 students and also houses a district Emotionally Handicapped classroom.

Missouri administers the Missouri Assessment Program, more commonly referred to as the MAP test. Williams Elementary has experienced peaks and valleys in its test data, and when interviewed, the teachers attributed the scores to the ability level of the students. In essence, a peak would indicate a "smart" cohort, and a valley would indicate a "struggling" group of students. Springfield Public Schools began administering several internal assessments and much data was being generated. However, the data were not being critically analyzed at the district or site level.

With a new school improvement process in place and the addition of six Instructional Specialists for School Improvement, the district administration placed high expectations on schools to meet the demands of the new No Child Left Behind legislation. Schools were to use the internal assessments to guide instructional practices and put into place a professional development system that provided ongoing teaching learning.

As a new Instructional Specialist, I served elementary schools on the north side of town. With the following assumptions in mind, I began to formulate a structure for helping schools with inconsistent achievement data move from what Douglas Reeves (2002) labels "lucky and losing" to "learning and leading."

There are two main underlying assumptions about professional development that guided my thinking toward facilitating school improvement in schools. These were:

- Professional Development is more effective when the leader takes an active role in developing and implementing that professional development
- Professional Development should contain trainings, collaboration times, and coaching experiences

THE BEGINNING DATA

At the end of the 2001–2002 school year, data began to pour into the Curriculum and Instruction office. As an Instructional Specialist, I began looking carefully at the data for the elementary buildings. Every elementary building was required to give an end-of-the-year reading assessment. The kindergarten assessment was the Early Literacy Survey. First grade gave the Daily Reading Assessment (DRA), and Grades 2 through 5 gave the Scholastic Reading Inventory (SRI). Each of these assessments contained either an oral or a written comprehension component.

The end-of-the-year data from Williams Elementary clearly showed a deficit in comprehension ability at every grade level. The data showed that:

- 46% of incoming first graders are scoring readiness according to the Early School Assessment
- 80% of incoming second graders are reading on grade level or above according to the DRA
- 48% of incoming third graders are reading on grade level or above according to the SRI
- 47% of incoming fourth graders are reading on grade level or above according to the SRI
- 56% of incoming fifth graders are reading on grade level or above according to the SRI
- 60% of incoming sixth graders are reading on grade level or above according to the SRI

COLLABORATION WITH THE PRINCIPAL

I knew there was need for improvement in reading comprehension at this building. I made an appointment with the principal to discuss the data and to plan out the professional development for the upcoming year. We began by asking what the data clearly showed. Then, we tried to look deeper. The principal, Lynne, could provide insight into the teaching and learning that the data couldn't reveal. Being more data driven, I could balance out the personal perspective that Lynne brought to the conversation.

I came to the meeting with Lynne with the notion that I was tired of doing one-shot workshops in schools and then not seeing any implementation of the material presented in teachers' classrooms. I wanted to develop a more in-depth approach to site staff development, and I needed a leader to collaborate with and to help put the plan into action.

Creating the Blueprint

I knew that in order to make the gains that were required in reading comprehension, the focus had to be on structures that created time for practice and refinement of new strategies. Also, time was required for the teachers to reflect, learn from their mistakes, and work with colleagues as they gained new information on best practices.

Consequently, I proposed a three-year plan for Williams that included acquiring new knowledge, implementing that new knowledge, and assessing the impact of the new knowledge on student learning. Year one would focus on the "content" of reading comprehension strategies that could be taught in the "context" of every classroom. Year two would focus on redesigning the "process" of how reading was taught in the classroom by providing a rationale and training in reading workshop. After the transformation to the reading workshop took place, year three would then focus on teaching writing in a writing workshop. So, now that the plan was set, Lynne and I had to create the structure required to ensure success for both teachers and students.

Understanding the Parts to Create the Whole

Professional Development in the school in the past had been organized at the district level. Typically, teachers were given a menu of workshops to choose from based on their interests. During the school year, workshops had been offered beyond contract time, on weekends or holidays when students were not in school. Teachers were required to attend large-group training sessions but were not held accountable for implementing any of the information. They were, for the most part, "putting in their time." A workshop was perceived as worthwhile if the speaker was entertaining or if one good idea was gained from the session. Most teachers complained that these staff development days were a waste of time and they would rather be working in their rooms.

New educational reform had placed more pressure on teachers to change practices and on the school to be the vehicle responsible for facilitating the change. Educational reform required teachers not only to update their skills and information but also to totally transform their role as a teacher.

Leading staff-development researchers around the country have focused on designing structures that help districts support teachers' moving forward in the profession without funding. DuFour (2001) states that

> The most significant contribution a principal can make to developing others is creating an appropriate context for adult learning. It is context—the programs, procedures, beliefs, expectations, and habits that constitute the norm for a given school—that plays the largest role in determining whether professional development efforts will have an impact on that school. (p. 14)

During the previous year, the Springfield Public Schools embarked on a new school improvement system that had included a job-embedded plan for professional development. During this year, the Whole-Faculty Study Group System was introduced as an option for leaders to consider as a vehicle for making their school improvement plan a "living, breathing document." Initial training was provided, and many schools chose to begin. Lynne, however, firmly believed that it was important to "start slow in order to pick up speed" and felt that it would be beneficial to observe the implementation of this new model for the first year and begin implementation the next year.

One of the strengths of Williams Elementary is that it has a culture of operating as a "team." Helping each other out and working together were not new concepts. So, the idea of collaboration was nonthreatening. But, is this truly collaboration? DuFour (2003b) speaks to leaders about defining collaboration in narrow terms: the systematic process in which we work together to analyze and impact professional practice in order to improve our individual and collective results. However, collaboration by invitation is doomed to fail. Lynne and I knew that we had to find a way to provide not only time for collaboration during the day, but also a structure for teams to "work on the work." We knew that these teachers would require new information about reading comprehension strategies as well as information about how to be more effective with children with limited literacy backgrounds who were lacking in resources.

FACILITATING THE WHOLE-FACULTY STUDY GROUP SYSTEM

Lynne and I decided that the Whole-Faculty Study Group (WFSG; see Murphy & Lick, 2005) System could provide many of the processes we were considering putting into place at Williams. WFSGs offer one of the most preferred structures for implementing a professional learning community within a school. In schools that use study groups effectively, every certified staff member joins a study group that meets weekly, or at least every other week (Murphy & Lick, 2005). Because these study groups were new to this school, we created a combination approach that consisted of (a) monthly training that provided new information to use and practice in classrooms and (b) monthly meeting times for WFSGs to meet, create lessons, and look at student work around the new concepts. We also implemented peer coaching within the building. Each teacher did a peer coaching session with three other teachers around the implementation of one of the new reading strategies.

Although I had the vision of what this would look like as a whole, Lynne had the organizational skills to put it all into place. I knew the "content" of what we would study and the "process" of how we would study it, but Lynne had to fit it into the school "context." We created a theme for the year, provided notebooks for teachers to track their work, and designated the faculty lounge as the place to make the work public by creating a public display board to house the action plans, logs, and principal's feedback. The two of us were truly a mismatched pair, and we were dedicated to learning from each other and to making this partnership work in order to begin improving students' literacy at this school.

Observable Changes in Year One

During the first year, the most noticeable change that took place was that there was now a common language among teachers about reading comprehension strategies. It was really the specialty teachers, art, music, and P.E., who began to see the common language take form. Since these teachers were involved in the study groups and had contact with every student in the school, they were the first to notice that when they used terminology learned in an "expert voice" session, students instantly knew what they meant. This common language helped redirect conversations from a focus on what students couldn't do to what they could do.

Another change was a feeling of empowerment. This empowerment stemmed from Lynne and trickled down to teachers and students. To this day, Lynne will attest that she was the one who learned the most this first year. It is great motivation to continue to learn when the leader acknowledges that she is learning right along with the rest of the Williams community. The expert voice sessions gave her the knowledge to be able to respond to the study-group logs in a meaningful way. She also had a foundation of strategies to look for when doing walk-throughs in classrooms. Teachers now had specific strategies to teach to students. But, most important, students now had strategies to use when confronted with difficult text.

Muddying the Waters in Year Two

Carlene Murphy (Murphy & Lick, 2005, p. 137) affirms that the "content" of the study groups is at the heart of the learning that takes place. In year one, the comprehension strategies were the content of the study groups. But, in year two, the new learning went deeper. It was no longer about putting in a few new strategies. It was now about transforming how we teach and taking a very close look at restructuring the time spent on literacy. Anytime there is a switch from the "what" to the "how," challenges lie ahead. And indeed they did in year two of our study-group work. The focus was on implementing a reading workshop framework that included independent reading time with teacher conferencing, guided reading, and shared reading. To say this framework was a shift for the staff is an understatement. So, the learning curve went from a slight incline to a steep hill. Lynne and I spent most of our time observing teachers in classrooms to determine if there was genuine implementation of this new structure. The logs gave some evidence that teachers were trying to restructure their time and their teaching, but they were vague. So, we would read and respond to logs together and then do observations during literacy time to determine who was really utilizing this new approach.

If we all felt we were on the same page in the first year, the opposite was true in year two. The level of implementation was "all over the board"; but we did find some key staff members who seemed to grasp this new way of teaching and learning. We began to bring these teachers to the forefront and had them share their results with the entire faculty during the expert voice sessions. Although it seemed uncomfortable for these teachers to share at first, it was time to institutionalize the guiding principle of "the work is public." We continued to share the connection between teachers who were implementing a workshop structure and student achievement results. There was definitely a positive correlation between the two. This notion of making the work public was the premise that guided year three.

Gaining Momentum in Year Three

As we entered year three, we were still not achieving the results we had hoped for after two years of intense teaching training in literacy instruction. With the reading workshop model in place after year two, it seemed natural to begin the implementation of writing workshop as the final piece of the three-year literacy plan. Because the teachers had a strong foundation in the workshop model, the implementation of a writing workshop seemed relatively seamless and smooth. It was also time to begin shifting the focus from being primarily on teacher learning to being focused on tracking student learning. Beginning to make the student learning more public than ever before has been a challenge this year. We have begun a systematic format for benchmarking student learning in both reading comprehension and writing that includes tracking students' growth over time. Collaborative time is being spent talking about where we are in terms of grade level and where we are as a staff in terms of reaching our achievement goals. Lynne and I met with each grade level and discussed successes and gaps in the benchmark data. This close examination of data was a new process for the teachers at this school. We spent time analyzing data, discussing surprises in the data, and formulating plans for how to make changes in our teaching practices to address these deficiencies. For the first time, we were truly engaging in authentic data-driven decision making. We used the data as a spring-board for conversations around what must take place in the expert voice sessions and during study-group time. Lynne went deeper in her responses to the logs by asking more questions, challenging thinking, and raising the expectation for results.

Beginning to Win the Race

It is the beginning of our fourth year of learning together, and the data are finally beginning to show increases in student achievement. Although there was no doubt in anyone's mind at the school that major gains had been made in literacy achievement over the past three years, it was important to everyone that the state test scores reflect improvement. Scores in the past had shown the majority of students achieving in the bottom two levels. This year, the majority of students scored in the top three levels, leaving a very small percentage of students still in the bottom two. This was data worth celebrating! But, it was a real sign that reflection was now ingrained in the school when teachers immediately began to plan instruction based on the deficiencies that were still present. No, this group was not going to sit and gloat for long for there was work to be done. Finally, the understanding is that it isn't about the "ability level" of a cohort of students, but about "our ability" to teach all children at a high level of achievement.

Learning Worth Sharing

The principal of the Williams Elementary School taught me that timing is everything. The Whole-Faculty Study Group process helped me understand that learning is really all about time. Providing time, structuring time, and honoring time is truly what is essential when engaging in school improvement. Finding time during the day for groups of teachers to work not only on "the work" but on "their work" is what motivates teachers to want to improve practice. Structuring the time with expert voice sessions, action plans, logs, and protocols was what made the collaboration productive. Valuing the expertise of teachers and allowing them to design their own learning path honored them as professionals and as the "lead learners" of their school. Even though this school has a long road ahead in improving student achievement on state tests, one thing was clear: Everyone was learning and will continue to be learners at Williams Elementary, which is fundamental for progressive future achievement.

CONCLUSION

So, as it begins with data, it ends with data. And, cyclically, it begins with data again. It is the data that facilitate the collaborative dialogue that forces us to grow, change, listen, and reflect. School improvement is not easy, nor does it truly ever come to an end. It is a continuous learning process that evolves from learning new practices, engaging students in those new practices, and then having open and honest conversations with colleagues about the success of the new practices. It is about understanding—understanding that if we are not rigorous in our own learning, we can't be rigorous with our students' learning.

26

Activating a Professional Teacher Evaluation Model

Jill Potts

Jeff Zoul

Expectations for public schools are increasing as the demands of the information age challenge traditional ideas of knowledge and education. As the paradigm shifts for teaching and learning, so do the processes that monitor the quality of education, including evaluation of instructional practice. In the new standard, all components of instruction are evaluated in the context of student success. Teachers must possess many skills to be effective practitioners, and these aren't limited to performance in the classroom. Yet teacher performance has traditionally been the singular source for evaluating teacher effectiveness.

Teachers are the greatest determiners of student achievement. The quality of the work they give to students and the effectiveness of their instructional practices have more impact than any other factor on the degree to which students succeed. Teacher evaluation in a bureaucratic model of supervision is dependent on a checklist of behaviors that emphasizes individual, rather than collective instructional practices.

The concept of teacher evaluation as a solely supervisory function does not promote professional growth. Sustained professional growth requires shared instructional leadership that incorporates coaching, reflecting, and problem solving. Introducing a collaborative model for professional growth and improved instruction without also introducing a complement for teacher evaluation undermines the effectiveness of teacher collaboration.

This chapter introduces a model that incorporates teacher evaluation into a model of sustained teacher collaboration. In this model, the process by which teachers are appraised naturally integrates the expectations for self-directed professional growth and the elements of shared instructional leadership. Successful integration of collaboration and teacher appraisal empowers both processes and provides a consistent and cohesive focus for increasing student achievement.

Whole-Faculty Study Groups and Teacher Appraisal

The Whole-Faculty Study Group (WFSG; see Murphy & Lick, 2005) System emphasizes and interweaves professional growth and increased student achievement. The culture of teacher collaboration, meaningful review of student work, and purposeful instruction must be cultivated in the school environment in order to improve student learning. Most components of the WFSG process are incorporated into school improvement plans and mission statements across the nation because the concepts embedded in the process are universal and widely accepted as best practice. While the WFSG concept is a clear, systematic, and proven program for increasing student achievement, its primary strength is its focus and reliance on practitioner collaboration. Educational practitioners know that people, not programs, determine the success of students. The WFSG process weds the two: It is a program that emphasizes people.

One of the many components of the WFSG model is its innate application for teacher appraisal. The evaluation of teachers in many school systems is disconnected from what they do daily in their classrooms, and does not always reflect the professional growth they gain from collaboration and interaction with peers. Often, teacher evaluation is based on a single classroom observation. Teachers may not be held accountable for or encouraged to pursue professional growth opportunities in areas that will ultimately benefit students. This narrow perspective on teacher performance does not promote meaningful change in instructional practices that will ultimately have the greatest impact on student achievement.

How might the WFSG process include the appraisal of teacher effectiveness? Following is a case study of one elementary school that implemented the WFSG process and incorporated it into an existing model of teacher evaluation. It offers a structure for implementing a cohesive and relevant method of teacher appraisal that promotes the ideology of WFSGs.

The Setting

Coal Mountain Elementary School is one of fourteen elementary schools in Forsyth County, Georgia, a suburb thirty miles northeast of Atlanta. The school opened in 1981 and serves students in kindergarten through fifth grade. The student population fluctuates from 680 to 750 students predominantly from middle- to upper-middle-class homes. The free and reduced lunch population represents approximately 15% of the school, 14% are classified as students with disabilities, and 3% are identified as Limited English Proficient (LEP). The student population includes 97% Caucasians and 3% Hispanics. Coal Mountain offers a gifted program, ESOL (English for Speakers of Other Languages), special education programs, and an early intervention program for students who are below grade level in reading and mathematics.

The number of schools in Forsyth County tripled in the past ten years. For several years in the 1990s, Forsyth County was named the fastest growing community in the nation. Its main artery, Georgia 400, is known as the "Technology Corridor," as dozens of high-tech businesses are located in communities that cluster around the state highway that extends northeast out of Atlanta.

As Forsyth County steadily changed from rural to suburban, so did the expectations of the residents for the schools. Within a ten-year period, Forsyth County morphed from existing as one of the poorer counties in Georgia to thriving as one of its most affluent. The public schools enjoy tremendous community support; schools within Forsyth County have at their disposal vast resources to offer a world-class education to all students in kindergarten through twelfth grade.

THE PROFESSIONAL APPRAISAL CYCLE

In 1995, the Georgia state legislature withdrew the mandated use of the state teacher evaluation instrument. School systems in Georgia were then free to create and implement their own structures for teacher evaluation. Forsyth County teachers and administrators created an evaluation model, the Professional Appraisal Cycle, a process that was approved and adopted by the Board of Education in 1996 and fully implemented in 1997.

The Professional Appraisal Cycle, known as PAC, incorporates all aspects of professional growth and accountability, including appraisal of teacher performance. PAC is built on the foundation of four standards that describe and outline expectations and responsibilities of teachers in designing quality work for students.

Professional Appraisal Cycle Standards

Standard 1: The teacher is a leader.

Standard 2: The teacher manages time, people, space, assessment data, and technology in order to improve the quality of student work.

Standard 3: The teacher designs quality knowledge work that actively engages students in learning.

Standard 4: The teacher monitors and adapts the work provided based on student engagement to achieve desired results.

Certain essential questions drive the standards:

- What is it that I am trying to involve others in doing, and what reasons might they have for doing these things?
- How might I help others see the need, importance, or value of participating with me in learning activities?
- How will we know our work is focused on improving student achievement?
- How does the action agenda we have planned facilitate the intended results?
- How can we rethink and improve our work to foster higher student achievement?

Each of the four standards includes indicators that illustrate what the standards look like in practice. The indicators are organized into a rubric that scales on three levels the requirements for each standard. The minimum expectations are on Level 1, while mastery of each standard is described on Level 3 (see Table 26.1).

The primary responsibility of educators in Forsyth County is to design high-quality work that engages students. Student gains occur when educators focus on improving the quality of work provided to students rather than focusing directly on "fixing" the student. The PAC procedures support educators as professionals and leaders as they assess their own performances and work collaboratively with other professionals to employ reflective practices that are focused on improving the quality of the work provided to the students.

The PAC views teachers as designers of quality knowledge work for students. Quality knowledge work is defined as the ideas, concepts, symbols, and observations used by people in an information-based society. The schoolwork that educators develop must be compelling and engaging so that students learn what the school system, community, and society at large deem to be of academic value. Students are engaged when they are interested in the work, challenged by the work, satisfied with the work, persistent in the work, and committed to the work. The critical result of student engagement is that students learn what is important for them to learn.

Stages of the Professional Appraisal Cycle

In the first stage of the PAC process, teachers complete an individual self-assessment in which they reflect on their practices in the context of the Forsyth County Schools' Educator Standards and Indicators. Teachers are encouraged to use a reflective conversation with a colleague to assist in completing the self-assessment. The second stage of the PAC process is a formal, structured conversation with a school administrator. The teacher and administrator discuss the teacher's self-assessment of his or her work and activities in order to assist the teacher in forming potential growth goals. The conference is a time to encourage reflection and promote new understandings. The conference serves to clarify professional growth goals for the teacher and determine placement of the teacher on a

Table 26.1   Professional Appraisal Cycle Summary Rubric

Standard 1: The teacher is a leader.	Engages in collegial activities and self-reflection. Participates in school- or districtwide activities.	Takes a leading role in some aspect of professional activities. Encourages others' self-improvement. Volunteers to participate in schoolwide activities.	Contributes extensively to student, school, and districtwide activities. Contributes to peer development. Perceived by others as a leader of leaders.
Standard 2: The teacher manages time, people, space, assessment data, and technology in order to improve the quality of work.	Consistently uses time, people, space, assessment data, and technology in designing quality work.	Designs student work incorporating effective use of time, people, space, assessment data, and technology. Seeks resources needed to provide quality work.	Designs student work by employing a variety of means of using time, people, space, assessment data, and technology. Assists others in using these resources.
Standard 3: The teacher designs quality work that actively engages students in learning.	Creates student work using design qualities.	Designs student work using a variety of design qualities.	Demonstrates and assists others in planning student work with many of the design qualities of knowledge work. Makes quality knowledge work a part of overall unit planning. Involves students in planning their own quality work.
Standard 4: The teacher monitors and adapts the work provided based on student engagement so desired results are achieved.	Analyzes student learning and adapts re-teaching for student success. Maintains records of student achievement.	Uses student assessment data to plan work with alternatives so students can be monitored and guided into successful activities. Provides formative feedback to students.	Assesses student needs and designs quality work with initial modifications for those specific needs. Assists students to self-reflect and monitor their own progress.

Professional Growth Team. Professional Growth Teams are made up of teachers who have similar goals.

The third stage of the PAC process involves placing teachers in appropriate Professional Growth Teams in which teachers work together toward achieving goals in similar areas. The fourth stage of the PAC process is the development of a professional growth plan by each teacher that reflects the goals for the cycle and is supported by the work of the Professional Growth Team. It is in this stage that teachers are reminded that the purpose of the appraisal process is professional growth. Growth does not occur without risk taking and stretching. The fifth stage of PAC includes the planned meetings of Professional Growth Teams to establish goals and reflect on practice.

The sixth stage of PAC is a summative conference between the teacher and an administrator to review the professional growth of the teacher and the accomplishment of student achievement goals set out in the teacher's action plan. Purposes of the summative evaluation include the following determinations:

- Did the teacher meet minimum requirements in the four standards?
- Did the teacher meet the goals on the stated action plan?
- Did the teacher successfully execute the strategies designed to improve student achievement?

While the implementation of PAC as the primary structure for teacher appraisal in Forsyth County has met with favorable response, many educators in the system felt that something different was needed to genuinely wed professional development and student achievement. At Coal Mountain Elementary School, that proved to be Whole-Faculty Study Groups.

Whole-Faculty Study Groups and the Professional Appraisal Cycle

The introduction of the Whole-Faculty Study Group System to the teachers at Coal Mountain Elementary School presented a framework that activated and enhanced the Professional Appraisal Cycle. The objectives of the PAC align with the objectives of WFSGs, in that teachers are responsible for their professional growth, and that growth and increased student achievement can be accomplished only through common focus and collaborative effort. The WFSG process sharpens the focus on specific areas of student achievement that are identified through extensive data analysis. The stages of the PAC, including teacher appraisal, are easily transferable to the WFSG process.

After being introduced to the WFSG methodology, the administrators at Coal Mountain Elementary School decided to use the WFSG process to enact the Professional Appraisal Cycle. A team of administrators and teachers attended training sessions to learn about the WFSG practice. This initial team mapped out a plan to merge the stages of the PAC to the processes of WFSGs. The standards of the PAC were incorporated into WFSGs so that the requirements for teachers' satisfactory performance could be justified and defended in the context of the WFSG process.

As stated in the WFSG literature, a framework for designing professional development has three major components: context, process, and content. The context addresses the culture in which the study groups exist; that is, how safe individuals feel to take risks and whether it is standard practice to work in isolation or with peers. The WFSG process promotes a culture favorable to collaboration and collegiality in that it instills organizational and cultural factors that facilitate progress toward intended results, such as a shared vision and norms of continuous improvement and collegiality.

With PAC, the structure used to share vision and establish and continue norms may not be consistent from school to school. WFSGs streamline and standardize this structure so that maximum results can be achieved at any school.

The process component of WFSGs aligns with the PAC in that it provides a system for teaming teachers in collaborative groups. With PAC, the formation of the groups is random and not necessarily connected to goals in student achievement. The WFSG process incorporates teacher collaboration into the shared purpose of school improvement.

The school improvement process may be streamlined into the work of WFSGs. The Professional Growth Teams of the PAC and school improvement teams are two separate entities, with two different sets of procedures. At Coal Mountain, the study groups are school improvement teams, and the action plans of the study groups are the foundation of the school improvement plan. The WFSG process combines the objectives of teacher professional growth *and* school improvement goals geared toward increasing student achievement. This strategy also connects student achievement with teacher evaluation.

The third component of WFSGs, content, is what study groups *do.*

"High-performing study groups do intellectually rigorous work, meaning that content is substantive enough to sustain and challenge the members as they strive for deeper understanding of what they teach" (Murphy & Lick, 2001, p. 41). In their study groups, teachers use data analysis to identify student needs, they develop action plans in which they agree on specific areas to address, and they work in their groups on instructional strategies that will improve student achievement in these areas. In study groups, teachers do what students need them to do.

The focus on academic content and specific, measurable attainment of student achievement goals defines a purpose for study groups. By narrowing the objectives for the PAC Professional Growth Teams to connect with specific student achievement goals, study groups are able to concentrate on activities that result in quantifiable student achievement in target areas.

Teacher Appraisal and the Whole-Faculty Study Group System

The incorporation of the WFSG System into the Professional Appraisal Cycle at Coal Mountain Elementary provides a means for the evaluation of teachers based on their effectiveness as that relates to their attainment of specific student achievement goals. Movement through the stages of PAC reflects the work of the teachers in their study groups.

During the initial conference, teachers work with an administrator to examine potential professional growth goals based on the four standards of the PAC. These goals are formed through the teachers' self-assessment and analysis of student achievement indicators. The teacher and administrator review the teacher's class profiles, which include test scores, grades, and other data to determine areas of instructional strengths and weaknesses. The teacher and the administrator then work together to finalize the plan for the teacher's professional growth.

The WFSG process begins after the initial teacher conferences. Administrators plan meetings with the faculty to analyze schoolwide student achievement data. Through this analysis, student needs are identified, categorized, and prioritized. The categories for student needs become the topics for study groups (Professional Growth Teams in PAC terms). Once the categories are identified, administrators review the topics along with the teachers' professional growth plans from their initial conferences. Administrators use the teachers' individual growth plans to place teachers in appropriate study groups.

Once the study groups are formed, they follow the protocol of WFSG meetings. Groups establish meeting norms, they develop action plans with measurable student achievement goals, and they engage in collaborative activities that concentrate on their specific targeted area of student achievement. The WFSG meetings encompass all the requirements of the Professional Growth Team meetings; however, the WFSG meetings include important components that Professional Growth Team meetings lack. The WFSG meetings have a designated protocol with a standard log for reporting the results of meetings. The minutes of WFSG meetings are public and are reviewed and monitored by administrators who give feedback to the groups. WFSG meetings are focused on accomplishing identified student achievement goals.

WFSGs: Changing the Structure and Culture of Appraisal

At Coal Mountain Elementary School, significant change occurred immediately after implementing the WFSG concept. While much of this change was directly related to the critical examination of both teacher practices and student work, another powerful change involved the appraisal of teacher performance. The change that occurred in this area included both structural and cultural transformations. An extremely specific structure was implemented whereby teachers were organized into collaborative professional development communities. As a result, attitudes and practices began to change. A culture of collegiality and collaboration became the prevailing norm. Teachers served as critical friends to each other in order to support, not inhibit, risk taking as a way to enhance instruction.

A major component of the summative teacher evaluations conducted at the culmination of the first year using the WFSG System included the work each individual engaged in as a member of a WFSG. Teachers presented portfolios, both individually and as a group, containing evidence of student achievement within their targeted area of student need. All teachers presented a narrative chronicling the extent to which the work they did within their WFSGs impacted student achievement.

CONCLUSION

The WFSG approach to improving student achievement, while simultaneously promoting collaborative professional development, can be adopted and incorporated by any elementary, middle, or high school. Because the aim of WFSGs is to increase student achievement, it is also effective for assessing and refining teacher performance. The success of incorporating teacher evaluation into the WFSG process depends upon several key factors:

• Teachers must be able to view the WFSG process as a vehicle for more effectively doing those tasks they are already doing, including school improvement practices, data analysis, instructional planning, and curriculum design and development.

- Expectations for participation in WFSGs must be clearly communicated and linked to teacher evaluation.

- Teachers must understand that much of their evaluation depends on their own reflections and self-assessments: Evaluation is not something that is done *to* them.

- Although it is tempting at times to "tweak" the system to suit individual styles and preferences, the WFSG concept is most effective when it is implemented exactly as described by Murphy and Lick (2005). Weekly meetings are critical; to meet less often interrupts momentum, and progress toward group goals wanes, resulting in less effective collaboration and planning.

- Teachers must be allowed the freedom to take risks without fear of administrative reprisal. While not every idea imagined by every study group results in success, knowing that they have the freedom to experiment and explore new approaches to instruction motivates teachers to take seriously the work they engage in with their group members.

- Teachers and administrators must realize and accept the fact that the benefits of WFSGs will not be immediately obvious. The administrators and group leaders at Coal Mountain found some initial teacher resistance and periodic setbacks in the first months of WFSG implementation. Over the course of that first year, however, WFSGs gained momentum as teachers gleaned insights into what students needed and how to best meet their needs.

With the continuation of the WFSG cycle at Coal Mountain Elementary School, increased collaboration is anticipated, with teachers observing in each other's classrooms and providing critical feedback. The WFSG System has proved to be an ideal way for teachers to engage in self-appraisal and peer appraisal. It has evolved into the primary vehicle for improving student performance; in addition, it is the primary tool for evaluating and improving teacher performance.

PART VII

State and National Initiatives

Earlier sections have related the field experiences of mostly individual schools or school system efforts. These efforts have added immensely to our knowledge base and will continue to be valuable to our schools well into the future. However, the potential for even greater impact comes when statewide and national initiatives for school improvement and student performance achievement enter the picture.

This section of the Fieldbook, *State and National Initiatives*, presents four chapters that deal with such efforts, three involving a state or state-related agency and one reflecting an important national initiative. These chapters: (a) unfold the story of how Louisiana and educators throughout the state are implementing in 170 schools, through their Learning-Intensive Networking Communities for Success (LINCS), an effective multidimensional professional development process to support improved teacher and student performance; (b) tell how Georgia, in cooperation with business and nonprofit organizations in the state, created the Georgia Leadership Institute for School Improvement, providing unique approaches to leadership development, policy influence, and research and development that are positively affecting systematic changes with long-term implications for student success; (c) relate insight into the roles and responsibilities of the Georgia Department of Education and the significant potential it has to influence proper school development, where the critical ingredient is statewide dialogue followed by true, meaningful, long-term collaboration with and among all education stakeholders, particularly schools, unifying ideas to ignite and sustain the required change to perpetuate far-reaching, future-oriented school improvement; and (d) describe the National Whole-Faculty Study Group Center, whose mission is: "to ensure student achievement through the authentic application of the

WFSG System in schools worldwide," which will be accomplished through people (consultants, principals, teachers, researchers, district leaders, curriculum coordinators, and content specialists), programs (national conferences, special institutes, technical assistance, preparation assistance for projects and proposals, research, electronic support, and a worldwide network), and products and resources (implementation tools, books, articles and reports, protocols, portfolios, and lessons).

27

Going Statewide With Whole-Faculty Study Groups in Louisiana

Teri Roberts

This chapter unfolds the story of how educators throughout Louisiana are implementing an effective multidimensional professional development process to support improved teacher and student performance. You will discover how the Learning-Intensive Networking Communities for Success (LINCS) is the impetus for schools initiating and maintaining professional learning communities using the Whole-Faculty Study Group System and how this process is facilitated by regional coordinators, school content leaders, and school teams. Also, you will learn how to support teachers as they design and teach standards-based, technology-rich lessons, critique student work, analyze data, and create job-embedded learning experiences that have led to significant increases in teacher and student learning.

THE SETTING

State, district, and school staff development leaders in Louisiana have been active in programs of the National Staff Development Council (NSDC) for many years. At NSDC's 1998 Annual Conference, several of the leaders heard Carlene Murphy speak about Whole-Faculty Study Groups (WFSGs; see Murphy & Lick, 2005). As a result, Murphy was invited to conduct a workshop on WFSGs at the Louisiana Staff Development Council's (LSDC) 1999 Spring Conference. The LSDC workshop led to conversations between Murphy and state leaders regarding how WFSGs might be the main job-embedded professional development structure needed to establish a professional learning community for a new state initiative that would become known by its acronym, LINCS. The result of the conversations was to have Murphy present WFSGs at a state conference for schools that would be the first to implement LINCS. The conference followed the hiring of regional coordinators who would have the responsibility for guiding schools in the implementation of all aspects of the LINCS program. There are nineteen LINCS regional coordinators to serve eight regions in the state of Louisiana. The hiring of the coordinators preceding the conference meant that the new coordinators would be trained in the WFSG procedures as they were learning the full range of their responsibilities and would learn from Murphy how to integrate the LINCS content with the WFSG process. After the conference, there were ongoing communications between the state leaders and Murphy that were shared with the regional coordinators. A year later, Murphy returned to conduct another two-day WFSG institute for school teams from LINCS schools. During the third year, Murphy conducted a statewide video conference in which all school teams went to the Regional Service Centers to view presentations and participate in discussions about WFSGs, learning more about the implementation of effective study groups and benefiting from what was happening at WFSG sites in other states. In the fourth year, several LINCS regional coordinators attended the National WFSG Conference, returning to Louisiana to share what they had learned with their colleagues. During the fifth and current year, Murphy returned to Louisiana to do another statewide video conference, bringing everyone up to date on best WFSG practices. Through state leaders, there is a constant flow of information to LINCS regional coordinators that helps facilitate the ongoing work of WFSGs in all LINCS schools.

STATE LEADERSHIP

What is now being done in the schools of Louisiana could not be done if it were not for strong support, professional development, and continued guidance from leaders at the state level. As employees of the state, LINCS Regional Coordinators depend on state leaders to provide them with the professional learning opportunities and materials they require to support the schools they serve. It is absolutely imperative for state leaders to maintain commitment to programs in which schools and individuals throughout the state have made major investments of time, money, and energy. It is difficult for regional coordinators to ask schools for a commitment if the state is not going to maintain a high level of commitment to local schools. With the LINCS program and its WFSG core, there is a steady, even hand of commitment and support from state leaders. Just as schools take their lead from district leaders, district leaders take their lead from state leaders.

WHY WHOLE-FACULTY STUDY GROUPS?

LINCS is a whole-school professional development initiative, focusing on the improvement of teaching and learning in Language Arts, mathematics, and science. The WFSG system is a whole-school professional development process that includes at least all certificated personnel as members of study groups. In this way, the entire school is involved in "finding solutions to common school problems." Groups of three to six members are formed to study, learn, and work together for the school year.

After a thorough analysis of student data, the faculty selects the student needs to target, and each study group further specifies the one or two needs on which that group will focus. Murphy and Lick (2005) state that the major functions of WFSGs are to:

- Develop a deeper understanding of academic content
- Support the implementation of curricular and instructional initiatives
- Integrate and give coherence to a school's instructional programs and practices
- Study research on teaching and learning
- Monitor the impact of instructional initiatives on students
- Provide a time when teachers can examine student work together

The above functions reflect what WFSGs do in LINCS schools. After each group validates the instructional student needs that its study group will focus on, members of the study group determine what actions they will take when their study group meets to target those needs. Study groups share, at regular intervals and with the entire staff, effective practices and materials. Time is provided for study groups to create a study-group action plan (SGAP), do the designated work in the action plan, and record their efforts and outcomes in their action plan. WFSGs are both a vehicle and a means to the end goals: improvement in teaching and learning.

THE WHOLE-FACULTY STUDY GROUP SYSTEM

The WFSG System, when properly applied, has been shown to be one of the most effective research-based professional development designs for bringing about instructional improvement in schools. As such, the National Staff Development Council featured the WFSG System in its book, *Powerful Designs for Professional Development* (1999).

The WFSG System includes a seven-step Decision-Making Cycle (DMC) that schools use to determine student needs at the school, how the study groups will be organized, and what they will do.

The Decision-Making Cycle

A brief overview of the DMC follows:

Step 1: Analyze Data

Step 2: State Student Needs

Step 3: Categorize the Student Needs

Step 4: Form Study Groups

Step 5: Develop Study-Group Action Plans

Step 6: Implement the Plans

Step 7: Evaluate Impact of Study Groups on Student Learning

Steps 1–4 are implemented with the whole faculty by a school team that has been trained in the WFSG process. This takes place at the beginning of the school year in a three-hour meeting.

In Step 5, each group develops an action plan. Action plans are usually completed in the first two meetings of study groups. By the end of September, study groups, typically, are in Step 6, implementing the action plans by doing in their study-group meetings what members indicated and committed to do in their action plan.

Examples of study-group actions are:

- Design lessons
- Practice teaching lessons
- Model effective practices for peers
- Examine and/or score student work
- Discuss readings from professional journals
- Have a skillful person train the group in an effective strategy

Step 7, the last step in the continuing cycle, is an ongoing assessment of the study group's work throughout the school year to see its impact on student learning. In addition, at the end of the school year there is a meeting of the whole faculty to assess overall results and celebrate successes. During this Evaluative Summary meeting, each study group makes a presentation, describing its impact on student achievement.

THE LINCS PROGRAM

In Louisiana, schools can apply for a grant supporting school improvement from the Learning-Intensive Networking Communities for Success (LINCS) program. LINCS is a multidimensional professional development partnership in association with the Louisiana Department of Education (LDE), the Louisiana Systemic Initiative Program (LaSIP), and the Southern Regional Education Board (SREB). The purpose of the LINCS program is to build and strengthen the ability of K–12 classroom teachers to design and implement standards-based, technology-rich lessons in their daily instruction.

Components of the LINCS Program

The seven components of the LINCS program are:

- *LINCS Regional Coordinators:* LINCS regional coordinators, who are paid by the Louisiana Department of Education (LDE), work with schools, districts, universities, and LDE staff to ensure the faithful implementation of the LINCS process. The coordinators work in the LINCS schools in classrooms with participating teachers and LINCS content leaders to strengthen content knowledge, instruction, technology integration, and assessment practices to improve student achievement. LINCS regional coordinators assist schools with the implementation of the WFSG System and serve as "expert voices" for study groups.

- *LINCS School Content Leaders:* All schools and districts that participate in the LINCS process have a "content leader" for each school that is served. A content leader is a school- or district-based educator who is proficient in the content areas on which the school is focusing. The content leader's role is to work alongside classroom teachers, modeling lessons, coaching, and providing other feedback as needed to support the implementation of standards-based teaching and learning strategies.

- *LINCS School Team:* Each school in the LINCS process has a LINCS school team whose members will lead and support the entire faculty as it implements the WFSG process in the school. The principal and three teachers, one of whom is a special education teacher, are required members of the LINCS school team.

- *LINCS District Contact Persons:* LINCS district contact persons support schools in the district that are a part of the LINCS process. The state hopes that districts will begin to implement the process by themselves.

- *WFSG Process:* The "WFSG process," referred to above, is a schoolwide, content-focused, data-driven professional development process in which every faculty member is a member of a study group. The goal of WFSGs is to focus the entire school faculty on integrating effective teaching and learning practices into the school. The results are increases in teacher content knowledge, student learning, and positive student behavior.

- *University Professional Development Projects:* The content-professional development focus of LINCS/LaSIP university projects is determined by addressing the student-needs data collected from the LINCS schools. School team members, along with content leaders, participate in these twenty-day student-needs projects during the summer and academic year.

- *Comprehensive Evaluation Process:* The LINCS comprehensive evaluation process measures improvements in teacher practice and student achievement.

LINCS SUPPORT AND RESULTS

Results from earlier "comprehensive evaluations" reveal that intensive professional development, with sustained follow-up support that helps align curricula, instruction, and assessment with state/district standards, is a catalyst for enhanced student performance. Louisiana's results indicate that the LINCS model, involving the WFSG process, is an effective school improvement process when faithfully implemented.

Components of the LINCS process provide varying levels of support to assist schools in improving teachers' content knowledge and skills and increasing student achievement. As reported by a school survey conducted in the spring of 2004, LINCS program implementation appears to be reasonably strong. It was found that the amount of time the faculty engaged in collaborative work within the LINCS process was statistically significantly associated with the degree of gain in student achievement.

In addition, the LINCS professional development process improves the ability of K–12 students to perform at higher levels of competency, as evidenced by increased performance on standardized tests: Norm-Referenced Tests; IOWA Tests of Basic Skills (ITBS) in Grades 3, 5, 6, 7, and IOWA Tests of Educational Development (ITED) in Grade 9, and Criterion-Referenced Tests; Louisiana Educational Assessment Program (LEAP-21) in Grades 4 and 8, and Graduation Exit Examination (GEE-21) in Grades 10 and 11.

A LOUISIANA SNAPSHOT
OF LINCS AND WFSGs

In Louisiana, WFSGs are implemented as job-embedded professional development for participating schools. Study groups in schools meet for an hour every two weeks for the purpose of deepening content knowledge, becoming more skillful practitioners, collaborating on lesson development, and doing joint problem solving.

LINCS, now in its fifth year, has spread rapidly across the state of Louisiana since its inception in the 2000–2001 academic year. The growth of schools, which in turn increases the number of WFSGs, is reported in Table 27.1.

LINCS is providing schools with the framework and support through which teachers can develop the knowledge and skills they need to do the following:

- Participate in content-rich activities and projects in mathematics, science, and/or English language arts
- Enhance teaching with the integration of technology
- Develop and deliver standards-based lessons
- Implement WFSGs to develop a culture of high expectations and to strengthen teaching and learning

LISTENING TO WHAT
LOUISIANA LEADERS SAY

Over the past five years, numerous surveys have been conducted. One component of the surveys has been to get feedback on WFSGs. The following quotations from a LINCS principal, a LINCS district contact person, and a LINCS content leader are representative of the responses.

Whole-Faculty Study Groups at Simsboro High School created an opportunity for teachers to examine test scores and reveal strengths and weaknesses.

Table 27.1   A History of LINCS in Louisiana

YEAR	2000–2001	2001–2002	2002–2003	2003–2004	2004–2005 (No new schools accepted)
Schools (LINCS)	48	70	170	175	170
WFSGs (LINCS)	305	430	1040	1100	1075 (estimated)
Teachers (LINCS)	1800	2390	5370	5972	5842 (estimated)
Students (LINCS)	22,700	24,400	78,995	79,285	77,590 (estimated)
Regional Coordinators (LINCS)	8	8	16	18	19
Content Leaders (LINCS)	0	42	115	125	136
University Professional Development Projects (LaSIP)	0	0	17	18	17

This was a great way to introduce the concept of examining test scores to those who have been reluctant to study test data. WFSGs have also helped create a spirit of collaboration within grade levels that did not exist before.

—Tim Nutt, LINCS Principal
Simsboro High School, Ruston, Louisiana

Whole-Faculty Study Groups in the Madison Parish School District have made an effective, positive change on the teachers because they created conditions that have promoted teacher learning. The teachers now work as teams instead of independent grade levels. Their efforts are not focused just on their growth but on the growth of their students as well. Teachers now work together to study research, design teaching activities, examine student work, and explore ways to improve it. Their focus is strictly on student needs. Teachers state that "the time devoted to Whole-Faculty Study Groups is well worth the time out of the classrooms." This is what I have experienced in the four years that we have had Whole-Faculty Study Groups in our district.

—Patricia B. Chandler
LINCS District Contact Person/Elementary Supervisor
Madison Parish, Tallulah, Louisiana

Being a part of Whole-Faculty Study Groups at several schools in our district has been a wonderful learning experience and a continuous walk in my profession. Sharing knowledge, gaining information, and strengthening friendships have been a few of the positive rewards of this job-embedded professional development. Working and growing in your profession and seeing the positive effects on your schools makes the real reason come into clear sight—children learning, smiling, and enjoying the experience of being in school.

—Jan Murphy, LINCS Content Leader
Lincoln Parish, Ruston, Louisiana

CONCLUSION

As one of the LINCS Regional Coordinators, now serving in my fifth year, I am proud of the stand our state has taken to provide schools with the in-depth guidance and expertise required to improve the education of all students. LINCS is a courageous and labor-intensive approach. It is a massive attempt to touch every school in a deep, personal way.

It is our role as LINCS Regional Coordinators to foster the WFSG implementation as its designers intended. We can truly say that we are doing our best to assist and monitor the process by faithfully working in the LINCS schools on a daily basis and working to provide stronger follow-up to enhance the effectiveness of the design. In the WFSG process, LINCS Regional Coordinators assist teachers the majority of the time in Step 6: Implementation (DMC), by helping them to understand the cycle of Assessing/Researching, Planning, Acting/Implementing, and Reflecting on their actions.

We believe we are doing as well, or better, in maintaining the integrity of the program as any group has done in similar efforts sponsored by any state department of education. With continued support and guidance from our state and national leaders, we know Louisiana's students will be the beneficiaries.

28

Developing and Supporting Leaders

A New Day, A New Way With New Results

Deb Page

Gale Hulme

To improve student achievement, where should a state focus its efforts: on improving teacher quality or improving the quality of leadership in schools and school districts? Proponents of teacher support could argue that research indicates quality teaching has the greatest impact on student achievement (Haycock, 1998; Rice, 2003; Rivkin, Hanushek, & Kain, 1998; Sanders & Rivers, 1998). Those with broad organizational perspectives can make an equally strong case that teachers do not work in a vacuum. Rather, teachers perform within their district and schools' systems of teaching and learning and within the cultures created, led, and supported by district and school leaders. The system of work and culture, driven by district and school leaders, can either support quality teaching and learning or impede it. Research at the University of Minnesota and the University of Toronto (Leithwood, Louis, Anderson, & Wahlstrom, 2004) found that leadership, among school-related factors, follows teacher quality in its impact on student learning. In fact, their research shows that 20% of the impact on student achievement is attributable to leadership, precisely the difference between success and failure. The research does not settle the debate as to which is most important, building leadership capacity or teaching quality, but it does suggest another conclusion: Both are critically important to improving student achievement.

In 2000, when the state of Georgia intensified its focus on improving student achievement, state leaders came to the same conclusion: the state had to focus on both teacher quality and leadership quality if it were to improve student achievement to meet both newly set state mandates and the requirements of No Child Left Behind, which loomed on the horizon at that time.

The study pointed to methods for improving teacher quality, which guided the state to launch and accelerate initiatives to support teachers' development. However, the state's governance and stakeholders in public education recognized that leadership quality was a somewhat different and potentially more complex issue to address, largely because leadership of school improvement is not the role of one leader, or one type of leader, but instead is distributed within schools, school systems, school boards, and the community. As those who recognized the need to improve leadership as well as teacher quality in Georgia pondered the challenge and the options, a state study concluded that: *The degree and magnitude of change needed to improve and support educational leadership could not happen within the traditional structures in time to meet the needs of state and national educational reform mandates.*

The study, coupled with the state's dead-last SAT ranking and lagging student achievement results, especially among children of color and poverty, became a call to action, particularly to Dr. Jan Kettlewell, Associate Vice Chancellor for the Board of Regents of the University System of Georgia and Tom Upchurch, then president of the Georgia Partnership for Excellence in Education, a nonprofit organization devoted to education advocacy. The two were among the state's leaders who reviewed the results of the state study and stepped up to the challenge to create a solution. Using start-up funding from the Bill & Melinda Gates Foundation and the Wallace Foundation, the two assembled a team of stakeholders from K–12 public education, higher education, state government, the Southern Regional Educational Board (SREB), and the business community to design and implement an out-of-the-box solution to the state's educational leadership challenges: Georgia's Leadership Institute for School Improvement.

Three years later, the Institute's unique approaches to leadership development, policy influence, and research and development are influencing systemic changes with long-term implications for student success. This chapter will unfold the story of the Institute's launch and development and will point to the unique approaches that many say are creating for Georgia education "a new day, a new way . . . with new results."

Be warned, what lies ahead is not traditional. We hope that what you will read will cause you, gentle reader, to examine your mental models for equipping and supporting educational leaders to drive change for student success, and to embrace a blend of best practices from inside and outside education that are improving leadership and the effectiveness of schools and school systems in Georgia to better support teaching and learning.

THE BEGINNING

In 2000, Kettlewell and Upchurch, armed with private grants and matching state funds, recruited partners from state government, K–12, higher education, and the business community to form a shared governance structure to guide and oversee the solution they envisioned. They viewed this partnership of ownership as key to creating an organization that could function outside the traditional structures and without complete control by any one partner organization. They recruited leaders who shared a belief that strong leadership and organizational effectiveness at the district level, linked with capable, courageous school leadership and teacher engagement in team-based, data-driven improvement is needed to drive and sustain change for student success. They set out to design an Institute that could raise the bar for development of leaders, while incubating new ways to prepare leaders while advocating for changes to help the state attract and keep high-quality leaders.

Georgia's Leadership Institute for School Improvement

These visionaries had seen well-intentioned, traditional leadership academies come and go—with school leaders coming in "one-sies and two-sies" to hear experts' wisdom on school leadership. They determined that participants often learned a great deal and left inspired, but once they faced the challenges "back at the ranch," many admitted they were unable to transfer their learning quickly into practice. In academies that trained school-based leaders and their teachers, those leaders often found they lacked the structures, support, and common focus with their peers and district leaders to drive sustainable, long-term change.

The Vision

The founders of Georgia's Leadership Institute for School Improvement (GLISI) set their goals on a definably different and systemic solution: *An organization that would dare to break from traditional approaches to embrace a systemic model of performance-based leadership development, policy influence, and research and development.* They intended to link those core efforts to develop a new model and process for equipping and supporting leaders to drive change for student success that aligned with and supported the missions of the organizations these visionaries represented.

The Development

A diverse team from education, higher education, the Southern Regional Education Board (SREB), and executives in charge of leadership development for major businesses headquartered in the state was tapped to design the organization. The design team created a blueprint for a core leadership development program that would draw best practices from executive training in business and research on instructional leader development.

Although the original action plan was focused primarily on the core leader development program, the visionaries behind the organization developed an additional set of aspirations that had more far-reaching implications. Their goals included:

- Influencing changes in practices and policies for recruitment and selection of educational leaders
- Influencing changes in educational leader preparation with an emphasis on shifting to performance-based approaches that reduce time to competency
- Institutionalizing school leadership practices that merged best practices from educational research and business and engaged entire faculties in team-based learning and improvement, much like the Whole-Faculty Study Groups (Murphy & Lick, 2005)
- Piloting new practices for recruitment, selection, preparation, and development that make a case of changes in district, state, and university policies
- Creating a cadre of educational leaders from school districts and universities who would assume the role of change agent among their peers to drive change for student success
- Researching best practices of educational leaders and other organizational leaders to develop models and curriculum for the "new work of leadership of school improvement," for leadership performance coaching, distributed leadership, and other best practices
- Evaluating the effectiveness of training, pilots, models, and influence in equipping and supporting educational leaders to drive change for student success and improving the pipeline of new leaders and teacher-leaders

The newly formed governance team also appointed a nonpartisan Coordinating Board of the primary stakeholders in educational leadership in the state to ensure statewide alignment of efforts to support educational leadership, identify needs for support, and provide input on policies and issues related to educational leadership.

Creation

To execute the design and plan, the Institute hired an executive director with background in education and in business. Among the executive director's first hires was a director who had deep knowledge and experience in schools and school systems in professional learning, organizational learning, and leadership development. Together, they staffed the Institute primarily with on-loan, exemplary practitioners from Georgia school systems who had distinguished themselves as principals for their work in leader development, school improvement, organizational development, professional learning, and instructional leadership. One of the key team members had served as the project facilitator while the Institute was being designed and, thus, was instrumental in the transition from design to launch.

Once in place, the Institute team set out to execute the design. The Institute established two core values that would guide all work of the Institute:

1. To affirm the value of educational leaders

2. To use relationship development and value creation to influence the willing engagement of leaders at all levels and stakeholders in the Institute

The team committed its effort to building an organization that focused on creating high-performing schools and districts by leveraging the strengths of educators and their leaders, their commitment to their profession, and their values for making a difference for all children, rather than a deficit model focused on meeting improvement mandates. The team worked to establish a unique brand and a set of highly professional, high-value products and services that were definably, detectably different than potential participants' other options. It decided that both training and influence would be conducted leader to leader, to focus attention on credible leaders who would be role models for driving change for student success.

The Institute also acknowledged that its role in the state would at times be risky when it advocated for changes in mental models, practices, and policies within the organizations that made up its Executive Committee and Coordinating Board. The team chose the metaphor of "being the sand in the oyster" to characterize its role as a change catalyst that would ultimately cause its participants and partner organizations to collectively create the "pearl" of great value: *a non-partisan, systemic, aligned process for equipping and supporting educational leaders to drive change for student success.*

The team's first task was to develop and execute the core leader development process. The Institute used leader-to-leader influence to secure superintendent commitment for teams of district and school leaders to participate. The participating superintendents and their teams were then selected to create cohorts of diverse district teams that represented a wide range of demographics, geography, and economic resources.

Teams employed a business-based research, analysis, and instruction design process to develop "get and do" training sessions rather than traditional "sit and get" programs. The Institute interviewed more than seventy individuals who had led improvement of student achievement and established effective organizational cultures, structures and conditions, or who had led winning organizations outside of education. The process identified the performance required, the underlying knowledge and skills, desired outcomes, context variables, and other factors that impact performance. The practices were validated against educational research. The analysis lead to the development of a model, a Framework for Leadership of School Improvement© (see Figure 28.1), that indicated the work leaders must be able to do and the improvement support systems that require top-down focus and support.

The Institute designed its leadership development program's curriculum, its delivery, and the tools to train leaders to know what they should do back in their schools to scaffold that work and to equip leaders to achieve specific, measurable student achievement targets. The curriculum and its delivery model provide a unique blend of aligned information, communication, education, and motivation that drives the focus, alignment, and adaptation of best practices in school districts. Rather than being another "add-on" model, the Framework allows school and district leaders to compare whatever school improvement model they use with the education research-based and business-based best practices advocated in the Framework.

The Who, What, and How

Each class or "cohort" engages 12 to 14 district Change Teams, each led by its superintendent. These superintendents, along with nine district leaders, principals,

Figure 28.1 Framework for Leadership of School Improvement©

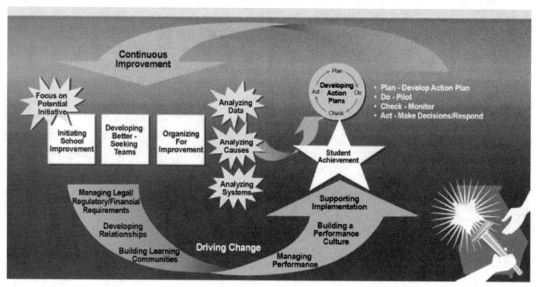

GEORGIA'S LEADERSHIP INSTITUTE FOR SCHOOL IMPROVEMENT

assistant principals, and teacher-leaders, participate in five days of intensive training over a three-month period. As the teams work together through the Institute Experience, they bond as teams and operate from shared beliefs, measurable goals, and tightly aligned improvement action plans. Individual team members become part of an empowered, passionate learning community and cross-functional change team.

The training process is split into three phases: a two-and-one-half–day session called "Leadership Base Camp," a two-and-one-half–day session termed "Leadership Summit," and a three-year action learning project that uses the skills acquired in the first two phases. The Institute purposefully adopted a delivery format that combines elements of an executive planning session, high energy music, and special effects typically used in sales training and high-quality, visually stimulating learning materials, in a highly professional retreat setting.

The start of the event is designed to send a signal to even the most seasoned leaders that this experience is meant to drive change. "Are you ready for this?" shout the lyrics of the jock-rock music that kicks off the Base Camp session. Within seconds audience members are on their feet, clapping and swaying to the beat. The anticipation is palpable as the teams watch the countdown to the beginning of the event on the giant projection screen. "Ten, nine, eight, seven, six, five, four, three, two, one!" roars the crowd, and explodes into cheers and applause. The time has come that these teams have been chosen for and are eagerly awaiting: the chance to learn, plan, and work together collaboratively to lead the "new work of leadership of school improvement."

The learning climate is intense, and throughout the experience it conveys the Institute's theme: "A New Day, A New Way with New Results." The curriculum, team-work time, and even a light-hearted talent night in which each district team teaches the others tenets of leadership for school improvement through music, drama, and even self-effacing humor, are all carefully designed to help participants learn and internalize a continuous improvement mindset.

Reading, Reflection, and Applied Learning

Just as mountain climbers prepare for the climb, Institute participants must also prepare for the school improvement journey ahead by completing advanced readings and reflecting on how these lessons apply to their leadership challenges and school improvement initiatives. To this end, the Institute staff provides relevant articles and books to our District Change Team participants as resources to enhance their learning during the training. These resources are distributed to participants at various times over their Base Camp and Leadership Summit experience by their Improvement Initiative Coordinator (IIC). A Leader Journal, another tool provided for reflection and response, provides structured opportunities for response and blank pages for reflection.

Prior to attending Base Camp, participants read these articles:

DuFour, Richard. (2002). The Learning-Centered Principal. *Educational Leadership*.

Haycock, Kati, Craig Jerald, & Susan Huang. (2001b). New Frontiers for a New Century. *The Education Trust*.

Haycock, Kati, Craig Jerald, & Sandra Huang. (2001a). Closing the Gap: Done in a Decade. *The Education Trust*.

Stiggins, Richard. (June 2002). Assessment Crisis: The Absence of Assessment for Learning. *Phi Delta Kappan*.

During Base Camp, District Change Team members analyze data and engage in uncovering root causes around their identified improvement focus, using quality tools for the analyses:

McManus, A. (1992). *The memory jogger for education: A pocket guide of tools for continuous improvement in schools*. Salem, NH: GOAL/QPC.

At Base Camp, District Change Team members also explored ideas developed in more depth in the following book; thus, at the conclusion of Base Camp, Institute staff members suggested teams later form study groups to continue their team reading, reflection, and application of team learning:

Davies, Anne. (2000). *Making Classroom Assessment Work*. Courtenay, British Columbia: Connections Publishing.

While no single school-improvement model is endorsed by the Institute, staff members bring in at least one keynote speaker who has been a turnaround leader and who is known nationally during each Leadership Summit to inspire hope and to share his or her promising practices. Dr. Gerald Anderson, coauthor of *Closing the Achievement Gap: No Excuses,* is one such speaker, who has been invited to tell the story of how one team-oriented district built on the effective schools research; applied total quality management concepts, strategies, and tools; and utilized the Plan-Do-Check-Act improvement cycle to identify and leverage identified best practices of Brazosport Independent School District teachers in developing and implementing The Eight-Step Process to improve adult and student learning and performance. After the keynote address, a panel of Georgia practitioners who have adapted or adopted the Brazosport model and who have documented positive student achievement results share their challenges and successes. To ensure that everyone has the same knowledge base, participants read the keynote speaker's book prior to hearing the presentation:

> Davenport, Patricia, & Gerald Anderson. (2002). *Closing the Achievement Gap: No Excuses.* Houston: American Productivity and Quality Center.

Participants also read the following book in preparation for a module on driving change for student success at Leadership Summit:

> Kotter, John P., & Dan S. Cohen. (2002). *The Heart of Change: Real Life Stories of How People Change Their Organizations.* Boston: Harvard Business School.

Through powerful "real-life" leadership stories, hands-on activities, tips, tools, focused conversations, and relevant readings with opportunities to reflect in their Leader Journals, District Change Team participants dig deep and apply what they are learning before, during, and after Base Camp and Leadership Summit.

The District/School Commitment

Once initial training is complete, individual school-based leaders prepare to return to their schools to form and lead "Better Seeking Teams" composed of their entire faculty and staff. The school leaders focus their teams' efforts on specific student achievement targets derived from analysis of school data, root causes, and the systems of teaching, learning, and support. Everyone who participates in the Institute Experience continues to work together as the District Change Team to create and sustain the momentum for change.

Each district team participant signs a three-year engagement commitment to pursue school improvement through these methods and documents his or her results in an electronic portfolio (e-Portfolio) that is shared with the Institute for research and evaluation purposes. An Improvement Initiative Coordinator (IIC), appointed by the superintendent and trained by the Institute, serves as project manager and coach to the team, and participates fully in the Base Camp and Leadership Summit training with the team.

Superintendents invariably ask to bring additional district teams to create a critical mass of leaders trained in the Framework for Leadership of School Improvement who are committed to driving school improvement. The participants are encouraged and equipped to reteach the Institute-supplied curriculum back in their schools to ensure the learning extends to leaders at all levels in their schools.

The Institute's Faculty

The instructors for the Base Camp and Leadership Summit are not paid consultants, but are teaching leaders with strong track records for improvement of student achievement who are drawn from local schools and districts. Instructors are not paid for their services, but serve for the recognition of their peers and the satisfaction of helping others improve their craft. The message underlying their practical, how-to advice and research-based content is: "If I can do this, you can do this provided you have the right beliefs, skills, and commitment." The peer leaders cultivate the confidence needed for change (Kanter, 2004). The staff of the Institute also teaches during the Institute Experience. The combination of capable, diverse, and seasoned leaders creates a dream-team GLISI faculty.

The Institute's staff also conducts follow-up research and evaluation for continuous improvement. The staff designs and develops tools and training materials to support continued learning with performance tools. Designated staff members, known as Performance Consultants, provide follow-up coaching and consulting services to participating districts and "coach the coaches." An Operations Manager with strong project management and financial skills runs a tight ship—keeping costs low, efficiency high, and events and products delivered on time with high quality. A tiny support team that calls itself "Educational Light and Magic" provides design, graphics, media, technology, and logistical support. The combined GLISI team models what it expects the leaders it trains and supports to do: *become high-performing teams that get results and that continuously improve products and services.*

Supporting Transfer of Learning and Systemic Change

The Institute closely monitors and evaluates three critical outcomes of its leadership development program:

1. The degree of transfer of learning into leadership performance

2. The levels of demonstrated leader proficiency in core leadership skills for school improvement

3. The student achievement results of the leaders' schools in comparison with other schools with similar demographics

By using a checklist of the skills and tools taught, the performance consultants determine whether participants are actually performing the skills learned in training. These transfers are seen as predictors of improved student achievement. When participants are not performing as they were trained, the consultants work with participants' Improvement Initiative Coordinator and their superintendent to determine the cause. The process provides rich feedback that informs curriculum redesign, identifies needs for additional training and support, and identifies both accelerators and barriers to improvement.

The factor that the Institute's research points to as critical to both the transfer of learning into practice and to improvement of results is the focused leadership of superintendents, combined with high expectations and support for their school leaders. As needs for additional training and support are identified, the Institute works with each district's superintendent to arrange for additional training and support, which is often provided by Institute consultants.

Following the initial training, superintendents and district staff continue to work in Communities of Learning and Achievement (COLAs) to continue learning, sharing best practices, and networking. By design, these learning communities are incubators of change, as the leaders align to drive specific changes for student success through shared learning and alliance. For example, one learning community of more than forty district leaders joined together to learn and share practices for improving achievement as evidenced in SAT scores statewide using the IBM Change Toolkit™. Another worked to design a Balanced Scorecard as a performance management tool for district leaders. One worked with consultant Carlene Murphy to explore professional learning communities and the application of the Whole-Faculty Study Group System to school-based teams. Yet another focused on designing a communication toolkit for school districts.

Supporting Leadership Development

Learning Expeditions sponsored by the Institute expose leaders to replicable leadership best practices across the state and nation. As leaders learn and travel together, they form strong bonds and alliances. Their collaboration has developed a strong core of leaders who are active in the Georgia School Superintendents Association (GSSA). These leaders are champions for systemic improvement and have the credibility to influence policy changes and gain support for educational leadership.

To support the Georgia Department of Education (DOE) in training leaders in all the schools in the state that need improvement, the Institute worked with the Southern Regional Educational Board (SREB) to develop four in-depth training modules that can be delivered regionally by school districts, Regional Educational Service Agencies (RESAs), colleges, and universities to ensure every school leader is fully trained in team-based leadership of improvement (led by the principal), use of data to lead change, aligning teacher assignments with standards, as well as prioritized curriculum, assessment, and instructional and leadership skills. The Institute trained trainers across the state to deliver the extensive curriculum to ensure that each leader in every school in the state had access to quality, in-depth training in leadership of school improvement that reflects national standards for effective professional learning (National Staff Development Council, 2001).

Influencing the Leadership Pipeline

The Institute is influencing the leadership pipeline as well. By working with the P-16 Initiatives of the Board of Regents of the University System of Georgia, the Institute is influencing improvements in its colleges and universities to be more responsive to district needs and to redesign their programs that prepare leaders. Using the Institute's research and analysis along with national best practices, public colleges and universities are redesigning their curriculums and partnering with districts engaged by the Institute to form "collaboratives" to ensure a pipeline of capable new leaders.

The Institute worked with the Board of Regents to coordinate an external review team to help each college and university that prepares leaders to identify its opportunities for change and improvement. A statewide policy review pointed out the systemic changes required for the state to better attract, hire, prepare, develop, and retain educational leaders. The external review and policy audit was the catalyst for a pilot preparation program, dubbed *Rising Stars.* This pilot was launched with the support of the Board of Regents and the Professional Standards Commissions. GLISI formed the Northern Georgia Consortium with North Georgia College and State University, Piedmont College, Reinhardt College, Brenau College, the Pioneer Regional Educational Service Agency, and local school districts that had participated in the Institute's Leadership Development cohort process (Base Camp and Leadership Summit). The group is testing performance-based preparation practices to ensure that new leaders can practice, demonstrate, and master specific school leadership skills before licensure and before assuming a formal leadership role in their schools. Special provisions were granted for the pilot to allow for the incubation of performance-based programs and to prove the need to shift traditional preparation programs to this more results-oriented approach.

Using a grant developed through Georgia's Partnership for Excellence in Education and provided by the Wachovia Foundation, the Institute is identifying and codifying coaching best practices and developing a leadership preparation coaching model with training for performance coaches to support new and aspiring leaders during preparation and induction. Grants from the Citigroup Foundation and the Wallace Foundation also supported the Institute in training teachers and their leaders to participate in distributed leadership as well.

The Results

Ninety-two percent (92%) of leaders who attend the Institute indicate that the Institute has accelerated their school improvement efforts. Over 87% report their school cultures change for the better after participation in Base Camp and Leadership Summit. The most common feedback the Institute receives from participants is that their participation has aligned and focused their district and school efforts and that the experience was the highest quality professional learning they had received in their careers. Early analyses of schools' results on state tests show schools led by Institute-trained leaders are making gains in student achievement that exceed those of nonparticipants. Follow-up observations indicate a high degree of transfer of learning into practice (closing the knowing-doing gap). The Institute is carefully monitoring participants' school and district results to determine how to continuously improve the Institute's programs, and to determine barriers to performance that must be addressed by policy change.

Dr. Steve Dolinger, current president of the Georgia Partnership for Excellence in Education, describes the Institute as "Georgia's best solution for improving student achievement." Dr. Jan Kettlewell, who continues to provide leadership as the Chair of the Institute's executive committee, is leading change teams at the 11 state colleges and universities that prepare new leaders to work with the Institute to find ways to help those leaders reach competency faster, and she says,

> The Institute is an incubator for best practices for leader preparation and for systemic changes which align the efforts of the Board of Regents and all the other state agencies and stakeholders in public education, particularly our state's Professional Standards Commission, Department of Education, the Governor's Office, and the Office of Student Achievement.

Table 28.1 Comparison of What GLISI *Is* and *Is Not*

What GLISI Is *Not*	What GLISI *Is*
Activities-based	Standards-based
Data-naïve	Data-driven
Individual-oriented	Team-oriented
Information-based	Performance-based
Intuitive-based	Research-based
Program-focused	Results-focused
Fragmented	Systemic

COMMITMENT TO SYSTEMIC IMPROVEMENT: LESSONS LEARNED

Staying the course for systemic improvement and avoiding being embraced by some or dismissed by others as a quick fix or "silver bullet" for school improvement has required the Institute to define and communicate its methods and the beliefs and research in which the approaches are rooted. Table 28.1 depicts what GLISI "is" and "is not" in terms of how it functions.

Educational leaders who participate in GLISI hear a consistent message: *Leaders of school improvement must be standards-based, data-driven, team-oriented, performance-based, research-based, results-focused, and systemic in their approach to school improvement if they are to engage, equip, and inspire their staffs to move the needle on student performance.*

Standards-Based

In addition to conducting our own research with exemplary practitioners who consistently achieve desired student achievement results, GLISI has conducted a "cross walk" of our curriculum against an array of standards, including the Interstate School Leaders Licensure Standards (ISLLC), SREB's Critical Success Factors, the Baldrige Criteria, and McREL's Balanced Leadership criteria to ensure that GLISI's training meets leadership standards. We further ensure that our training design mirrors national standards for effective professional learning (e.g., the National Staff Development Council's revised *Standards for Staff Development*, 2001). In addition, the Institute's Base Camp and Leadership Summit training support the Georgia Department of Education's focus on performance standards for instruction in schools. Rather than duplicating training conducted by the DOE, the Institute supports the emphasis on Georgia's Performance Standards, underscores the importance of unpacking standards, and provides an orientation in the need to balance "assessment of learning" (for reporting) with "assessment for learning" (for learning) in a standards-based environment. Continuing in many of these districts and some new ones in 2005–2006, the Institute is piloting yearlong, follow-up training in designated districts for three groups in each of the districts: assessment coaches, administrator leaders, and school-based leadership teams led by the principal. One of our GLISI team members has extensive training in assessment for learning and also has background working in a standards-based district, thus enabling the Institute to offer in-depth follow-up that will help these districts in the readiness phase of moving to a standards-based environment in Georgia.

Data-Driven

Many educational leaders are aware of the need to use data to make decisions; however, GLISI provides opportunities for hands-on experience guided by recognized peer expert practitioners. Through a series of break-out sessions, leaders disaggregate sample data sets and dig for root causes before diving into their own data. They experience sessions that help them balance qualitative with quantitative data from multiple sources and use the analysis of their own data sets to identify key indicators, a baseline, and targets for improvement over three years, and to set SMART (specific, measurable, attainable, relevant, and time bound) goals for improvement. They track one of these goals over the three-year course of their institute experience and report their progress in an electronic portfolio (e-Portfolio) that is shared with the Institute.

Team-Oriented

While district Change Teams attend the Base Camp and Leadership Summit cohort training, participants are charged to go back to their schools to engage Better Seeking Teams of teachers to drive their identified improvement initiative. The same is true for district team members who help their superintendent drive district change goals systemwide. The work of school improvement is simply too large and too complex to be handled by a single "superhero" principal. Participant leaders receive tips and tools for engaging and sustaining a distributed leadership approach that engages teachers as leaders in the important business of school improvement. The cohort experience is designed to help leaders reculture their schools to become more collaborative and to focus on powerful conversations, collective inquiry, and ongoing team learning. In this way, schools and districts become learning organizations (Lick, 2006; Senge et al., 2000) that focus on the continued learning of both adults and students.

Performance-Based

A critical difference in the GLISI cohort experience hinges on a "get it—do it" versus "sit and get" mentality. While the initial Base Camp and Leadership Summit cohort experience is grant funded (at approximately $2500 per participant), we remind participants that the training is not "free." The Institute expects participants to go back to their schools and districts to transfer their learning into practice. We provide high-quality materials, tips, and tools that scaffold the work; guide on-the-side support from the Improvement Initiative Coordinator (IIC); and provide focus from the superintendent that encourages transfers of learning. GLISI's performance consultants (PCs) conduct site visits to collect evidence of transfers, engage teams in reflective conversations around rubrics, and offer statewide recognition based on implementation of training with progress and results documented in an electronic portfolio (e-Portfolio). Further, Institute staff is developing performance-based modules that can be used for follow-up and with a GLISI-trained leadership performance coach to help participants develop and deepen skills related to Institute curriculum.

A Wachovia grant is funding research, development, and training for performance coaching that will result in a leadership performance coaching model, a training process, performance tools, and a Web-based knowledge management system, The Success Center, where coaches' learning can be shared and where tips, tools, and modules can be down-loaded for easy access.

Research-Focused

As Georgia Department of Education Deputy Superintendent Jeanie Weathersby (a former Institute staff member) says, "There are no silver bullets in school improvement work. There are, however, a number of research-based best practices that every educational leader should know and use." In keeping with this sage advice, GLISI's cohort training experience is based on educational and business best practices. As an example, participants complete a self-assessment of best practices in curriculum, assessment, instruction, professional learning, and technology for 21st-century learning environments. They then delve deeper by examining indicators of achievement that help them know what best practices look like in action. They go back to their schools and conduct the same self-assessment with a school-based team, conduct a "gap analysis" of where the team is in relation to where it wants to be, and develop a plan of action for implementation of selected best practices related to their improvement initiative. Through entries in their Leader Journal and through documentation of progress and results in an electronic portfolio (e-Portfolio), leaders capture and share their learning with the Institute.

Results-Focused

GLISI cohort training helps leaders begin with the end in mind by focusing like a laser beam on their results. Participants emerge from the five-day Base Camp and Leadership Summit training experience with clearly articulated SMART goals and chart their progress at yearly intervals over a three-year period. The Institute acclaims leaders who implement GLISI training and document progress and results as Educational Celebrities with recognition in front of peers. The Institute continues to report results of cohort participants to the Georgia Office of Planning and Budget. Our success is directly tied to the success of our participants; therefore, we are literally "all in this together" as we strive to improve the bottom line—student achievement and school improvement—across Georgia.

Systemic

The Institute team does not sugarcoat the fact that school improvement is hard work. Base Camp and Leadership Summit programs launch a continuous improvement journey focused on organizational effectiveness and student achievement that is never-ending. As the old saying goes, "If this were easy work, anyone could do it." The successful leader is one who engages the hearts and minds of every person in the school and in the community in the climb toward ensuring high-quality learning for every adult in order to achieve high-quality learning for each student. Band-Aids, nips and tucks, and program-of-the-month approaches are neither adequate nor sufficient for sustained school improvement. In today's time of changing conditions and rising expectations, educational leaders must lead school improvement by engaging their entire staff in analyzing disaggregated data, setting learning improvement targets, analyzing learning processes and root causes of problems, monitoring learning improvement, leveraging tools and technology, and identifying and utilizing best practices to achieve desired student performance. More than that, educational leaders must inspire others, communicate with and engage others in achieving a shared vision, plan and develop strategy, access resources and organize structure, manage the change, coach performance, and nurture a culture that "leaves no child behind" in a complex and ever-changing environment. This heroic charge demands a systemic versus a fragmented approach—one that invites all stakeholders to engage in the critical work of improving our schools and creating a future of hope and achievement for all students. Thanks to the visionary leaders from education and business who spawned the Institute design, GLISI takes an out-of-the-box, systemic approach that equips, supports, and inspires Georgia's educational leaders to drive change for student success.

RECOMMENDATIONS

For those who wish to leave the beaten path and explore out-of-the-box solutions for improving leader quality, we first recommend that you align your efforts with other like-minded partners willing to create and share governance of an entity outside traditional structures that can be nimble, innovative, and adaptive. Next, create a process for development of curriculum and performance support that focuses not on competencies, but on the best practices of exemplary educational leaders. Glean those practices from those who have actually led achievement of improved student success in their schools or who have developed and led winning organizations outside education.

Tap leaders willing and able to teach and coach others, who are consciously competent in what leaders must do, and who can teach and influence others to do the work well. Affirm, affirm, affirm school and district leaders and those who prepare new leaders, and challenge, challenge, challenge them to move beyond excuses and blaming to create school and university cultures that support measurable success for all—all students, all teachers, and all leaders.

Be a model of what you teach, treat those you serve as customers, and decide and communicate the value you can provide. Work as hard to codify and share new knowledge as you do to develop leaders who are solid performers; create networks of leaders who will support each other and partners who will sponsor your causes and influence needed policy changes.

Most important, recognize the mantle of leadership you are taking on personally if you choose to implement such an out-of-the-box solution and embrace the work. Remind yourself every day that your job is to develop leaders who will in turn develop the minds and talents of students. In doing so, you will find, as have those who work together for Georgia's Leadership Institute for School Improvement, that you will never work a single day of your life that is not devoted to this cause. Every day will be an opportunity to do what you love and were called to do.

For further information on Georgia's Leadership Institute for School Improvement, contact Deb Page, executive director, at deb.page@galeaders.org or Dr. Gale Hulme, director of strategic initiatives, at gale.hulme@galeaders.org

29

Improving Schools Through Statewide Collaboration

Stephen M. Preston

The traditional roles and responsibilities of State Departments of Education (SDOEs) must be transformed if large numbers of schools are going to develop the capacity to sustain successful innovation and improvement. State Departments of Education are somewhat like chelating molecules in inorganic chemistry. Alone they are inert; they can do little on their own, but they have a tremendous capacity to attract and bond with other molecules to make more complex and useful compounds in response to their environment. SDOEs must use that capacity to meet the ever-changing needs of their states' children and youth.

This chapter provides insight into the roles and responsibilities of State Departments of Education and the powerful potential they have to influence school improvement—if they take it. The case is made for the critical ingredient being a statewide dialogue followed by true, long-term collaboration with and among all education stakeholders, particularly schools. It argues that such a statewide approach is the best assurance we have to date for encouraging sustainable long-term school improvement in most schools. And, perhaps most important, an argument is offered for the absolute necessity of a unifying idea to ignite and sustain such change.

THE NECESSARY ROLES FOR SUCCESS

The three most critical roles of State Departments of Education are:

- Leadership
- Resources
- Regulation

SDOEs have traditionally operated primarily as regulatory agencies, either directly or indirectly administering state and federal funds through specified programs. This is done through state laws; state board rules; and SDOE regulations, guidelines, and guidance, including the provision of various resources. Even when SDOEs provide technical assistance, workshops, seminars, drive-ins, implementation guides, and detailed guidance, it is most often to carry out state law, state board rules, or SDOE regulations. While it is true that most of the laws, rules, and regulations are believed to encourage and support good, statewide education, research and experience have long demonstrated that regulating with laws and rules, or even enticing with funding and programs alone have had, at most, spotty impact on school improvement. Perhaps most problematic, this regulation is often confused with leadership, but it is not. It is still regulation, benevolent though it may be. SDOEs must keep this role to a minimum—only to the extent necessary to physically and emotionally protect children and to husband the resources of the state provided by taxation. This can be done with a fraction of the staff available to most SDOEs. Building capacity within schools to sustain effective practice that results in success for all students is, however, much more labor intensive and the proper emphasis of the SDOE.

Resources are an extension of regulation. Most often regulation has to do with the allocation, distribution, and uses of resources, particularly funding. Perhaps, however, the most important resource that is traditionally provided by state agencies is personnel. One of the keys for successful school improvement in a state lies in how that state chooses to deploy those personnel—and the resources that accompany them. If they are all employed in regulation and monitoring, little improvement can be expected. If, however, they are employed as leaders in support of a clear mission supporting a collaboratively established vision of high levels of learning, improvement is more likely. Many state and federal programs in Georgia are currently undergoing this transformation from regulating resources (and therefore practice), to using those resources to lead large-scale improvement. The process is difficult, however, and will take time because the personnel hired to carry out regulations and monitor expenditures are often not necessarily those with the knowledge, skills, or experience to carry out the much more complicated and demanding role of leading change. Leading statewide change is not the same job as running a state or federal program.

Leadership is, of course, the most important of the three roles. Leadership at the state level cannot be just the Superintendent, Deputies, and the state board. It must be everyone in the SDOE. State leadership, defined as the whole-state team, must *inspire, encourage, challenge, and champion a common, attainable vision.* Above all, SDOEs must enable local districts and schools to *build the capacity to sustain research-based change that has been proven to increase student success.* Regulation and resource allocation alone have never accomplished this. There are, however, strategies, attitudes, and a state culture that can accomplish *high-quality, sustained school improvement by building administrator and teacher collaboration concentrating on the actual work of their students!* Resources and regulation *must* support the leadership role. This may best be done by limiting such regulation. To be successful, leadership must be flexible, able to respond to changing conditions in a timely manner. Laws, rules, and regulations are, by definition, long term and difficult to change. Therefore, effective leadership requires the most open-ended rules and regulations within the context of state law. If the bureaucracy is allowed to dictate policy in the name of "requirements," responsive leadership will be thwarted.

CONNECTING THE DOTS

For too long, individual state and federal education programs within SDOEs have operated virtually independently, perusing their specific interests and perceived problems and serving esoteric customers. This is not only encouraged by the way state and federal education legislation is written, but even more so by the way the states and districts organize themselves and distribute resources. Most state staff members are responsible for a specific state or federal "program" or "title" created by different entities with different constituencies and different agendas. The SDOE must take the responsibility for making a coherent whole of all of the various goals, agendas, and budgets. This task must begin internally. The typical "turf guarding" and myopic vision of how to support school improvement must be given up in support of a transparent, truly collaborative, client-centered capacity-building approach to statewide support. Instead of the usual "How can my program (project, funding source, or responsibility) show the way to student achievement?" SDOEs must ask, with a single voice, "How can we pool our talents and resources to be of the greatest service to our clients, both directly and indirectly?" This may be the most difficult task of all for a SDOE. If education is classically slow to change, SDOEs are the slowest of the education entities to change for all of the reasons with which we are all too familiar.

Georgia has begun to address this task in several ways. First and foremost, Superintendent Cathy Cox began her administration by hiring SDOE leaders on the basis of their commitment to, and skills in, building and sustaining a team approach to the work of the organization. As an illustration, the state's most important current initiative is the implementation of the Georgia Performance Standards, the curricular performance standards that must be the basis for any and all improvement in student achievement. This implementation is being led not by a single office, as would be the case in most SDOEs, but through the collaboration of the two offices most responsible for supporting schools and teachers in the classroom—Curriculum and Instruction (Division of Curriculum) and Teacher and Student Support (Division of School Improvement). These offices and their divisions are collaborating to lead the orientation and training of more than one hundred twenty thousand teachers and administrators in the delivery of a performance curriculum requiring almost all teachers and administrators to consider student learning and, more important, their role in that learning, in a completely new way—a daunting task that will take years but must, in part, start with the SDOE "getting its act together!"

More specifically, and with a potentially equal impact, is the department's commitment to a truly comprehensive, coherent approach to service to districts and schools. This is being actualized, in part, in the form of a District Comprehensive School Improvement Plan. Districts will be expected to identify and prioritize their district and schoolwide needs first and then consider all state and federal resources to meet those needs. In order for districts to do this, the program managers at the state level must first agree what they will have to do within and among their own spheres of influence to facilitate this planning approach. This is a departure from "standard operating procedures" in that the program managers will have to consider the larger mission first and then any requirements of their own programs second, instead of the reverse, which is most often the case. The Georgia SDOE has committed itself to a year of planning and organizing in pursuit of this approach.

SDOE solidarity is necessary but not sufficient to ensure success for Georgia's students. Leading by example, SDOEs must pull all other agencies, entities, and stakeholders concerned with public education together to share the vision and mission. SDOE leadership is in a unique position to "connect the dots" for public education. For example:

• In the role of keeping abreast of ongoing research and development around the country, SDOEs are in a position to identify the ideas, trends, research, and individual nationwide visionaries and practitioners who can be drawn upon to add their unique piece to the puzzle of school improvement in their state or even in different regions and districts of their state.

• In their national and regional networking role, SDOEs can draw on personal and professional contacts with like-minded educators not only in other SDOEs, but at the federal level, in regional laboratories, professional associations, and leading universities for meaningful collaborative relationships, bringing research and experience from these entities into the state and their schools.

• Within its responsibility of representing and being responsible for the interests of education in each state lies perhaps the SDOE's most powerful role. First, the SDOE must use its power of funding and regulation not just to create and run programs, but to foster coordination and collaboration throughout the state. As a matter of fact, the only proper role of funding and regulation must be to foster collaboration at all levels among all stakeholders for student success. Second, most SDOEs have natural political and personal connections to the governor's office, the legislature, the university system, the state regional education support agencies, local schools and school districts, and the often overlooked private sector. These state-level informal networks can be a powerful leadership tool not readily available to most regional or district educators within the state.

All of these natural roles can be channeled and called upon to foster a statewide dialogue leading toward a collaborative vision. Each state stakeholder can then identify realistic missions for their particular niche in that vision. SDOE efforts cannot be just for narrow, short-term success, either; these efforts must be for broad, long-term *sustained* impact! Collaboration must span multiple governors, legislatures, university presidents and deans and superintendents, and state and local agencies over time. The state must use its power and position to facilitate a long-term, collaborative vision. To have a statewide testing program is not a vision; how schools work to increase their students' success on state tests can be a vision. The advantage of a state bureaucracy with a powerful vision of student learning is that it can influence statewide leadership, from school leadership teams to the governor, by organizing around success and ensuring that succeeding generations of the bureaucracy and the body politic understand, share, and sustain the dream in its most active, practical version from year to year—influencing education leadership at all levels as it changes over time. This requires a tremendous vision and a cooperative combination of leaders to get such a journey under way, with just the right combination of internal and external forces and pressures. This country, and this state in particular, have such a combination now. It is a chance none of us can afford to let slip through our grasp. It is the best chance that has come in thirty years, and it may be another thirty years before it comes again. With drivers like No Child Left Behind and the Georgia Performance Standards, and with enablers like new and vibrant leadership and "the right people on the bus in the right seats" (Collins, 2001), Georgia (and the nation) has a chance like never before.

To take advantage of this opportunity, state leadership must become *transformational*. Leadership may be described as "transformational leadership" or "transactional leadership." Both are useful and necessary in particular circumstances. *Transactional leadership* strives to take what is there and make it better by improving it, strengthening it, and reorganizing it. This has been the traditional leadership approach assumed by SDOEs—"we must dedicate ourselves to making schools better!" Since this approach to leadership is all in the realm of known practice, it is "low-risk" change. *Transformational leadership*, on the other hand, strives to take what is there and improve it by making it into something different—"We must dedicate ourselves to envisioning and creating a different kind of school!" A transformational twist on the old adage, "If you keep on doing what you are doing, you will keep on getting what you always got," would be, "Even if you do a better job of what you're doing in schools, you still may get only the schools (or results) you always had." Since this leadership strategy enters the realm of the unknown, it is "high-risk" and, therefore, outside the comfort zone of the timid leader. Evidence in Georgia shows that "more/better of the same" has not brought significant increases in student learning.

The case of professional development in Georgia illustrates this well. According to Annual Program Reports (see http://public.doe.k12.ga.us/tss_school_prolearning .aspx), Georgia spends more than $30,000,000 a year of state allocated funds on professional development. In 2003, Georgia concluded an extensive evaluation of staff development in the state to ascertain to what end these funds were being spent. Georgia Law and Georgia State Board Rule indicated that the two main purposes of staff development in Georgia were to (a) increase the knowledge and skills of certified personnel and (b) support the recertification (license renewal) of teachers and administrators. The state evaluation not only demonstrated that there was overwhelming evidence that staff development in Georgia did both of those things, but that the workshops, seminars, courses, and conferences were generally of high quality and well received by the majority of participants when participants chose their activities and experiences. The Georgia Staff Development Program was meeting the expectations of the Georgia Legislature, the State Board, the SDOE, and consumers—teachers and administrators. Even so, the evaluation had to conclude that staff development was largely ineffective in Georgia! How could that be? How could a program that met the requirements of the law, state board rules, and the expectations of not only the providers but also the customers be unsuccessful? The facts were that the same evaluation was unable to find more than 5% to 10% of the staff development activities in the state in evidence in classrooms—therefore very low transference into classroom practice and negligible impact. The problem turned out to be simple and almost universal in every state. Staff development had always been based upon the assumption, "If you give them good stuff, they will use it." Much literature and research in the last several years has highlighted this "knowing-doing gap"—that just because we "know" what to do, it doesn't mean that we necessarily "do" what we "know" (Pfeffer & Sutton, 2000). So, Georgia realized that continuing to do a great job of something that wasn't working would be pointless. Staff development must be transformed in Georgia; the state must pursue a different kind of staff development, with different intentions and purposes and originating from a different stakeholder group than before if we are to expect different results. Georgia has come to call its transformation of staff development "Professional Learning." The state must understand and publicly communicate such transformations in its entire approach to school improvement, not just professional learning, to fulfill its leadership role and be successful. How might a state accomplish this?

BUILDING REGIONAL AND LOCAL CAPACITY

All too often, SDOEs believe that as instruments of the state, they are supposed to know what schools ought to do and that knowledge can best be expressed by creating just the right combination of programs, funding, and guidance that will lead to school improvement, the more "teacher proof" and "school proof" the better. Schools and school districts often ask for and encourage this—"just tell us (show us) what to do and how to do it." Unfortunately, SDOEs often try to comply. We now see that not only the problem but also the solution is best understood and addressed by the staff at the school and perhaps, at most, in conjunction with the staff at the district level. So what does that leave an SDOE to do? The answer is analogous to what we all know to be good teaching practice—*facilitate learning* rather than *direct learning.* The state must not "tell" or "show" systems and schools what to do, but must do all it can to *build the capacity* (i.e., both willingness and ability) of schools and school districts to identify and prioritize their own needs and to seek out and develop their own solutions, with accompanying knowledge and skills, for implementation. This is state leadership!

How do SDOEs then facilitate change and improvement rather than direct it? Among the keys to accomplishing this goal are a commitment to extensive, constant communications and to eliciting and using input from practitioners and sharing state decisions with them. The objective of such input must be increased decentralization and collaboration with education professionals across the state. Most critical, however, is the community development of vision, a powerful idea that can drive all action.

Communications

Effective communications are an important element of every relationship, especially a relationship as complex as a state. Everyone must feel the urgency and must feel a part of the solution, not a recipient of it: co-opt everyone. State leadership must ensure that the collaboration is a win-win situation for all stakeholders and that all stakeholders can see the actualization of their particular goals in the larger effort. In addition, this statewide dialogue must be ongoing among all stakeholders. Too often, busy stakeholders believe that working very hard to agree on a plan is enough; that once the agreed-upon plan is in place, everyone can go and do their own part. This will not work. The dialogue must be regular and continuous. Finally, communication must be by and between the appropriate individuals and groups—and timely. Technology and personal contacts are the keys.

Go to the Source

Ask practitioners what needs to be supported and encouraged and what needs to be changed—and why—from a practical point of view; people in schools know a lot more than SDOEs do about what's needed and what's possible. This does not mean that all the state has to do is turn around and do whatever the schools say they should do. The state's job is to find a way to use its unique position and point of view to translate what it learns from practitioners into successful state strategies that have the potential to be used successfully by the greatest number of schools and school districts. Again, using professional development in Georgia as an example, SDOE staff began their examination of state staff development in two ways. The first was to travel around the state, talking to groups of local educators (central office and school leadership) in Regional Education Service Agencies (RESAs) and state and regional professional association meetings. These conversations were basically, "What should the state continue to do that has facilitated your work? What can the state stop doing that is standing in the way of your improvement efforts?" And, "What is the state not doing that it should be doing to support your improvement efforts?" At that point, there was no definitive state vision or mission for staff development or school improvement. On the contrary, the point of these conversations was to help state leadership conceptualize a vision and mission. Second, the state established a Georgia Staff Development Advisory Committee made up of twenty of the state's most experienced Professional Development Directors from school systems and regional service agencies (RESAs). This advisory committee was asked to generate more specific recommendations based on feedback from the statewide conversations and their own extensive experience. Their recommendations were used to inform the state vision and mission and to formulate new and revised state rules and regulations that would facilitate the vision and mission and specifically address particular needs uncovered in the statewide conversations. The extensive statewide evolution of professional development validated these directions and provided details for specific emphasis by the state.

Share the Load, Responsibility, and Success (Decentralization and Collaboration)

The state should not give up its regulatory power; it must learn to use it as a tool to facilitate learning and build the capacity of schools and school districts. This can take the form of successfully *enabling* rules and regulations that *encourage and reward experimentation, innovation, and risk taking.* Experience at the state level in Georgia has demonstrated without a doubt that you cannot really *force* a school district to do anything that is going to last. State regulations typically *prevent* districts from acting or *require* districts to comply. Such regulations most often result in proforma compliance and are almost always a waste of everyone's time and energy. The state must support those who are ready to change, or willing to risk it, and sustain the rest by encouraging them to reach that level—all the while trying to be equitable and fair to all. Only in a few cases should it be necessary to use the power of law, board rule, and the budget to get some sort of movement, any sort of movement, on the part of a school district. Even then, if the rules allow alternative compliance, districts are more likely to genuinely meet expectations.

From the statewide conversations in Georgia and with the help of the Advisory Committee in Georgia, there emerged a series of modifications to state board rules that offered districts and schools the opportunity to go outside of existing regulations and propose alternatives that would better fit their needs. For example, the extensive state evaluation of professional development in Georgia demonstrated beyond any doubt that the heavy emphasis in staff development on renewal of their professional license (recertification) by measuring seat time hours was responsible, at least indirectly, for the experiences not being translated into the classroom. Teachers and principals were often more concerned with how many hours credit they were earning rather than applying what they had learned in the classroom. Many respondents even indicated that they never actually connected the work they were doing to gain recertification with any improvement or changed behavior in the classroom. One of the most promising ways to address that problem was to convert to a "performance-based" recertification process, thus shifting the purpose of professional development from counting hours for recertification to teacher learning activities and experiences based on the work they were actually doing with students—improving teacher knowledge and skills identified from the explicit needs of their students in the classes they are teaching now. Instead of passing Georgia State Board rules requiring this approach or requiring that approach in order to qualify for various state funds, the state modified its rules to allow systems that wished to pursue this idea to submit a plan for approval. The State Board rules allowing this alternative were left very open-ended to allow for as much individual differences in systems and schools as possible. These state rule changes, therefore, encourage and reward good practices without requiring them. A school or district, for example, is now encouraged through State Board rule to adopt a policy that doubles certification renewal credit if a teacher or group of teachers demonstrates use of the concept(s) in their classrooms; they can triple credit by also demonstrating measurable improvement in student achievement resulting from the professional learning experience. This is not required, but is offered as a rewarding alternative and an incentive to pursue effective practices—facilitate, don't regulate!

Just as the secret to optimum performance in an SDOE is dependent upon close collaboration between divisions and offices, so too is successful statewide improvement dependent on collaboration and a shared vision among all education stakeholders. As a matter of fact, without such statewide collaboration, student success is much less likely. The SDOE, or any other state education entity, can be well led, well organized, and effectively integrated—yet statewide success for children and youth may not be realized. Central to Georgia's school improvement initiatives is its commitment to involve all direct and indirect stakeholders in formulating and sharing the vision and collaborative pursuit of a common mission. Perhaps the epitome of this collaborative commitment in Georgia is the Regional Support Teams. These teams are currently focused on addressing Needs Improvement (NI) schools identified through No Child Left Behind (NCLB). The state is divided into five regions, and an intra-agency team made up of SDOE, Regional Educational Service Agency (RESA), Georgia Learning Resource Center (special education), and university staff serves each region. One of the strengths of these teams is that they are not centralized in Atlanta, but regionally based and made up of educators from that area who are familiar with regional schools. This level and extent of commitment and collaboration has never existed in Georgia before.

Promote Powerful Ideas: The Most Critical Task!

A catalyst, a unifying vision with a small collection of powerful but simple ideas, is necessary to transform a critical mass of schools in a state to the extent that sustainable, statewide school improvement can be expected. The transformation of education in a state can begin without the powerful ideas being articulated in detail, but all aspects of the organization, communication, and collaboration must, ultimately, have one or more powerful ideas to ripen into fruitful statewide impact that can be sustained and become "standard operating procedure." The transformational process, when pursued with vigor and honesty, will generate the powerful ideas if the leadership and the rank-and-file have the professional and political will.

The idea of "professional and political will" cannot be overemphasized. Transformational leadership in any organization requires a level of dedication and effort and a degree of serious risk taking that many leaders and organizations are not willing to pursue vigorously enough to realize success. Almost always such transformation requires a significant shift in the way organizations view their mission and, particularly, the appropriate ways to pursue that mission. Organizations change missions much more readily than they do the "way" they do business and the "why" (their culture). It is difficult to admit that the way you have done your job for twenty years may not be the best way to do it. This is particularly true in a profession like education where the job is so personal, so akin to one's beliefs about one's individual worth. If your mission throughout your career has been to help children, it is especially difficult to believe that you may have been doing an inadequate job all of that time. The same is true of the professionals in all of the education-stakeholder organizations, since most of the professionals in those organizations began their careers as teachers and still identify helping children as the motivation for their careers.

This is one of the main reasons why a really powerful idea is necessary to actualize any lasting transformation. You are asking people, often, to reconsider their closely held life beliefs. Beliefs and values, by definition, are very difficult to modify. Because of that, the notions that would suggest such changes must present the individual and the organization not only with a new idea, but with practical ways to make the idea a reality. Perhaps most important, the idea must describe a win-win scenario for those who buy into it. Instead, for example, of casting a new idea as something completely new and different, find a way to cast the idea as a logical, vibrant extension of or variation on what the group members are already doing. In that way, the last twenty years are not seen as a waste, and the new idea is just extended practice for what you always wanted to accomplish anyway! This, in essence, is making a transformational change (high risk) "feel" like a transactional change (low risk). Such a transformation may best be realized through real-life demonstration by the organization and its leadership. In other words, you must practice what you preach. If the idea includes professional learning teams and study groups, for instance, then the SDOE must model the idea at its level by generating appropriate types of learning teams that fit and advance the mission of the SDOE— and the practice must be sustained and demonstrate success. It may take time to convince some districts that you are actually going to continue to "walk the talk." Care also must be taken to ensure that the powerful ideas are not confused with, or seen through the lens of, the old regulations or guidelines. The absolute key is to avoid requiring too much; instead, offer creative ideas and reward those who pursue them. Through the application, then, of traditional and nontraditional state roles and the application of a few proven leadership practices statewide, pioneer school districts that are ready to consider a few unifying ideas that are powerful enough for statewide, sustained change can serve as the catalysts to begin the transformation across the state.

CONCLUSION: ONE POWERFUL IDEA AND ONE STATE

As an illustration, consider the following powerful idea and its state application.

To address statewide school improvement and respond to the concepts inherent in NCLB, the state has adopted and is nourishing a simple but powerful idea—that the crux of all school improvement lies with *teachers working in collaborative teams working on the work of the students.* And that's it. Nothing else is necessary. This is not a program, not a project, not a new federal title; this is not a new "Ivory Tower" concept. This is one of those big ideas that has grown out of school practices and been generated by building-level practitioners trying to solve the learning problems of real schools. This is what the Whole-Faculty Study Group System is all about! This idea is almost 180 degrees from the concept of school improvement pursued by professional educators for the past fifty years.

The emphasis has always been on improving teaching, or leadership, or resources, or organization, or structure. None of those approaches alone have ever worked. The approaches have worked only in so far as the personality of a powerful leader has made them work together. The continuous improvement of the people and organization that we have always identified as essential to the endeavor must continue, but we now know that the emphasis must be on learning—learning by everyone in the school, from students to teachers to administrators, and including all support staff— "a community of learners." By now the idea of a professional learning community has been researched and replicated extensively enough across the country to have gained our confidence.

Georgia finds itself in an ideal position to advance just such a high-impact, transformational idea. The state has been in the process of such a transformation for over two years. Like all other states, Georgia is being driven by the ideas of No Child Left Behind (NCLB). Regardless of how one feels about this legislation, in Georgia it has led many educators to reconsider perhaps long-held, even subconscious beliefs about whether *all children can, in fact, learn.* That all children can learn is the absolute, fundamental belief that must be held by every teacher and administrator in a school if that school is to be fully successful. Every teacher and administrator in a school must say, as Alan Blankstein (2004) says, "failure is not an option." We must do "whatever it takes" to ensure success for all students (DuFour, Eaker, Karhanek, & DuFour, 2004). We must expect, and demand, high levels of achievement and success for all students. This is truly a "powerful new but simple idea" for many educators.

If all children are to learn, research has shown us that the most important ingredient of all, at the top of Marzano's (2003) research-based factors for school success, is a "guaranteed and viable curriculum." Georgia is in the midst of a five-year introduction of performance-based curricular standards—The Georgia Performance Standards (GPS). A common, agreed-upon curriculum is absolutely essential to the idea of "collaborative teams of teachers working on the work of students" (e.g., see Lick, 2006). The isolation of teachers and their individual interpretations of the curriculum have long been recognized as a detriment to student and school success. Only when collaborative teams of teachers can (a) come to a common understanding of the curriculum in performance terms and (b) agree on periodic common assessments and use those assessments to compare student work, will high-quality, sustainable instruction ensure continuous student success. Only then can true "professional learning communities" be realized. It all starts with the standards-based curriculum and an effective context for delivering that curriculum—professional learning communities.

Georgia is also fortunate to have cooperative leadership at this critical time. The Governor's Office, the State Superintendent, and State Board are on the same page politically and fiscally. Added to this is the creation by the State Superintendent of a large, powerful, and well-led Office of Teacher and Student Support with a well-funded School Improvement Division collaborating with an experienced, well-led Curriculum and Instruction Division. This collaboration and leadership at the SDOE has nurtured alignment with all major education entities in the state, public and private. Perhaps for the first time in the history of Georgia education, these entities are speaking the same language, are heading in a common direction, and agree on simple but powerful means and ends. This has contributed to a significant statewide sense of optimism and hope. This latter cannot be overemphasized as a keystone factor in any success the state might realize in the next decade. That sense of the possibility of success, if we just have the personal and institutional will to pursue it, is perhaps the most important goal of good leadership.

So, we see in Georgia a combination of drivers and enablers that, taken together, can mean success for our state's children and youth. The combination of (a) the growth of a fundamental and necessary belief ("all children can learn") with a viable curriculum (Georgia Performance Standards) and (b) a powerful idea (teachers working collaboratively within the context of a professional learning community) supported by positive leadership and a legislature that trusts—and is willing to fund—this great leap forward in education in the state are the essential elements for success. Any state can lead in this way!

30

Establishing a Support Network

The National Whole-Faculty Study Groups Center

Carlene U. Murphy

As I look through my attic window at the haze, I wonder what readers envision when they see "National Whole-Faculty Study Groups Center." A slick office building? An executive suite? A foyer with a receptionist? Members of the staff at the water cooler? Most people seem to envision a physical facility with people who work within a designated area. How different reality can be! The National Whole-Faculty Study Groups Center is both a place and a concept. The place fits none of the previous descriptions. Maybe someday it will, but not today. Today it is the attic of my home, the third floor of a house that sits on a hill. I have a view of the city of Augusta as I look out the window in front of me. Just as I have a wide, spacious view of the city, I have an ambitious, long-term vision for Whole-Faculty Study Groups (WFSGs). My vision of the professional development system that my colleagues and I developed has grown from being "a part of a training design put in place in three schools in Augusta in 1987" to being "a system that

261

hundreds of schools are using today to connect teacher learning to student learning." The place or location of the Center could be anywhere, but, most important, the conceptual approach of the Center can benefit any school anywhere.

BRIEF HISTORY OF THE CENTER

Chapter 1 in the companion book to this fieldbook, *Whole-Faculty Study Groups: Creating Professional Learning Communities That Target Student Learning* (Murphy & Lick, 2005), gives the history, development, and evolution behind the WFSG System. A quick look backward establishes the context for the National WFSG Center. History is important. It tells how a people, an idea, or a procedure became a reality and how time and circumstances shape the present.

The WFSG System, in its current form, represents an approach that grew from many people and applications in many different contexts in many schools. As someone once said to me, "You weren't born five feet tall." The birthing of the WFSG System, or WFSGs, took hard, dedicated labor. Bruce Joyce and Beverly Showers, who based their research on how teachers implement what they have been trained to do, guided the beginning of the study-group work and established many of the WFSG procedural guidelines used today. The teachers in what we called the Models of Teaching schools in Augusta formed study groups, and, through them, we learned more about how to work with the groups so that student effects could be realized. After I retired from the school district in Augusta, I had to learn how to work with study groups when the content was not predetermined. In Augusta, all of the study groups were in various stages of training in how to use several models of teaching with students appropriately.

In Augusta schools, the content was "brought in" or predetermined. Schools in San Diego, California; Round Rock, Texas; Americus, Georgia; and Greeley, Colorado, were the primary places where we learned how to use a school-based process for determining what the study groups would do. The WFSG Decision-Making Cycle was a giant step forward in the evolution of the WFSG System. The next step in the evolution phase came when I began working with ATLAS Communities, one of the national comprehensive school reform program models. The five years I worked in ATLAS schools involved all areas of the country, especially the inner-city schools in New York City, Detroit, and Philadelphia, and proved that the WFSG System could be replicated in any elementary, middle, and high school. The burden of traveling becoming too great, I decided to spend more time at home in Augusta and establish the National WFSG Center. With the Internet and all the technologies of today, it is possible to be in touch with anyone anywhere. With a deep, experiential, and growing knowledge base and experts and consultants available in Augusta and around the country, the Center, as a physical place and as a concept, became a reality.

VISION OF THE CENTER

We envision the National WFSG Center as "the exemplary learning organization that provides systemic support for creating collaborative cultures ensuring student success." The key phrases in our vision statement are *learning organization, systemic support, collaborative cultures,* and *student success.*

As WFSG consultants work with faculties, we are conscious of what Peter Senge (1990) said in *The Fifth Discipline: The Art and Practice of the Learning Organization,* "Organizations that excel will discover how to tap people's commitment and capacity to learn at all levels of the organization." This means that the Center must help study groups design their own learning experiences to target the instructional needs of their students. Teachers' commitments deepen as they see that their leaders are not going to tell them what to do and how to do it. Leaders give study groups feedback while allowing groups to be self-directed. As commitment grows, individual capacity for new learning also grows. Not only are WFSGs tapping into the commitment and capacity of classroom teachers, they are giving equal attention to media specialists, counselors, coaches, special educators, and administrators. Everyone in the organization is expected to be a learner and to be respected as a learner.

Systemic support means touching every individual in the organization. WFSGs were conceived with "whole" as the central concept. We have insisted, from working with the first faculties in 1987, that every faculty member must be a member of a study group. In that way, every part of the school is influenced. As members of every group expand their capacities, the whole organization becomes more capable of fulfilling its mission. We believe, as our vision implies, that as individuals grow, the school progressively grows. "Whole" is nonnegotiable when the Center works with a school.

Building collaborative cultures takes time, but not as much time as we thought when we began organizing whole faculties into study groups. Once study groups are in place and groups are doing substantive, meaningful work, we see shifts in the culture. Everyone is talking more about learning, their own learning and their students' learning. There is more sharing of resources. The ground rules change. For example, when once the conversation in the teachers' lounge focused on Friday night football or how bad the kids are, it now is okay to talk about teaching and learning. Norms that study groups establish become norms for faculty meetings. The WFSG System creates changes in roles and relationships among the staff. Faculties need support as "all teachers are leaders" is actualized, and status, in terms of experience and certification, becomes minimized. Often, WFSG consultants spend as much time strengthening these new interrelationships as they spend supporting the actual work of the study groups.

Student success is why we do what we do. As educators, our primary goal is student success. In the WFSG System, students are first, and our students help us determine what we need to do. For example, students not mastering basic computation skills are telling their teachers that they may need to identify or develop more effective strategies for teaching mathematics. WFSG consultants routinely ask, "What are your students learning and achieving as a result of what you are learning and doing in your study groups?"

MISSION OF THE CENTER

The mission of the National WFSG Center is: "to ensure student achievement through the authentic application of the WFSG System in schools worldwide." The key words in the mission are *student achievement, authentic application,* and *worldwide.*

The WFSG System is based on what students need others to do. The *grounding questions* are: What do students need teachers to do so teachers will be more knowledgeable about what they teach? What do students need teachers to do so teachers will be more skillful in how they teach? The process of determining what students need begins with looking at student achievement data. On study-group action plans, groups hold themselves accountable by what students learn as a result of the actions that teachers take in their study groups.

Authentic application of the WFSG System is the Center's greatest concern. The fact is that once the system is described in print (e.g., in WFSG books by Corwin Press, i.e., Murphy & Lick, 1998, 2001, 2005) and shown on video (e.g., produced by Video Journal of Education) and these materials are distributed worldwide on the open market, the Center cannot control how faculties apply the system in schools. Some purchasers of the book may read only a part of the book, lessening their chances of understanding how all the parts fit. Purchasers of the first edition may not purchase later editions and not be aware of how the system has been modified to increase the effectiveness of the system. WFSG book readers may interpret the aspects of the system themselves and apply the information as they understand it. The Center would have no knowledge of interpretations or how the information was used. A principal or other leader may purchase the video, view parts of it, and implement only part of the system. The Center has no control over who purchases the materials or how the materials are implemented.

One caution we have taken is to have the term, Whole-Faculty Study Groups®, registered in my name in the U.S. Patent and Trademark Office. The notification letter stated that we are now privileged to use the "®" symbol and/or the notation "Registered—U.S. Patent and Trademark Office" in connection with the term. We submitted the application so that no one else can use the term and apply a different definition and set of procedures. This will not ensure authentic application of the WFSG System, but it will hopefully give us some control over the use of the term or name.

The surest path to authentic application is to have a WFSG consultant work with a school through the initiation, implementation, and institutionalization stages. Arrangements for such consultants can be made through the Center. Such consulting can be done directly or through a combination of on-site/off-site planning. *Authentic application* means that Steps 1–4 of the WFSG Decision-Making Cycle are followed when making decisions about what study groups will do and how the groups will be organized, and that Steps 5–7 are followed once the study groups are formed. It also means that the fifteen WFSG procedural guidelines are properly enacted. For example, one guideline is that study groups meet weekly for about an hour or every other week for a longer period of time. We hear faculties say that they are implementing WFSGs, yet their study groups meet only once a month. Such schools are not authentically applying the WFSG guidelines. As stated earlier, the National WFSG Center has no way of monitoring the hundreds of schools that implement most or all of the WFSG System. Experience has shown, however, that if the WFSG System is not authentically applied, the results are diminished, sometimes significantly. The Center's Advisory Board has discussed certifying schools that meet the authentic application standard; however, we have not yet determined the best way to do it.

To have "worldwide" in the mission statement may seem overly ambitious. Our efforts in this direction have already started. There are schools in Canada implementing

WFSGs. The Center is currently reaching out to K–12 international schools and their professional organizations to explore opportunities for implementing the WFSG System in schools serving students from many different nations. We are beginning a partnership with RubiconAtlas, which is serving schools worldwide in the area of curriculum mapping (see http://www.rubiconatlas.com). RubiconAtlas is adding to and modifying its systems to accommodate WFSGs, which means schools implementing WFSGs can post action plans and logs on the Web site as well as connect study-group work to curriculum and performance standards adopted by individual states and countries.

ACCOMPLISHING THE MISSION OF THE CENTER

The National WFSG Center will accomplish its mission through people, programs, and products and resources.

People

WFSG Consultants. The Center has no staff in Augusta other than me as the Director. Currently, there are four WFSG consultants who live in different sections of the country. The WFSG consultants work full- or part-time for the Center in schools that are in various stages of implementing WFSGs. I have twenty years of experience working with study groups, two consultants have twelve years experience, one has eight, and one has five. The consultants initially went through formal training experiences and worked alongside me in schools before working on their own in WFSG schools. They have been members of WFSGs, have supported study groups in various ways, and have worked in WFSG schools reflecting different demographics and all grade levels. These individuals have demonstrated exceptional ability in working with whole faculties, small groups, and individuals. They understand the change process and how to support school teachers and leaders.

In addition to the consultants, there are teachers and principals who are "on call" and will provide limited service when a school specifically requests a teacher or principal who is currently working at a WFSG school. WFSG consultants have learned their craft by doing the work in schools with teachers and leaders. As I think about the work we do in schools, I am reminded of what Bruce Joyce once shared with me after talking with a superintendent. The superintendent looked directly in his eyes and asked, "Have you ever gotten dirty?" What the superintendent was asking was, "Have you ever worked in real schools and struggled in the dust and dirt of new learning?" I often think of that question when I read how different authors write about professional learning communities.

Principals. Principals make what happens in their schools happen. The principal is usually the person who contacts the Center for information. Prior to beginning any WFSG work, the principal is sent a variety of information so he or she can speak knowledgeably to the faculty. Often a principal will hear about WFSG from a district leader, by attending a conference, or from reading a book or journal. In talking with principals, we stress that the principal is the key factor in the initiation, implementation, and continuation of WFSGs. It is expected that the principal will be the key *sponsor* for the school's WFSG efforts and a member of its Focus Team, which introduces the faculty to WFSGs and organizes the faculty into groups. We expect the principal to attend and fully participate in all training and organizational events. We do so because we know that it is the principal who legitimizes WFSGs in the school and determines what structures are in place, how time is utilized, how resources are distributed and managed, and what behaviors are acceptable. Of these things, legitimizing WFSGs—that is, strong sponsorship—and finding and protecting the time for study groups to meet are probably the most critical, especially in the beginning. We believe that it is the principal's job to "create the conditions that make it possible for all faculty to be members of study groups that meet routinely for the improvement of student learning." WFSG consultants work more directly with principals than any other individuals in the schools or districts. Principals need to be coached on how to support study groups. When the first action plans are sent to the principal, the principal usually sends the plans to the school's WFSG consultant, who reviews the plans and gives the principal feedback on each plan. The principal chooses how he or she will use the feedback. This process may also be followed when principals receive the first few logs. The consultants will do as much handholding as principals need and are willing to accept. We know that if the principal is not alert to the ups and downs of study-group work, the groups will get stuck and not move beyond what members already know. WFSGs are a sure path to the principal becoming the school's instructional leader.

Teachers. As former classroom teachers, WFSG consultants know that teachers make what happens in their classrooms happen. Teachers decide what they are going to do or not do. When the teacher closes the door to the classroom, it becomes the teacher's world. If persons external to a teacher's classroom have not had sufficient influence, expertise, or power to impact what the teacher will do, they have no chance once the door is closed. As WFSG consultants work with faculties, we try to communicate effectively in all we do and to respect the work teachers do. If teachers feel respected and respect the individuals working with them, they will do or try to do what is right to the best of their abilities. I firmly believe this is true. In the WFSG System, teachers experience how decisions are made regarding what study groups will do, select for themselves the student needs most descriptive of the students they teach, form groups around the needs, and decide what actions they will take when their study groups meet and are left to do what they say they are going to do. Principals may give feedback, but no administrator sits in a group and monitors its work. Logs are used to support the work and not to evaluate the work. In these ways, teachers most often see WFSGs as self-directed, job-embedded professional development learning experiences. These attitudes are not automatic. The principal and other leaders of the WFSG System must facilitate and shepherd teachers' understanding of the process. Many teachers are disillusioned from experiencing many initiatives that held promise but did not meet expectations and because support did not materialize as originally committed. WFSG consultants are first and foremost teachers. Everyone working through the Center has been a public school teacher; for example, I began as a fourth-grade classroom teacher in 1957. We respect and honor all teachers for the work they do every day. We also remember, from our own teaching days, how difficult the work is and that only teachers can do it.

Researchers. I am listing "researchers" separate from "teachers" so that the role of teachers as researchers can more fully be developed. The Center's position is that teachers are researchers, and it is one of the primary roles of WFSG consultants to help teachers see themselves as such. Yet, most teachers do not consider themselves as researchers. A teacher's research laboratory is his or her classroom. WFSG consultants have to show teachers how they can be researchers and how important that role is to the WFSG System. When working with faculties, we are deliberate in showing how study groups conduct *action research* (see Lick, 2006). We stress the Plan-Act-Assess-Reflect cycle. When we look at logs and coach principals on how to look at logs, we look to see how, over several meetings, the groups are: (1) diagnosing the current status of student needs being targeted, (2) identifying strategies and materials to address needs, (3) planning lessons, (4) sharing the actions they took in their classrooms, (5) looking at student work based on the lessons, and (6) reflecting on student results. Teachers generally perceive researchers as being individuals not connected to public school classrooms, such as those in higher education institutions or businesses. When talking to teachers, I often compare what I see in public schools with what I see at the Medical College of Georgia. At MCG, there are physicians who treat patients and physicians in laboratories who test medical procedures. The clinical physicians and the laboratory physicians listen to what each other has to say. Teachers in schools are the clinicians, collecting data to document best practices in their classrooms. Relative to research, WFSG consultants have two challenges: help teachers see themselves as effective researchers and encourage them to use external research that documents best practices from data collected in many schools.

District Leaders. We define district leaders as the superintendent, the associate and assistant superintendents, directors of departments, and coordinators of curriculum and instructional areas. District leaders have strong influence with principals and, depending on the position of the leader, have power over principals. District leaders often attend a variety of national conferences and have access to information that principals may not have. In that way, district leaders most often give principals information about how to contact the Center. When a school faculty decides to implement WFSGs, especially if there is more than one school in a district planning to begin WFSGs, a district leader is identified as a contact person. When schools are sent electronic messages and information, the e-mails are copied to the district person. When WFSG consultants visit schools, arrangements are made to see the district contact person who, most often, visits the schools with the consultant. Exit interviews with principals and district leaders are requested when consultants schedule visits to a district. One key role that district leaders have is securing and protecting funds for school initiatives. District leaders need to understand that it takes up to three years for WFSGs to become routine in schools and that the initial training is only the beginning.

Curriculum Coordinators and Content Specialists. Even though these individuals are also considered to be district leaders, content specialists serve a unique role and are essential to the successful institutionalization of WFSGs. One of the first tasks of a WFSG consultant in a school is to identify the curriculum and instructional programs that are in place in the school. WFSGs are a process, a set of procedures, a structure, a vehicle, a place to work. Content must be put into the process, the structure, the vehicle. If the content is not substantive and focused on specific student needs, the process or the structure or the vehicle is empty of value. The truck that delivers gas to a gas station can be a magnificent machine; yet if when the truck gets to the station it has no gasoline, the magnificent machine has no value to the station. Curriculum specialists not only make sure there is gas in the truck, they make sure it is the right kind of gas. They are absolutely key to the development of the content of study-group work. They provide expertise, information, materials, and training. WFSG consultants identify the content specialists in a school and district and connect their work to the work of the content initiatives or instructional programs being implemented in schools.

Programs

National Conferences. The Center sponsors the National WFSG Conference each year in February. There are two primary purposes of the conference: (a) a forum for sharing and building community among the schools implementing WFSGs and (b) an opportunity to further educate participants on effective strategies and skills groups require to continually deepen the work so that student benefits are assured. The 2003, 2004, and 2005 conferences were held in Augusta, Georgia, as will be annual conferences in the foreseeable future. Schools implementing WFSGs are encouraged to send each year at least one faculty person to the conference, more if possible. The conference provides one or two general sessions and sets of concurrent sessions. The concurrent sessions focus on strategies that effective study groups use. Teachers, school leaders, researchers, and WFSG consultants are presenters. One feature of the conference is the organization of participants into study groups. These groups meet at least four times during the conference and focus on how they are going to use the content of the conference to deepen the work of their school's study groups.

Institutes. The Center sponsors training institutes at different times during the year, most often in February (preceding the WFSG Conference), June, and July. An institute is a two- or three-day in-depth, formal training program. A Level I WFSG Institute prepares focus teams and individuals to introduce and launch WFSGs. A focus team is usually five representatives, including the principal, from a school that will work with the whole faculty in getting the study-group process started. A Level II WFSG Institute is for representatives from schools that have begun WFSGs and want an array of strategies for deepening their work. Institutes on other specific strategies are also offered, such as "Looking at Student Work." In the latter, participants learn how to use protocols to study, reflect on, and learn from student work.

Technical Assistance in Schools. WFSG consultants travel to districts to work with faculties, principals, and district leaders. Consultants can conduct Level I WFSG Institutes in the local area upon request. There are many services that can also be offered to schools and districts on site. One especially valuable service to schools is when a consultant arranges a meeting that includes one person from each study group. Through the sharing and interventions offered by the consultant, all groups can benefit.

Preparation Assistance for Comprehensive School Reform (CSR) Proposals. For schools wishing to write a CSR program proposal that includes WFSGs, the Center has an application template with inserts that describe how the professional development component (WFSGs) is linked to the other ten components. The school will need to describe its curriculum, parent involvement, and classroom management components. WFSG consultants are also available to assist schools in writing other proposals that include the WFSG System.

Electronic Support. The Center is connected to every WFSG school through the Internet, especially through electronic messaging systems. In many cases, the Center has a "Group in Outlook Express" for every study group at a school. In that way, communications can be direct. In such cases, the principal always receives a copy of any exchange. WFSG consultants regularly assist principals with timely tasks and offer support for other identified tasks.

Worldwide Network. September 2005 ushered in a new service of the Center. Through RubiconAtlas, all WFSG schools that elect to become members of that Web site will be connected. Schools can share action plans and logs. A study group focusing on Reading Comprehension can see what other groups focusing on the same topic or concern are doing. Resources can be shared. Lessons developed by one study group can be shared with another study group.

Research. The WFSG Center collects information and data from WFSG schools and those implementing WFSGs. I feel this is one of the most critical functions of the Center and the most difficult to accomplish. Collecting, interpreting, and reporting what happens in schools as a result of implementing WFSGs is the Center's greatest challenge. We have to depend on the schools to provide us with the information. WFSG schools are in different districts in many states that have different assessments, assessment procedures, and ways of interpreting results. We can only look at one school and compare where that school was when it began implementing WFSG and where it is after one or more years of implementation. The question is: "Did WFSGs cause student learning to increase?" The most critical factor in determining the answer to the question is, "What did the study groups do?" WFSGs are only a structure to facilitate what teachers do about what they teach and how they teach. If the structure is filled with meaningless work, the groups will be meaningless. The content of a group's work is what ultimately determines whether student results are meaningful. That is, when determining whether WFSGs increase student learning, we have to assess what the groups did. It is the intention of the Center to be more active in the area of research. In the future, we will (a) pursue ways to track schools authentically implementing WFSGs, (b) track student performance over time, (c) follow WFSG schools beyond the time the Center usually provides direct assistance, (d) determine the impact of leadership transitions at school and district levels, and (e) discover the types of content that best fit the WFSG System.

Products and Resources

Implementation Tools. The Center provides examples of action plans from elementary, middle, and high schools. Sets of logs from an illustrative study group are available to show how groups evolve over a period of time. The WFSG Rubric (see C. Murphy, Chapter 10 in this volume) is offered to schools for study groups to use to determine the levels of implementation of WFSGs in its three major components: context, process, and content. A dozen different tools are available to assess group work. There are checklists to cover an assortment of the major tasks. For example, there is a checklist of "to dos" for the first three study-group meetings. For focus teams that want their faculties to have a workbook as they go through the steps on the WFSG Decision-Making Cycle, a workbook is available. There are many documents available electronically pertaining to WFSG work upon request.

Books. Three editions of the basic Whole-Faculty Study Group book have been published by Corwin Press: *Whole-Faculty Study Groups: A Powerful Way to Change Schools and Enhance Learning* (Murphy & Lick, 1998); *Whole-Faculty Study Groups: Creating Student-Based Professional Development* (Murphy & Lick, 2001); and *Whole-Faculty Study Groups: Creating Professional Learning Communities That Target Student Learning* (Murphy & Lick, 2005). Each builds on the preceding edition and includes new perspectives, findings, and strategies. Also, their resource sections contain different examples and illustrations of work from schools. Other books that include chapters on WFSGs are also available, such as the National Staff Development Council's *Powerful Designs for Professional Learning* (1999), which has a chapter on WFSGs and a companion CD.

Articles and Reports. More than two dozen articles and reports on WFSGs have been published in major professional journals, and information about them is available by contacting the Center. From time to time the Center produces a report. An example is "High Schools and WFSGs" (available from the Center; see chapter end for contact information), which gives a brief summary of the WFSG work in twenty-two high schools.

Protocols. There are many protocols to assist study groups in using a structured process for having conversations around a piece of student work, teacher work (such as a lesson), and readings (such as an article or book chapter). Protocols are also available through the Institutes that teach the proper use of these protocols.

Portfolios and Lessons. The Center has begun collecting electronically examples of study-group portfolios and lessons developed around a specific student need.

Videos. The Video Journal of Education has produced a two-tape video program on WFSGs titled, "Whole-Faculty Study Groups: Collaboration Targeting Student Learning." It can be purchased through www.TeachStream.com. Other short video clips are available that were not professionally produced.

OPERATION OF THE CENTER

The operation of the Center revolves around four basic functions:

1. Respond to requests for information
2. Arrange technical services to schools and districts

3. Develop, offer, and follow-up on National WFSG Conferences and WFSG Institutes

4. Prepare publications and reports

As Director of the Center, my primary responsibility relates to the above functions and interactions with the Center's Advisory Board.

The Center is not financially supported by grants or gifts from any individual, group, agency, business, or organization. It receives no state, federal, or private funds. There are no salaried employees. Operational costs, such as materials, copying, office equipment, and utilities, are built into the registration fees to the National WFSG Conference and WFSG Institutes. Schools and districts are not charged for the Center's administrative or overhead expenses. WFSG consultants are paid fees plus expenses for their services. All fees and expenses are paid directly to the WFSG consultant assigned to a school or district. Fees and expenses paid to consultants are not routed through the Center, and consultants do not pay a percentage or any portion of their fees to the Center. In the future, we may have to restructure our financial approach. As long as I continue to host the Center and serve as its Director, I do not expect any changes.

SUMMARY

As I return to my attic window and view the city of Augusta with more clarity in the afternoon light, I see the future of the National WFSG Center with more clarity after writing this chapter. I see the Savannah River over the treetops. I see the river connecting Georgia and South Carolina, rather than separating the two states. In a similar way, I see WFSGs and the National WFSG Center as connectors. Whole-Faculty Study Groups are a structure in schools that connects teachers to each other, to each other's students, and to student success. The National WFSG Center is a place that helps connect and support faculties implementing this structure in their schools. The future of both will depend on how we connect both the WFSG structure in schools and the Center to meaningful and measurable student success.

The National Whole-Faculty Study Groups Center can be contacted at: 706-736-0756 or CarleneMurphy@comcast.net

PART VIII

An Overview of School Reform

School improvement and reform are both "significant local, state, and national issues," *and* "truly global issues." What happens in this global arena will become a critical part of the foundation for the long-term future growth and development of each member-nation in the world community. This situation is one of those "good stories" and "bad stories" for us. On the "good side" is the fact that we have many relevant and meaningful improvement initiatives going on in our schools and school systems today, such as those discussed in the chapters of this Fieldbook. On the "bad side," our general, systemic state and national school improvement and reform efforts are neither adequate nor doing especially well, and we appear to be continuingly slipping in comparison to many of our competitor nations around the world!

The single chapter in this section presents a big-picture perspective for school reform by discussing both sides of the school improvement and reform issues and then illuminating the positive and negative factors and circumstances for us for today and tomorrow, as we attempt to prepare our people and country for the long-term future.

31

Improving Schools

Seeing the Big Picture

Dale W. Lick

Carlene U. Murphy

"**E**xcellence in education" should rank among the highest priorities for our fifty individual states and the nation. It should be obvious, even though many don't see and appreciate it, that our future way of life in the United States, in the long term, is directly dependent on the quality of our educational systems.

IMPORTANCE OF THE FIELDBOOK INITIATIVES

The initiatives discussed and illustrated in this fieldbook represent an impressive and broad array of the kinds of school-improvement efforts that should be going on in every school and school system across the country. For example, Chapters 5 and 25 tell the story of successful efforts to significantly improve the quality in the Springfield (Missouri) Public Schools.

The total score for 2000–2001 found the Springfield (Missouri) Public Schools only one point above the cut-off for "provisional accreditation" on the Annual

Performance Rating of the Missouri accreditation process. They then implemented a major improvement process in approximately 90% of their schools, with the Whole-Faculty Study Group (WFSG) System (Lick, 2006; Murphy & Lick, 2005) being a central feature. On their last three annual accreditation reports, the district scored 100 out of 100 points on their Annual Performance Rating and earned the state's coveted "Distinction in Performance" award. "This award is unique and demanding, because it requires districts to demonstrate growth and progress across the board. Districts must show improvement or high performance at every level—elementary, middle, and high school," said Commissioner of Education D. Kent King. Almost all of the schools in the Springfield Public Schools are now WFSG schools!

The "critical elements" in the successes of the initiatives in this fieldbook are the same "key elements" implemented in the WFSG System. What these initiatives, and other similar improvement efforts in successful schools around the country, have shown is that the WFSG System, when properly implemented, has been unusually successful in facilitating schoolwide change and improvement and enhancing student learning (see, e.g., Koenigs, Chapter 7, this volume; Joyce, Murphy, Showers, & Murphy, 1989; Murphy, 1992, 1995; Murphy & Lick, 1998, 2001, 2005).

REQUIRED FOR SCHOOL CHANGE AND SUCCESS

The fundamental characteristics required in any effective school reform model are essentially the same as the "key elements" found in the WFSG System.

A driving force in an effective school reform process will be its self-directed, synergistic comentoring learning teams (see Murphy & Lick, Chapter 1 this volume; Lick, 1999a, 2000, 2006; Murphy & Lick, 2005, chap. 9). Such teams creatively:

1. Produce learning communities and set common goals, support member interdependence, empower participants, and foster active participation.

2. Plan and learn together.

3. Engage broad principles of education that modify perspectives, policies, and practices.

4. Construct subject-matter knowledge.

5. Immerse everyone in sustained work with ideas, materials, and colleagues.

6. Cultivate action researchers, producing, evaluating, and applying relevant research.

7. Struggle with fundamental questions of what teachers and students must learn, know, and apply (see Chapter 1 this volume, and Murphy & Lick, 2005, p. 13).

A focusing question for study groups in any effective school reform approach is: "What is happening differently in the classroom as a result of what you are doing and learning in study groups?" With that vision, "study groups are motivated, work harder and take responsibility for the successful implementation of required processes and procedures" (Murphy & Lick, 1998, p. 18). The benefits include the following:

- Improvement in the student needs areas that study groups target
- Culture shifts from isolation to collaboration
- Data are prominent in making instructional decisions
- Principals are more instructionally focused
- New teachers are in comentoring groups surrounded by support
- Teachers see themselves as action researchers
- New instructional initiatives are implemented sooner and more thoroughly
- Multiple initiatives are more coherent and integrated for maximum effects
- All teachers are viewed as leaders
- Behavioral norms for faculty become standard
- Looking at student work in collaborative settings becomes the norm
- Teachers take full responsibility for students represented in a study group

The WFSG process, centered around multilevel synergistic comentoring study groups, is, in fact, a massive change-creation process, as any meaningful school reform model should be. It is one of the most practical and effective change-creation approaches presently available in the literature (Lick, 2006; Murphy & Lick, 2005).

In particular, the WFSG process dramatically increases:

1. *Focus on imperative changes,* as determined by school personnel.

2. *Change sponsorship effectiveness,* both project and schoolwide.

3. *Preparation of change agents,* including the principal, faculty, and others.

4. *Commitment of change targets and the reduction of their resistance.*

5. *Positive advocacy,* including that of the school board, superintendent, principal, faculty, students, parents, and the general community.

6. *Individual, group, and school resilience,* enhancing stakeholders' change-adaptability.

7. *Knowledge of change and change principles* for stakeholders.

8. *Organized processes for transition,* including integrated, cocreative learning experiences that are teacher- and student-centered, experimental and research-oriented, reflective, supportive, and inspiring.

9. *Group synergy, comentoring, and learning team development,* setting new school operational and relationship norms for action research and improving learning systems (Lick, 2006; Murphy & Lick, 2005, chap. 9).

10. *School and educational culture modification,* allowing a critical reexamination of basic assumptions, beliefs and behaviors, and required learning systems and practices (Lick, 2000; Mullen & Lick, 1999).

The WFSG process, or any effective school reform method, through the above ten elements for creating desired change, generates a collective and inspiring vision and creates a high level of synergy and comentoring, allowing substantive learning, change, and continuous improvement to become the norm in the school workplace and culture.

And finally, the major system fundamentals of the WFSG approach are, as any effective school reform model should be, the following:

- *Standards-Based* (e.g., see M. Murphy, Chapter 3 in this volume; also National Staff Development Council, 2001)

- *Data-Driven* (e.g., priorities are set by the actual relevant school data; see Roberts, Chapter 14, and Clauset, Parker, & Whitney, Chapter 15, both in this volume)

- *Team-Oriented* (e.g., study groups become learning teams, providing the foundation for the development of learning communities within the school; see Lick, 2006; Murphy & Lick, 2005, chap. 9)

- *Performance-Based* (e.g., expectations are based not on acquiring information, but on genuine performance—not just knowing, but being able to do)

- *Research-Based* (e.g., professional development and processes are based on the best educational and organizational practices and research; Lick, 2006)

- *Results-Focused* (e.g., success is based on actual results relating to school improvement and student achievement)

- *Systemic System* (e.g., the WFSG System is a massive school-change system, dealing collectively with the various subsystems of the school as a whole)

- *Culture Modifying* (e.g., sufficient changes are successful and connected in the school to provide a strong enough foundation to sustain the changes and, as a result, shift key elements of the existing culture; see Rothman & Walker, Chapter 12, and Potts & Zoul, Chapter 13, both in this volume)

STATUS OF SCHOOL REFORM IN THE UNITED STATES

The school initiatives in this fieldbook and the discussions above assure us that there are many wonderful school improvement and effective school reforms going on across the country. On the other hand, it is fair to say that school reform in the nation, in general and in total, has not been very successful. As we said, this doesn't mean that there haven't been many successes, because there have been. However, the successes have been "more isolated and spotty" than "systemic and cutting across most schools and school systems." Frankly, the results over the past twenty years, even with loudly shouted statewide and national initiatives such as No Child Left Behind, have been basically minimal, and there is no accepted, broad-based, effective approach to general school reform, even now, on the horizon.

Why? Because either leaders or leadership entities didn't really know what was required or their initiatives settled for partial systems that met their particular fancy. The fact is that no major, powerful statewide or national entity has truly accepted this monumental challenge and embarked on a massive change plan that has adequate strength and breadth and could be sustained over a long-enough time period for systemic change and reform to take place and take hold in America (some of the best initial state and national change efforts are those discussed in Chapters 27–30, in this volume).

The politics, the culture, the funding requirements, the educational personnel and institutions, the educational stakeholders, and so many other factors that should be involved have never jelled to the point of meaningful collaboration to create new state and national vision and mission statements for education in this country—ones that are meaningful, effective, acceptable, compelling, inspiring, and broadly enough supported for the vital focus that will be required.

The truth is that significant and real reform across a state or the nation represents one of the most massive change efforts ever undertaken in this country. As of now, we are far from such an endeavor. The longer it takes us to get there, and we will be painfully forced to get there someday, the more ground and competitive edge we will lose to our competitors around the world. You see, in the long run, it is not "us against us," it is "us continuing to let our comparative educational advantage slip away to those more progressive in education in other countries." This slippage has been going on for the last twenty years and is accelerating today. For example, while we have some of the best technology in the world, we continue to use it mostly in the old learning systems of the past and fail to use it in new, creative approaches to learning to advance real school reform and substantially increase educational productivity and quality (Lick & Kaufman, 2005).

CONCLUSION

What is required? The closest we have come in this country to what is broadly required of us are initiatives like the ones illustrated in this fieldbook. Nonetheless, even though these reflect significant, valuable, and progressive efforts in the right direction, our states and nation must require and deliver much, much more! Frankly, what is required is that national, statewide, community, and school entities truly accept the monumental challenge of visionary and scientifically valid school reform (such as described in this fieldbook), generate the policy and support base for the related school reform approaches, and create environments that inspire and advance authentic and meaningful new change, transforming schools and assisting teachers in their local, day-to-day efforts toward school improvement and the enhancement of student learning.

References

Argyris, C. (1959). The individual and organization: Some problems of mutual adjustment. *Administrative Science Quarterly, 2*(1), 1–24.

Argyris, C. (1992). *On organizational learning.* Cambridge, MA: Blackwell.

Aspinwall, M. (2003). *Early intervention for reading difficulties using best practices and teacher training.* Unpublished doctoral dissertation, Argosy University, Sarasota, FL.

Atwell, N. (1998). *In the middle: New understanding about writing, reading, and learning* (2nd ed.). Portsmouth, NH: Boynton/Cook.

Ball, D. L., & Cohen, D. K. (1999). Developing practices, developing practitioners. In L. Darling-Hammond & G. Sykes (Eds.), *Teaching as the learning profession* (pp. 3–32). San Francisco: Jossey-Bass.

Barber, B. R. (1998). *A place for us: How to make society civil and democracy strong.* New York: Hill and Wang.

Baron, D., & Averette, P. (n.d.) *The final word protocol.* Retrieved June 28, 2004, from The National School Reform Faculty Web site: http://www.nsrfnewyork.org/articles/The FinalWord.doc.

Barth, R. S. (2002, May). The culture builder. *Educational Leadership, 59*(8), 6–11.

Beatty, B. R. (2000). Teachers leading their own professional growth: Self-directed reflection and collaboration and changes in perception of self and work in secondary school teachers. *Journal of In-Service Education, 26*(1), 73–97.

Beck, I., McKeown, M., & Kucan, L. (2002). *Bringing words to life.* New York: Guilford.

Blankstein, A. M. (2004). *Failure is not an option: Six principles that guide student achievement in high-performing schools.* Thousand Oaks, CA: Corwin Press.

Blythe, T., & Associates. (1998). *The teaching for understanding guide.* San Francisco: Jossey-Bass.

Bryk, A., & Schneider, B. (2002). *Trust in schools: A core resource for improvement.* New York: Russell Sage.

Calculated success. (2003). Boston: Project for School Innovation.

Caldwell, M. (2002). *The tipping point: How little things can make a big difference.* Boston: First Back Bay Books.

Chen, J-Q., Salahuddin, P. H., & Wagner, S. L. (2000, Sept.). Turning standardized test scores into a tool for improving teaching and learning: An assessment-based approach. *Urban Education, 35*(3), 356–394.

Clark, D. L., & Astuto, T. A. (1988). Paradoxical choice options in organizations. In D. E. Griffiths, R. T. Stout, & P. B. Forsyth (Eds.), *Leaders for America's schools* (pp. 112–130). Berkeley, CA: McCutchan.

Collins, J. (2001). *Good to great: Why some companies make the leap . . . and others don't.* New York: HarperCollins Business.

The concerns-based adoption model (CBAM): A model for change in individuals. Retrieved March 10, 2006, from http://www.nationalacademies.org/rise/backg4a.htm

Conner, D. (1993*). Managing at the speed of change.* New York: Villard.

Connors, N. A. (2000). *If you don't feed the teachers, they eat the students.* Nashville, TN: Incentive Publications.

Connors, R., & Smith, T. (1999). *Journey to the Emerald City: Achieve a competitive edge by creating a culture of accountability.* New York: Prentice Hall.

Covey, S. (1990). *The 7 habits of highly effective people: Powerful lessons in personal change.* New York: Fireside.

Cronan-Hillix, T., Gensheimer, L., Cronan-Hillix, W. A., William, S., & Davidson, W. S. (1986). Students' views of mentors in psychology graduate training. *Teaching of Psychology, 13*(3), 123–127.

Curwin, R., & Mendler, A. N. (1988). *Discipline with dignity.* Alexandria, VA: Association for Supervision and Curriculum Development.

Daniels, H. (2001). *Literature circles: Voice and choice in book clubs & reading groups* (2nd ed.). Portland, ME: Stenhouse.

Danielson, C. (2002). *Enhancing student achievement: A framework for school improvement.* Alexandria: Association for Supervision and Curriculum Development.

Darling-Hammond, L. (1992). *Building learner-centered schools: Developing professional capacity, policy, and political consensus.* New York: Teachers College, National Center for Restructuring Education, Schools, and Teaching.

Darling-Hammond, L. (1997a). *Doing what matters most: Investing in doing what matters most: Investing in quality teaching.* New York: National Commission on Teaching and America's Future.

Darling-Hammond, L. (1997b). *The right to learn.* San Francisco: Jossey-Bass.

Darling-Hammond, L., & McLaughlin, M. W. (1995). Policies that support professional development in an era of reform. *Phi Delta Kappan, 76*(8), 597–604.

Davies, A. (2000). *Making classroom assessment work.* Courtenay, British Columbia, Canada: Connections Publishing.

Davenport, P., & Anderson, G. (2002*). Closing the achievement gap: No excuses.* Houston, TX: American Productivity and Quality Center.

Deci, E. L., & Flaste, R. (1995). *Why we do what we do: The dynamics of personal autonomy.* New York: G. P. Putnam.

Dewey, J. (1916). *Democracy and education.* New York: Free Press.

Dewey, J. (1927). *The public and its problems.* New York: Holt & Co.

Dewey, J. (1944). *Democracy and education.* New York: Free Press (reprint edition).

Dewey, J. (1994). *Democracy and education: An introduction to the philosophy of education.* New York: Free Press.

Drucker, P. (1985). *Innovation and entrepreneurship: Practices and principles.* New York: Harper & Row.

Duck, J. D. (2001). *The change monster: The human forces that fuel or foil corporate transformation and change.* New York: Crown Business.

DuFour, R. (2001, Winter). In the right context. *Journal of Staff Development, 22*(1). Retrieved March 10, 2006, from: http://www.nsdc.org/library/publications/jsd/dufour221.cfm

DuFour, R. (2002, May). The learning-centered principal. *Educational Leadership, 59*(8), 12–15.

DuFour, R. (2003a). Building a professional learning community. *The School Administrator, 60*(5), 13–18.

DuFour, R. (2003b, Summer). Leading edge [Electronic version]. *Journal of Staff Development, 24*(3). Retrieved March 10, 2006, from http://www.nsdc.org/library/publications/jsd/dufour243.cfm

DuFour, R., & Eaker, R. (1998). *Professional learning communities at work: Best practices for enhancing student achievement.* Alexandria, VA: Association for Supervision and Curriculum Development.

DuFour, R., Eaker, R., Karhanek, G., & DuFour, R. (2004). *Whatever it takes: How professional learning communities respond when kids don't learn.* Bloomington, IN: National Educational Services.

Eaker, R., DuFour, R., & Burnette, R. (2002). *Getting started: Reculturing schools to become professional learning communities.* Bloomington, IN: National Educational Service.

Easton, L. (Ed.). (2004). *Powerful designs for professional learning.* Oxford, OH: National Staff Development Council.

Ebmeier, H. H., & Nicklaus, J. (1999). The impact of peer and principal collaborative supervision on teachers' trust commitment, desire for collaboration, and efficacy. *Journal of Curriculum and Supervision, 14*(4), 351.

Flower, J. (1995). *A conversation with Ronald Heifetz: Leadership without easy answers.* Retrieved October 8, 2004, from: http://www.well.com/user/bbear/heifetz.html.

Fountas, I., & Pinnell, G. S. (2001). *Guiding readers and writers.* Portsmouth, NH: Heinemann.

Fullan, M. (1991). *The new meaning of education change* (2nd ed.). New York: Teachers College Press.

Fullan, M. (1995). The school as a learning organization: Distant dreams. *Theory Into Practice, 4*(34), 230–235.

Fullan, M. (2002, May). The change leader. *Educational Leadership, 8*(59).

Fullan, M. (2005). *Leadership and sustainability: Systems thinkers in action.* Thousand Oaks, CA: Corwin Press.

Gardner, H. (1993). *Multiple intelligences: The theory in practice.* New York: Basic Books.

Gardner, H. (2004). *Changing minds: The art and science of changing our own and other people's minds.* Boston: Harvard Business School Press.

Gibson, S., & Dembo, M. (1984). Teacher efficacy: A construct validity. *Journal of Educational Psychology, 76*(4), 569–582.

Hall, G. E., & Hord, S. M. (2001). *Implementing change: Patterns, principles, and potholes.* Needham Heights, MA: Allyn & Bacon.

Haycock, K. (1998, Summer). Good teaching matters . . . a lot: Thinking K–16. *Education Trust,* pp. 3–14.

Haycock, K., Jerald, C., & Huang, S. (2001a, Spring). Closing the gap: Done in a decade. *Education Trust,* pp. 3–21.

Haycock, K., Jerald, C., & Huang, S. (2001b, Spring). New frontiers for a new century. *Education Trust,* pp. 1–2.

Heifetz, R. A., (1994). *Leadership without easy answers.* Cambridge, MA: Belknap/ Harvard University Press.

Heifetz, R. A., (1994) & Linsky, M. (2002). *Leadership on the line: Staying alive through the dangers of leading.* Boston: Harvard Business School Press.

Hiebert, J., Gallimore, R., & Stigler, J. W. (2002). A knowledge base for the teaching profession: What would it look like and how can we get one? *Educational Researcher, 3*(31), 3–15.

Hord, S. M. (1997). Professional learning communities: Communities of continuous inquiry and improvement. *Southwest Educational Development Laboratory.* Retrieved July 15, 2002, from http://www.sedl.org/pubs/change34/5.html

Hoy, W. K., & Woolfolk, A. E. (1993). Teachers' sense of efficacy and the organizational health of schools. *Elementary School Journal, 93,* 356–372.

Jenkins, T., & Baber, L. (1998). *Editing checklist.* Augusta, GA: Instruction.

Joyce, B., Murphy, C., Showers, B., & Murphy, J. (1989). School renewal as cultural change. *Educational Leadership, 47*(3), 70–77.

Joyce, B., & Weil, M. (1986). Models of teaching (3rd ed.) Englewood Cliffs, NJ: Prentice Hall.

Joyce, B., Weil, M., & Showers, B. (1992). Models of teaching (4th ed.) Boston, MA: Allyn and Bacon.

Kansas State Department of Education. (n.d.). Statistics K–12. Retrieved June 11, 2003, from http://www.ksde.org/Welcome.html

Kanter, R. M. (2004). *Confidence: How winning streaks & losing streaks begin & end.* New York: Crown Business.

Kaplan, R. S., & Norton, D. P. (1996). *The balanced scorecard: Translating strategy into action.* Boston: Harvard Business School Press.

Knowles, M. S., Holton, E. F., & Swanson, R. A. (1998). *The adult learner* (5th ed.). Houston, TX: Gulf.

Koenigs, A. E. (2004). *The affects of whole-faculty study groups on individuals and organizations.* Unpublished doctoral dissertation, Wichita State University, Kansas.

Kotter, J. P., & Cohen, D. S. (2002*). The heart of change: Real life stories of how people change their organizations.* Boston: Harvard Business School Press.

Kouzes, J. M., & Posner, B. Z. (2002). *The leadership challenge.* San Francisco: Jossey-Bass.

Kruse, S. D. (2001). Creating communities of reform: Continuous improvement planning teams. *Journal of Educational Administration, 39*(4), 359.

Lambert, L. (2003). *Leadership capacity for lasting school improvement.* Alexandria, VA: Association for Supervision and Curriculum Development.

Lambert, L., Walker, D., Zimmerman, D. P., Cooper, J. E., Morgan, D. L., Gardner, M. E., & Szabo, M. (1995). *The constructivist leader.* New York: Teachers College Press.

Lee, V., Dedick, R., & Smith, J. (1991). The effect of the social organization of schools on teachers' efficacy and satisfaction. *Sociology of Education, 64,* 190–208.

Leithwood, K., Louis, K. S., Anderson, S., & Wahlstrom, K. (2004). *How leadership influences student learning.* Center for Applied Research and Educational Improvement, University of Minnesota and Ontario Institute for Studies in Education at the University of Toronto, Commissioned by The Wallace Foundation.

Lesson Study Research Group. (n.d.). *What is lesson study?* Retrieved February 23, 2006, from Columbia University, Teachers College Web site: http://www.tc.edu/lessonstudy/whatislessonstudy.html

Lewin, K. (1948). *Resolving social conflicts.* New York: Harper & Brothers.

Lewin, K. (1951). *Field theory in social science.* New York: Harper & Brothers.

Lick, D. W. (1999a). Proactive comentoring relationships: Enhancing effectiveness through synergy. In C. A. Mullen & D. W. Lick (Eds.), *New directions in mentoring: Creating a culture of synergy* (pp. 206–207). London: Falmer Press.

Lick, D. W. (1999b). Transforming higher education: A new vision, learning paradigm, change management. *International Journal of Innovative Higher Education, 13,* 75–78.

Lick, D. W. (2000). Whole-faculty study groups: Facilitating mentoring for school-wide change. *Theory Into Practice, 39*(1), 43–48.

Lick, D. W. (2003). *Developing learning teams.* Keynote Address given at the Small Learning Communities Conference, Pinellas County Schools, Florida.

Lick, D. W. (2006). A new perspective on organizational learning: Creating learning teams. *Evaluation and Program Planning, 29*(1), 88–96.

Lick, D. W., & Kaufman, R. (2000). Change creation: The rest of the planning story. In J. Boettcher, M. Doyle, & R. Jensen (Eds.), *Technology-driven planning: Principles to practice* (chap. 2). Ann Arbor, MI: Society for College and University Planning.

Lick, D. W., & Kaufman, R. (2005). Change creation for online learning and technology. In C. Howard, J. Boettcher, L. Justice, K. Schenk, G. Berg, & P. Rogers (Eds.), *Encyclopedia of distance learning.* Hershey, PA: Idea Group.

Lieberman, A. (1995). Practices that support teacher development: Transforming conceptions of professional development. *Phi Delta Kappan, 76*(8), 591–596.

Littky, D., & Grabelle, S. (2004*). The big picture: Education is everyone's business.* Alexandria, VA: Association for Supervision and Curriculum Development.

Marzano, R. J. (2003). *What works in schools: Translating research into action.* Alexandria, VA: Association for Supervision and Curriculum Development.

Meier, D. (1995). *The power of their ideas: Lessons from a small school in Harlem.* Boston, MA: Beacon Press.

McManus, A. (1992). *The memory jogger for education: A pocket guide of tools for continuous improvement in schools.* Salem, NH: GOAL/QPC.

Mohrman, S. A., & Tenkasi, R. (1997, May). *Patterns of cross-functional work: Behaviors and benefits.* Paper presented at the University of North Texas Symposium on Work Teams, Denton, TX.

Moore, G. A. (2002). *Crossing the chasm: Marketing and selling high-tech products to mainstream customers.* New York: HarperCollins.

Mullen, C. A., & Lick, D. W. (1999). *New directions in mentoring: Creating a culture of synergy.* London: Falmer Press.

Murphy, C. U. (1991). Lessons from a journey into change. *Educational Leadership, 48*(8), 63–67.

Murphy, C. U. (1992). Study groups foster school-wide learning. *Educational Leadership, 50*(3), 71–74.

Murphy, C. U. (1995). Whole-faculty study groups: Doing the seemingly undoable. *Journal of Staff Development, 16*(3), 37–44.

Murphy, C. U., & Lick, D. W. (1998*). Whole-faculty study groups: A powerful way to change schools and enhance learning.* Thousand Oaks, CA: Corwin Press.

Murphy, C. U., & Lick, D. W. (2001). *Whole-faculty study groups: Creating student-based professional development* (2nd ed.). Thousand Oaks, CA: Corwin Press.

Murphy, C. U., & Lick, D. W. (2005). *Whole-faculty study groups: Creating professional learning communities that target student learning* (3rd ed.). Thousand Oaks, CA: Corwin Press.

Murphy, C., & Murphy, M. (2004). *Study groups: Powerful designs for professional learning.* Oxford, OH: National Staff Development Council.

Murphy, J., Murphy, C., Joyce, B., & Showers, B. (1988). The Richmond County school improvement program: Preparation and initial phase. *Journal of Staff Development, 9*(2), 36–41.

Nagin, C. (2003). *Because writing matters: Improving student writing in our schools.* San Francisco: Jossey-Bass.

National Staff Development Council. (1999). *Powerful designs for professional development.* Oxford, OH: Author.

National Staff Development Council. (2001). *Standards for staff development* (Rev. ed.). Oxford, OH: Author.

National Staff Development Council and Southwest Educational Development Laboratory. (2003). *Moving NSDC's staff development standards into practice: Innovation configurations.* Oxford, OH: Author.

Newmann, F., Bryk, A., & Nagaoka, J. (2001). *Authentic intellectual work and standardized tests: Conflict or coexistence?* Retrieved April 29, 2004, from http://www.consortium-chicago.org/publications/p0az2.html

Newmann, F. M., Rutter, R. A., & Smith, M. S. (1989). Organizational factors that affect school sense of efficacy, community and expectations. *Sociology of Education, 62,* 221–238.

Niven, P. R. (2000). *Balanced scorecard step-by-step: Maximizing performance and maintaining results.* New York: John Wiley.

Perkins, D. (2004). Knowledge alive. *Educational Leadership, 62*(1), 14–18.

Perry, T., Hilliard, A. G., & Steele, C. (2004). *Young, gifted, and black: Promoting high achievement among African-American students.* Boston: Beacon.

Peters, T. (2003). *Re-Imagine!* New York: Penguin.

Pfeffer, J., & Sutton, R. I. (2000). *The knowing-doing gap: How smart companies turn knowledge into action.* Cambridge, MA: President and Fellows of Harvard College.

Platt, A. D., Tripp, C. E., Ogden, W. R., & Fraser, R. G. (2000). *The skillful leader: Confronting mediocre teaching.* Acton, MA: Research for Better Teaching.

Reeves, D. (2002). *The daily disciplines of leadership.* San Francisco: Jossey-Bass.

Rice, J. K. (2003). *Teacher quality: Understanding the effectiveness of teacher attributes.* Washington, DC: Economic Policy Institute.

Rivkin, S., Hanushek, E., & Kain, J. (1998, January). *Teachers, schools, and academic achievement.* Paper presented at the annual meeting of the Econometric Society, Chicago.

Rosenholtz, S. J. (1991). *Teachers' workplace: The social organizational of schools.* New York: Teachers College Press.

Ross, J. A. (1994, June). *Beliefs that make a difference: The origins and impacts of teacher efficacy.* Paper presented at the annual meeting of the Canadian Association for Curriculum Studies, Calgary, Alberta, Canada.

Routman, R. (2004). *Writing essentials: Raising expectations and results while simplifying teaching.* Portsmouth, NH: Heinemann.

Sagor, R. (2000). *Guiding school improvement with action research.* Alexandria, VA: Association for Supervision and Curriculum Development.

Sanders, W. I., & Rivers, J. C. (1998). *Cumulative and residual effects of teachers on future students' academic achievement.* Research Progress Report, University of Tennessee Value-Added Research and Assessment Center, Knoxville, TN, p. 9.

Schein, E. H. (1992). *Organizational culture and leadership* (2nd ed.). San Francisco: Jossey-Bass.

Schein, E. H. (1996). Kurt Lewin's change theory in the field and in the classroom: Notes toward a model of managed learning. *Systems Practice, 9*(1), 27–47.

Schlechty, P. (1993). On the frontier of school reform with trailblazers, pioneers, and settlers. *Journal of Staff Development, 14*(4), 46–50.

Schmoker, M. M. (1996). *Results: The key to continuous school improvement.* Alexandria, VA: Association for Supervision and Curriculum Development.

Senge, P. (1990). *The fifth discipline: The art and practice of the learning organization.* New York: Currency.

Senge, P., Cambron-McCabe, N., Lucas, T., Smith, B., Dutton, J., & Kleiner, A. (2000). *Schools that learn: A fifth discipline fieldbook for educators, parents, and everyone who cares about education.* New York: Doubleday.

Senge, P., Scharmer, C. O., Jaworski, J., & Flowers, B. S. (2004). *Presence: Human purpose and the field of the future.* Cambridge, MA: Society for Organizational Learning.

Showers, B., Murphy, C. U., & Joyce, B. (1996). The River City program: Staff development becomes school improvement. In B. R. Joyce & E. Calhoun (Eds.), *Learning experiences in school renewal: An exploration of five successful programs.* Eugene: University of Oregon Press. (ERIC Document Reproduction Service No. EA0266996)

Sparks, G. (1983). Synthesis of research on staff development for effective teaching. *Educational Leadership, 41*(3), 65–72.

Sparks, D. (2002). *Designing powerful professional development for teachers and principals.* Oxford, OH: National Staff Development Council.

Steelman, L. C., Powell, B., & Carini, R. M. (2000, Winter). Do teacher unions hinder educational performance? Lessons learned from state SAT and ACT scores. *Harvard Educational Review, 70*(4), 437–466.

Stiggins, R. (2002, June). Assessment crisis: The absence of assessment for learning [Electronic version]. *Phi Delta Kappan.* Retrieved March 10, 2006, from http://www.pdkintl.org/kappan/k020sti.htm

Sullivan, S., & Glanz, J. (2000). *Supervision that improves teaching.* Thousand Oaks, CA: Corwin Press.

Tichy, N. M., & Cardwell, N. (2002). *The cycle of leadership: How great leaders teach their companies to win.* New York: HarperBusiness.

Tichy, N. M., & Cohen, E. (1997). *The leadership engine.* New York: HarperCollins.

Tschannen-Moran, M., Hoy, A. W., & Hoy, W. K. (1998). Teacher efficacy: Its meaning and measure. *Review of Educational Research, 68*(2), 202–248.

U.S. Census Bureau. (2000). *Quickfacts.* Retrieved June 11, 2003, from http://quickfacts.census.gov/qfd/states/20/20159.html

U.S. Department of Education. (2002). *No child left behind.* Retrieved July 22, 2002, from http://www.nochildleftbehind.gov

Vanzant, L. (1980). *Achievement motivation, sex-role acceptance, and mentor relationships of professional females.* Unpublished doctoral dissertation, East Texas State University.

Webb, R., & Ashton, P. T. (1987). Teachers' motivation and the conditions of teaching: A call for ecological reform. In S. Walker & L. Burton (Eds.), *Changing policies, changing teachers: New directions for schooling?* (pp. 22–40). Philadelphia: Open University Press.

Wiggins, G., & McTighe, J. (1998). *Understanding by design.* Alexandria, VA: Association for Supervision and Curriculum Development.

Wilms, W. (2003). Altering the structure and culture of American public Schools. *Phi Delta Kappa International, 84*(8).

Wong, H. (1998). *The first days of school.* Mountain View, CA: Harry Wong.

Zmuda, A., Kuklis, R., & Kline, E. (2004). *Transforming schools: Creating a culture of continuous improvement.* Alexandria, VA: Association for Supervision and Curriculum Development.

Action Research-Related Resources

R esources that have proved to be especially helpful to the work of study groups in the areas of action research, assessment and rubrics, Japanese Lesson Study, Looking at Student Data, and Looking at Student Work include the sources below.

Action Research

Glanz, J. (1999, Summer). Action research. *Journal of Staff Development, 20*(3).

Sagor, R. (2000). *Guiding school improvement with action research.* Alexandria, VA: Association for Supervision and Curriculum Development.

Sagor, R. (2004). *The action research guidebook.* Thousand Oaks, CA: Corwin Press.

Assessment and Rubrics

Exemplars: K–12 standards-based performance assessment. (n.d.). Available online at http://www.exemplars.com

Goodrich Andrade, H. (2000). Using rubrics to promote thinking and learning. *Educational Leadership, 57*(5), 13–18.

Association for Supervision and Curriculum Development. Available online at http://www.ascd.org/portal/site/ascd/menuitem.a4dbd0f2c4f9b94cdeb3ffdb62108a0c/

Japanese Lesson Study

Lewis, C. (2002). *Lesson study: A handbook of teacher-led instructional change.* Philadelphia: Research for Better Schools.

Richardson, J. (2004, February/March). *Lesson study: Teachers learn how to improve instruction tools for schools.* Alexandria, VA: National Staff Development Council. Retrieved March 10, 2006, from http://www.nsdc.org/library/publications/tools/tools2-04rich.cfm

Lesson Study Research Group. (n.d.). Available online at Teachers College, Columbia University, Web site: http://www.tc.edu/lessonstudy/whatislessonstudy.html

Looking at Student Data

Bernhardt, V. L. (1998). *Data analysis for comprehensive schoolwide improvement.* Larchmont, NY: Eye on Education.

Schmoker, M. (1999). *Results: The key to continuous school improvement.* Alexandria, VA: Association for Supervision and Curriculum Development.

Looking at Student Work

Web site for looking at student work developed by an association of educators and supported by the Harmony School Education Center: http://www.lasw.org

Allen, D., & Blythe, T. (2003). *A facilitator's book of questions: Resources for looking together at student and teacher work.* New York: Teachers College Press.

Blythe, T., Allan, D., & Powell, B. S. (1999). *Looking together at student work.* New York: Teachers College Press.

Langer, G. M., Colton, A. B., & Goff, L. S. (2003). *Collaborative analysis of student work: Improving teaching and learning.* Alexandria, VA: Association for Supervision and Curriculum Development.

McDonald, J. P., Mohr, N., Dichter, A., & McDonald, E. C. (2003). *The power of protocols: An educator's guide to better practice.* New York: Teachers College Press.

Index

**CORWIN
PRESS**